Database Principles
For
Personal Computers

Database Principles For Personal Computers

Richard F. Walters

Prentice-Hall Inc.
Englewood Cliffs, New Jersey 07632

Library of Congress Cataloging-in-Publication Data

Walters, Richard F. (date)
    Database principles for personal computers.

    Includes bibliographies and index.
    1. Data base management. 2. Microcomputers–
Programming. I. Title.
QA76.9.D3W35 1987   005.26   87-2358
ISBN 0-13-197294-4

Editorial/production supervision
and interior design: Sophie Papanikolaou
Cover design: Lundgren Graphics, Ltd.
Manufacturing buyer: S. Gordon Osbourne

© 1987 by Prentice-Hall, Inc.
A division of Simon & Schuster
Englewood Cliffs, New Jersey 07632

Printed in the United States of America

10 9 8 7 6 5 4 3 2 1

ISBN 0-13-197294-4   025

Prentice-Hall International (UK) Limited, *London*
Prentice-Hall of Australia Pty. Limited, *Sydney*
Prentice-Hall Canada Inc., *Toronto*
Prentice-Hall Hispanoamericana, S.A., *Mexico*
Prentice-Hall of India Private Limited, *New Delhi*
Prentice-Hall of Japan, Inc., *Tokyo*
Prentice-Hall of Southeast Asia Pte. Ltd., *Singapore*
Editora Prentice-Hall do Brasil, Ltda., *Rio de Janeiro*

To *Loren, Glen* and *Ray*
who helped me on the way

Contents

3   *Personal Computer Environments*   59

1

Introduction

1.1 PURPOSE OF TEXT

Database Management Systems (DBMSs) have been available on large mainframe computers for many years, supporting the information needs of corporations, hospitals, and other institutions able to afford them. With the advent of personal computers, packages have been designed to perform the same function for the personal computer environment. The success of personal computer DBMSs is evident from the number of articles and advertisements describing the many packages commercially available. One company is said to have sold over one million copies of such a package.

There are important differences between database packages running on personal computers and those that are designed for mainframes. To begin with, most personal computers are single user systems, although multiuser versions such as the IBM AT are starting to appear. An individual using a personal computer must be familiar with all phases of its operation, something that is not required of the team member working on a large database application. Some features of large DBMSs are lacking on single-user systems, such as security and integrity provisions. The responsibility of providing these safeguards falls on the shoulders of the individual user, and many users are unprepared to accept this responsibility.

Another change that has occurred at the same time that personal computers were becoming widely available is the rapid advances made in the principles of database management. These concepts have revolutionized the field, introducing new models for data storage and retrieval. For the most part, these techniques have not yet been widely adopted for applications running on mainframes even though a few packages are available. However, DBMSs based on the new concepts are incorporated in most personal computer DBMSs sold today. Professionals used to working with conventional systems have not yet been obliged to learn about these new concepts, so they may be unprepared to make the decisions imposed by new data models.

Finally, the personal computer itself is a relatively new form of architecture. It is a technology that is evolving rapidly, with changes in processors, peripherals, and interconnections appearing at rates far exceeding the evolution of larger systems. Operating systems for personal computers are different from those running on larger systems, and they require a different approach to design and implementation of database applications. Although many people have become familiar with the operation of personal computers, few have studied their operation as it affects the database environment.

The purpose of this text is to provide an introduction to the use of DBMSs on personal computers. It is aimed at the serious user who wants to understand the principles of design and operation in this environment, not just to know how to use a particular package. The author assumes that the reader has an introductory knowledge of computers, but does not assume advanced levels of understanding of database systems, microprocessors, or personal computer operating systems. Since each of these areas is covered in sufficient depth to bring out its significance to the use of DBMSs on personal computers, experts in any one of these areas who lack knowledge of the others may benefit from the material presented. Mainframe DBMS users will find the details of personal computer operation explained in a way that translates their previous background to this new environment. The experienced personal computer user will learn principles of database systems as taught in computer science courses today and discover which features of personal computers affect the implementation of such principles. Students who have taken courses on database systems will learn how these principles must be modified to adapt to the personal computer environment. In short, this text should prove useful to a wide range of computer literates who want to take advantage of DBMS packages on personal computers.

After reading this text, one should understand basic principles of database systems as they apply to the personal computer environment. The text will also prepare the reader to design a database application for personal computers, evaluate available commercial packages in light of those design considerations, and develop an implementation plan that meets both short-term and long-range goals.

1.2 ORGANIZATION OF TEXT

The text presents fundamentals necessary to the operation of database applications on personal computers, and then illustrates these principles with hypothetical real-world examples. Next, it reviews measures of performance and evaluation of DBMS packages, and concludes by speculating on the evolution of database applications from their present-day, single-user state to integrated multiuser systems in a rapidly evolving technological environment. The material is presented in a cumulative fashion, with references in each chapter to material previously presented.

Chapter 2 introduces fundamentals of database systems as they have developed over the past decade. The material presented includes a survey of indexing techniques and a description of typical file structures, and then presents structural and conceptual models of database systems as they have evolved in recent years.

Chapter 3 presents an introduction to personal computers in the context of their use for DBMS applications. The principal families of microprocessors are contrasted, noting reasons why one group of processors is better suited to database operations than another. The next section describes disk storage systems, noting factors that affect database performance. The chapter concludes with a review of operating systems available on personal computers, describing in particular pertinent features of the IBM PC DOS operating system.

The next chapter applies the principles developed in the preceding two chapters to a specific example, using student records of the fictitious Maverick University to illustrate concepts of design and implementation of a database application. The chapter describes interviews with key personnel, development of a basic design, and selection of a model to represent these data. It then outlines the implementation of this design, using two commercial DBMS packages. Chapter 4 concludes with an analysis of the implementation examples, presenting generalities derived from these systems as they would impact other applications.

Chapter 5 presents practical considerations of performance and evaluation. The approach taken is unconventional, beginning with an analysis of the resources required to implement such a system including personnel, physical environment, and finally the necessary computer hardware and software. Performance measures are presented in the context of their importance to database operations. The examples also illustrate how these measures should be interpreted. Illustrations are taken in part from the two database packages described in Chapter 4.

The final chapter discusses the evolution of DBMS packages on personal computers. The presentation begins with a review of the consequences of moving from a single-user system to one that is shared by more than one user, and proceeds to distributed databases, noting the increasing levels of complexity introduced at each level. Next, Chapter 6 considers the potential effect on database applications of the introduction of technological advances in personal computers. It concludes with an analysis of current research in database systems and related computer science topics, noting the probable effect of this research on the evolution of current DBMS packages.

Examples used throughout this text are selected to illustrate a variety of real-world situations. The packages used to illustrate the basic principles, DATAEASE and dBASE III, represent two of the most widely distributed DBMS products currently available on personal computers. They also illustrate sharply contrasting design philosophies that further emphasize the basic concepts treated in the text.

An annotated list of references at the end of each chapter guides the reader to supplemental material. The references are taken from classical texts on database systems as well as current periodicals dealing with personal computers. Guidelines to the use of current literature are included in these reference supplements.

1.3 GUIDELINES FOR USE

This text presents principles of database management systems in a logical sequence, each section building on material presented previously. Readers who are familiar with various aspects of the material covered may still find it useful to skim those sections to make sure that they have not missed features that will be used later in the text. The material on personal computers, for example, points out features specific to database applications that are often skipped in conventional discussions of this material.

Perhaps one of the best ways to read this text is to do so in conjunction with the preliminary design of a real database application. In this setting, the material in Chapters 2 and 3 should prove helpful during the initial design. Chapters 4 and 5 will help during the actual implementation phase, and Chapter 6 will serve as a reference for future planning.

1.4 ACKNOWLEDGMENTS

A text of this sort is usually based on the author's experiences. In this case, the author has worked on database applications in the medical environment for over eighteen years and has taught principles of database systems for over a decade. Contacts with students and users of databases during these years have proved invaluable in helping select the concepts to be presented. To all of these persons, remembered or forgotten, the author owes a heartfelt debt of gratitude.

The actual writing was aided by several key individuals. John Lewkowicz, director of the Computer Facility at New York State College of Veterinary Medicine, was by far the most important contributor to this effort. He spent many hours painstakingly reviewing the text, discussing concepts that required clarification or elaboration with the author, and encouraging the author when the process slowed down. The text has also benefitted from the reviews of C. J. Bontempo, Ivan Gavrilovic, Frederick Lochovsky, and Dana Marks. Michael Shulman, microcomputer consultant at the U.C. Davis Computer Center, was extremely helpful in modifying dBASE III programs and writing additional examples for inclusion in the text. Scott Burger and Jeff Roberts, software consultants with Software Solutions, provided assistance on one DATAEASE program. Tracy Jones and Jill Rojas were especially helpful in reviewing portions of the text for grammatical and typographic accuracy.

One of the difficulties of creating examples for a text such as this lies in selecting names and data that, while being fictitious, will still appear reasonable. Friends and associates of the author may find their names appearing in slightly modified form; each of these disguised references in fact acknowledges support given in one way or another to this work.

Finally, I would like to express my sincere thanks to Karl Karlstrom, who first suggested that this text be prepared and who suffered through the delays inherent in its final production. Without his patience, this text may never have seen the light of day. I am also indebted to John Wait, who assumed responsibility for the text following Mr. Karlstrom's retirement and who assisted greatly in its final production.

2 ⸗ Principles of Database Management Systems

2.1 INTRODUCTION

It is unfortunate that we use the term *computer* to describe the electronic tools that have so profoundly changed our society in the last few decades. The most common uses of computers today involve organizing, sorting, and manipulating data rather than computation. Hence, the French term *ordinateur* better captures the flavor of the use made of these machines in database applications.

This chapter presents basic principles of database systems, with an emphasis on aspects that are particularly relevant to personal computers. The intent of the chapter is to provide the database designer with working tools and an understanding of the common pitfalls encountered in the design process.

Nearly everyone deals with many different types of databases as a part of daily life. It is perfectly natural, therefore, to assume that knowledge of the principles of database management is equally widespread. Unfortunately, it often happens that, while a person may be familiar with the content of one or more information systems, the principles governing organization and manipulation of these systems are not well understood. The reason may lie in the apparent simplicity of the topic, which is easy to take for granted and equally easy to use improperly.

No information system is designed correctly the first time. This comforting assumption will surprise some who may have felt that their own small failures were unique. In all probability, the process of developing computer support for an information system will itself change the system that is being automated, so that the initial assumptions will no longer hold; hence the design process involves serving a moving target. This type of design can be likened to trying to change a flat tire on a moving car, and it is no wonder that most initial designs prove inadequate.

Mechanical aids for data systems have been around for nearly a century, ever since Herman Hollerith developed the punched card for the 1890 census. Tab machines were the bread and butter of the companies that merged in 1914 to become the Computing Tabulating Recording Company, which later changed its name to International Business Machines (IBM). These devices were used until the 1950s, when they were gradually replaced by computers. While the skills associated with manipulating business data go back a long way, the influence of computer science in this field is much more recent. Despite the long history of data processing, the techniques used were unimaginative. Batch computing techniques were basically similar to tab machine processes. Computer science departments tended to concentrate on more glamorous aspects of the discipline, and it was not until the 1970s that the field of Database Management Systems began to take on an air of legitimacy. Since then, however, growth and change in this field have been dramatic. New architectures and new understanding of the underlying principles have appeared at an accelerating pace, and now most university computer science departments have at least one specialist in this area.

The number of textbooks on Database Management Systems is growing as the interest in the field expands. The references cited at the end of this chapter give a sampling of some of the better texts currently available. This chapter is intended to provide an introduction to the material rather than to provide complete coverage.

2.2 BASIC DEFINITIONS

Every discipline has its own jargon, sometimes using common English words with slightly different meanings. The field of Database Management Systems is no different. In the remainder of this chapter, we will introduce some special terms, giving definitions as we proceed. There are, however, a few terms that will be used throughout that require definition at the outset.

First, we must distinguish between the *logical* versus the *physical* levels of these systems. At the logical level, we are concerned with the organization, relations, and conceptual structure of the database. At the physical level, we deal with the actual manner in which the database is stored in an automated system. There may be several physical structures that will serve a single logical design, but the DBMS designer should be aware of the benefits and drawbacks of the different options.

At the physical level, there are several terms commonly used with specific meaning. A few are:

Data Elements: Data elements are the individual facts, observations, or items that are contained in a database system. Data elements might include such items as name, age, telephone number, and color of part.

Field: Data elements are stored in a single *field* in a database system. We will use both data element and field in this text. When we use *field*, we mean the computer storage location in which an element is to be placed.

Record: A record is a collection of facts about an individual, part, or other entity described in a database. It is the aggregate of all elements describing that entity, stored in a series of fields that define a single logical record on the computer.

File: A file is a collection of records that together describe all available entities of a particular type.

These physical components of a database form the basic tools used to create a logical design. At the logical level, we deal with the following two components:

Database: A database is a collection of one or more files that together describe the total information necessary for a given application. An organization may maintain more than one database (e.g., marketing and research). Each database will, however, be capable of dealing completely with questions involving the particular application.

Database Management System (DBMS): A DBMS is a package of computer programs designed to define, create, manipulate, and summarize databases.

2.3 DATA TYPES

Database systems deal with data elements that must be collected and organized in such a way that they can be interpreted to present *information* that was not obvious from the individual elements. There is a real difference in the meaning of *data* and *information* as used in the discipline of database management. For example, a Social Security number can be regarded as a data element. However, knowledge about the manner in which Social Security numbers are assigned can provide information about the individuals represented by those numbers. In general, Social Security numbers beginning with 0 or 1 were assigned in East Coast locations, whereas the initial digit 5 was reserved for the West Coast. Persons with Social Security numbers starting with the digit 6 were all enrolled through the railroad unions. As yet, no numbers are assigned that start with 7 or 8, and the starting number 9 is sometimes used for a foreign citizen with temporary visa status in this country. This type of information represents an extension of the simple data element. It is typical of many cases in which meaningful information can be extracted from raw data. A person can look at a list of Social Security numbers and perhaps know a little more about those individuals on the basis of this type of interpretation. "Knowing more" is the key to the information content of a system. We sometimes use the term *meaningful information* to convey this concept.

The difference between a database and a Database Management System is the ability of the latter to accommodate programs that extract meaningful information from the former. Learning to *design* a database to be used by a DBMS is a skill that can only be acquired with knowledge of principles coupled with experience, and experience is probably the more important component of this pair. The design process, which is illustrated in Chapter 4, involves a study of the *process* that is to be served by the proposed database and the *information flow* that serves that process. One effective means for determining the data required for a system is to analyze the uses anticipated for the database. What reports will be required, and what data are needed to prepare these reports? Although these answers may not be precise, they may help in excluding items of doubtful value, thereby reducing the overall cost of the system. This concept can best be illustrated by example, as we will see in Chapter 4.

When we look at facts in the world, they seem to be impossibly varied and incapable of classification. However, from the DBMS point of view, it is necessary only to group these facts into sets that have one thing in common: the manner in which they will be *processed* by the computer. Looked at from this point of view, the notion of *data types* becomes more tractable. The clue to the way in which data will be stored lies in knowing how the data will be used. Different forms of internal storage can be manipulated in different ways by a computer. To illustrate, let's consider an example of a personnel file. What information might such a file contain in order to answer questions about individual workers in a company? Here are some typical items:

> Identification Number
> Name
> Address (street, apartment, city, state)
> ZIP code
> Date of birth
> Sex
> Job classification
> Current department
> Current salary
> Date hired
> Previous position(s)
>> Date started
>> Department
>> Date transferred
>> Job classification
> Seniority level
> Confidential evaluation record
>> Date of review
>> Reviewer's ID number
>> Evaluation rating
>> Comments

Many elements could be added to this set, but it illustrates options for classification of facts into data types. Examining this list, we see that there are several obvious groupings. First, we have several elements that are *numeric*. In this listing, ID number, ZIP code, salary, and evaluation rating might all consist of numbers. Yet, when we think about the numeric content of these data fields, we realize that fields use numbers in different ways. It makes no sense to perform calculations involving ZIP codes or ID numbers. True, we might want to sort these fields in numeric order, but it is not necessary to add, subtract, or multiply them. On the other hand, salary is something that requires numeric computation in most databases.

The key to classification of data then is not simply the types of characters that appear in the field, but the use that is intended for the field. A *numeric* field may be appropriate for these data elements, but on the other hand, storing ID numbers and ZIP codes as *text* is also a valid approach.

From this first examination, we arrive at two major data types: numeric and text, and we see that classification of individual data fields will depend on proposed use. What about dates (date of birth, date hired, etc.)? They are, or can be expressed, as numbers, but the calculations involving dates are going to be different from other numeric calculations. For this reason, many DBMSs have a separate data type *date,* processed according to special rules.

The data type *text* is perhaps the most common in databases. Special techniques may be required to extract important information (such as last name from total name), but the actual number of characters stored in free text data types may vary, and the permitted characters might include punctuation, alphabetic characters, and even numeric characters as shown in the ZIP code example. Many of the fields in our list, such as name and address, are likely to be stored as free text.

What about a data element such as sex? It is usually represented by an alphabetic character, but in this case, the choice must be either M or F (ignoring biological anomalies). This is, therefore, a different data type, a *set*, or an *enumerated set*. Sets may be simple, such as M or F or perhaps academic degree(s) received, or they may be multiple choices including the ubiquitous "none of the above." This data type differs from "free text" in that the choices are limited to a controlled (enumerated) set, and a computer program can easily determine whether a new entry falls within the permissible set and can create lists of individuals whose records contain a particular set of attributes. As such, it qualifies as a unique data type.

There are several ways in which a data element such as department or job classification might be recorded, including either the set or even free text classifications. However, it might make more sense to use a code number for this type of field. There may be additional information about either a department or a job classification, information that is important to the total DBMS, but that need not be repeated under every employee's record. In cases of this type, a different data type called an *identifier* is often used. This data type is a code number that identifies a record in another file where further information about that element is stored. This technique has the advantage that it saves space in the personnel file. In addition, changes in information on *job classification* need only be made in one file, rather than each time a particular job is referenced in the personnel file. Identifiers of this type are used in almost all DBMSs, although they may have different names in different packages, such as "indices," "pointers," or "keys." The use of identifiers requires that more than one file must be present, but this is a desirable feature of many DBMSs since it helps the designer to treat independently information about different topics in his or her total system.

One more data type can be derived from examination of the foregoing hypothetical personnel file. The element "seniority" is clearly a moving target, whose value is *calculated* from an historic date and the current date. Now, it might be that a company would decide to calculate such a figure once a year (the way racehorses' ages are calculated on New Year's Day), but the results would be less accurate. If age of the employee were a data element, it would probably be important to calculate age more frequently to be certain that some milestones such as retirement or eligibility criteria are strictly observed. For this reason, a data type called *calculated* is added to the list of data types. In some DBMSs, calculated data are never actually stored; instead, the formula used to calculate them is stored in its place, and the current value is generated each time the element is requested. Salary to date, total FICS contributions this year, age, percent time worked on a given project for one month's time sheet — these are all candidates for data elements whose value is calculated.

At this point, we have pretty much taken care of every element in our hypothetical database. One way or another (the choice is ours), we can assign every fact in that file into one of the categories described thus far. Furthermore, if we select almost any other body of information likely to be incorporated into a database, we probably are going to be able to assign those values to one of these categories. This is not to say that there are not many differences between the data elements in such files, but rather that, from a computer processing point of view, we have exhausted the common alternatives. True, there are some hybrid data types that we might consider. For example, in word-processing applications it may be useful to embed special identifiers in a standard form letter that access other data such as amount overdue, city of recipient's residence, and so on, but these elements can ultimately be treated as composites of the foregoing classifications (in this example, free text and pointers).

To summarize, the following data types are required to define most anticipated types of elements in a database:

Numeric
Date
Free text
Set
Identifier
Calculated

2.3.1 Data Type Descriptors

Classifying data elements in one or another of the categories listed is one important step in creating a database. However, the data definition process is not yet over. Not only is it important to tell the computer about the type of data that will be used for a particular element — it is also vital to know several other facts about each field in a DBMS.

2.3.1.1 Field Length

Storage on computers is not infinite. Furthermore, for reasons of efficiency in processing, it often is important to have every data element start at a consistent boundary in a record. It is therefore necessary in most (not all) DBMSs to specify the space that must be reserved for a given data element.

Selection of size is a two-edged sword. A field length too short to accommodate some addresses may result in generation of invalid mailing labels; a field that is too large wastes space because once a file size is specified, all entries will occupy that space regardless of the actual values. The cost of going back later to expand a field may be prohibitive in time and reprogramming (although some systems are more forgiving in this respect), so it is wise to select a reasonable size and test it on a sampling of data before the final database is generated.

Some systems can accommodate variable-length fields. The physical storage required for a variable-length field will be less than a fixed-length field (since the fixed-length field must always assume the maximum length for a data element). This difference can have a major effect on the size of a file in which names and addresses are stored. The major drawback of variable-length fields is their inefficiency in processing each record. Since the size of the fields vary, it takes more time not only to process each record, but the address of each record may not be readily calculated, so random access is more difficult to accomplish.

2.3.1.2 Required Field

In every data record, there will be some data elements that must be completed. At a minimum, the *primary key* must be present in order for the record to be filed. The primary key of a record is defined as the data element (or elements) that uniquely identifies the record. It is used to search the file for specific records, and it often is used to sort the file, so that more rapid searches based on the primary key may be performed. A primary key usually is a value such as a Social Security number, a part code number, or some other field that is more fully described by other data elements in the record. It stands to reason, therefore, that a record without this "key" value could not be stored in a file that searches for records based on that key. The primary key, therefore, is considered to be a *required field*, one that must be present if the record is to be filed.

In addition to the primary key, other values may also be required in order to provide some consistency in the database. If a personnel record uses the Social Security number as the primary key, it may also require that the name of the employee also be present. The *name* field may not be unique (there may be two John Smiths in the company), so it is not a primary key, but it is nevertheless mandatory that the name be filed with the individual's Social Security number. The person defining a database will need to determine which fields must be entered for each record. Many systems will assume that, although the primary key is required, other fields are optional unless they are specifically identified as mandatory.

2.3.1.3 Controlled Value Options

Some other options used in defining data elements are useful in improving the overall value of the database. For example, if an order form calls for entering the part number from a catalog, the DBMS should check to make sure that the part number actually exists. Some systems will allow the user to require that a field be checked against an existing dictionary prior to acceptance. This form of controlling options is similar to the pointer data type.

There is, however, another form of control, based on entry of new values under some authorization control. For example, it may be that certain individuals (the marketing supervisor, for instance) are authorized to enter the name of a new client whereas other individuals such as store clerks must enter orders only for existing clients. This type of control can be selectively assigned, as described later in Section 2.3.1.6. For all other users, the values stored are the only ones that will be accepted at data-entry time.

2.3.1.4 Error Checks

There are many ways in which errors can be detected during the data-entry process when a clerk is adding new records to a file. Some errors can be detected even before the record is filed. In the case of numeric values, a minimum and maximum range may be specified. Sometimes dates are restricted to values reasonable for that particular data element (e.g., no date of birth before 1880 or after the current date for a living individual). Some numeric values have built-in error correction codes. Credit-card numbers, for example, use a special method of summing up all digits in the card to obtain a "check digit," which appears as the final digit and is used to verify that all previous digits were correctly typed.

There are also possible error checks of other data types. One might require a name to be entered in the format of last name, comma, first name. Any entry that did not contain a comma between two sets of alphabetic characters (possibly containing other punctuation) would not be considered valid. Some systems may require dates to be entered "mm/dd/yy," rejecting any other format. A calculated field may require presence of the values used to determine its value. These types of error checks improve the reliability of the database, and many DBMSs offer multiple options for error checking.

2.3.1.5 Multiple Entries

In the foregoing personnel file, there were some entries for which multiple values could be expected. History of employment, for example, might include several previous positions, and the confidential evaluation information has a new set of entries each time the employee is evaluated. These fields may be identified as *multiple entry fields*. They are among the most difficult elements that occur in database definition. A person familiar with a given body of information often may neglect to inform a database designer that a field may have more than one legitimate value. If the designer fails to provide for multiple entries, the value of the system may be compromised. When a field has been recognized as potentially being multiple, it will require special treatment. The degree of flexibility permitted in this category varies from one system to another, and the manner in which these fields are processed also varies, so it is essential to identify this data type during the design process.

2.3.1.6 Access Restrictions

Referring to our personnel example, it is likely that access to the employee evaluation portion of this file should be limited. Access restrictions can take many forms, the simplest ones being to permit a group of users to (a) read and modify a file; (b) read a file without changing it; or (c) not have access to a file either for reading or modifying. This type of access may be controlled at the file, record, or individual entry level. In the foregoing example, the fields relating to employee evaluation might be restricted even though the remainder of the record is available to be viewed by many users. Access restrictions are less important in single-user systems, since it is often possible to remove and lock up floppy disks with confidential data. However, access control may be important even on personal computers. We will return to this topic in Chapter 4.

These types of additional specifications to data elements are often available in personal computer DBMS packages. They may be defined by "default." A default value is one that is used automatically unless the user specifies a different one. For instance, a field may be defined as "required," but unless the user explicitly makes this choice, the default will be to make the field "optional." The security level for a data element may also be assigned a default value of "read only," meaning that the data element once entered would be open to read access by all, but it could not be changed by anyone but the operations supervisor. The importance of each characteristic will vary, but the availability of these options may be an important factor in determining the acceptability of one package over another.

2.4 INDEXING AND CLASSIFICATION

In the previous section, we defined the concept of a primary key, which is useful in searching for records in a file. Primary keys are representative of a larger problem associated with database design: *indexing* a file, or in a broader sense *classifying* the data elements that will become a part of the file. Ordinarily, we think of indexing and classification as problems associated with libraries. Large bibliographies should be indexed so that a person searching the file can retrieve information more rapidly. However, the problem can be extended to many other databases, and the techniques that have been developed for effective indexing represent another facet of DBMS implementation that should be understood by a database designer.

The process of computerization means, at the lowest level, placing pieces of data into forms that can be accessed and manipulated electronically. Even if we create a well-structured set of records, they may have no specific sequential organization other than occurring in the same sequence used to enter the data. Such a file has its merits, but it is evident that searching for information in a file of this type will require reading the entire file to make sure that all appropriate records have been located.

The alternative is to *index* the records or fields in a file. Indexing may seem to be a relatively straightforward process that "anyone can do." Often, however, the problems associated with indexing can be technically difficult and lead to operational situations that are totally unacceptable. The science of indexing techniques is also making progress as we learn more about information science in general. Some of the following notions may not appear immediately applicable to the DBMS environment, and yet each technique has been used and has its appropriate niche.

2.4.1 Example of an Indexing Problem

Let us consider an indexing problem with which most people are familiar: an office correspondence file. The subjects will vary in complexity and are more complicated if the office serves several different functions. A single item of correspondence often will include references to several topics, some of whose importance will change with time. The primary need for indexing may be to serve the objectives of a company, but on some occasions the same file needs to be searched to answer legal questions or perhaps to document fiscal actions questioned by outside sources (such as the Internal Revenue Service). The basic nature of many businesses tends to evolve over time, changing the emphasis that guides indexing strategies.

What is the most common solution to the correspondence indexing problem of an office? Each reader may have a different answer, but some of the typical responses are (a) to create multiple copies of correspondence, placing a copy in each of several locations; (b) to create one or more "daily boards," in which outgoing letters are filed chronologically (not always with the companion message that generated the need for the letter); (c) to assign an office supervisor the task of creating a single filing system, complete with file folders of different colors, numbers, an index book, and a training manual. When a system of this type exists, new employees must learn to index, file properly and promptly, retrieve completely and quickly, and solve new filing problems that the system addressed either ambiguously or not at all.

Most manual filing systems are unsatisfactory. It takes little imagination for most of us to recall the panic and confusion that occurred when a vital piece of correspondence could not be located; or the indispensability of one "old hand" who designed the system in the first place and kept the accurate, updated key to classification in his or her head; or the "GOK" file (God Only Knows what's in it); or the exponential increase in file storage as new cross references were required.

What if a file of this type were automated? Supposing (as has happened) that an entire file cabinet is microfilmed, and a computer-stored index of the microfilm reels is to be generated. What would that index file look like? What fields would it contain? How would a manager want to use that file to find the right microfilm reel and then get to the right image on that reel? One might come up with many answers to this question — some useful, others less so. But what tools have been developed to make this process easier? In the following section, we briefly describe some of the techniques developed (primarily by librarians) for indexing and classifying.

2.4.2 Indexing Techniques

In our correspondence file example, we have many forms of data that could be indexed in different ways. The selection of a choice depends on the way in which the file is likely to be accessed. The first thing that must be determined in deciding on an index scheme is to define the types of answers that might be required in searching the file. As a guide to the options described in this section, we will relate these techniques to hypothetical retrieval requirements from this file.

One of the most important principles to observe in indexing is to separate the index from the items being indexed. An index usually says as much about the needs and priorities of the person who created it as it does about the information being classified. Another indexer may have different perspectives and therefore classify things in another way, but the items themselves have not changed. Since the viewpoint of the classifier may change, it is important to keep it separate from the data file itself, so that, if necessary, new viewpoints can be introduced.

2.4.2.1 Numeric

Numeric values can be used in many different ways. If we include dollar values and dates as "numeric," there may be benefit in classifying our file according to one or more of these criteria. The fields date sent, date received, dollar amount of contract, sales volume, and other fields might be important to be used for rapid retrieval of particular documents.

2.4.2.2 Hierarchical

Perhaps the most common form of indexing in the world today is the hierarchical index, the outline form used in most books (including this one), the phylogenetic classification of living forms, the structure of the typical company, university, or government. In our correspondence file cabinet, there are probably major headings on drawers, and inside there may be two or more nested levels of subcategories for file folders. Clearly, a hierarchical structure is one that may serve a very useful purpose in classifying our database.

One of the benefits of hierarchies lies in retrieval strategies. It is possible, by using a very detailed hierarchical specification, to retrieve "granular" elements in a database. On the other hand, it is also possible to retrieve all elements dealing with a broader area of classification by specifying only the higher level of the hierarchy, allowing the retrieval to display all lower hierarchical elements within that portion of the tree. If we use a numeric classification, we might ask for all items between 3.0 and 3.62, for example, without knowing how many subcategories exist in that range.

Hierarchies have many advantages, but they also have disadvantages. In the correspondence file previously alluded to, adding a new topic may upset the structure of the existing file (what if the company decides to start a new product line?). The option of starting over is always available, but it may be impractical. Depending on the rate of change in an operation, the hierarchical scheme will sooner or later become outdated or will not be sufficiently precise to enable the user to get at a specific item in the file.

Due to this apparent limitation and since hierarchies necessarily represent only one viewpoint, other alternatives have been used to classify some types of information. Some of the more important approaches are described next.

2.4.2.3 Subject Headings

Subject headings differ from hierarchical indexes in having no implication of a subordinate classification. Each subject heading is equally important, and there are no subheadings in a strict subject heading index. The terms permissible are restricted by original design or approved modification, but there is no inherent "pecking order" in the nature of these headings. In our correspondence file cabinet example, we might decide not to subdivide our drawers more than one level, although this approach is rare. It is more likely to use subject headings when a file is more consistent in its contents. One might have a personnel file cabinet in which each individual has one file folder. In this case, an index would simply list the names of the employees, and there would be no hierarchical subdivisions.

Indexing by subject heading is usually simpler, less structured, and easier to maintain than hierarchies. It lacks precision, which in some cases is a desirable feature. In the personnel file, for example, it would be easy to add a new name.

2.4.2.4 Key Words

One of the more popular forms of classifying many documents (research papers, articles, technical documentation, etc.) is through the use of key words. Key words differ from subject headings in that several key words may be used to describe a single document. In our file cabinet, we might want to define several topics discussed in the correspondence, and index a letter multiply if several of these topics were discussed. By controlling or limiting the selection of key words accepted in a classification scheme, the chances of synonyms is reduced and the probability of accurate retrieval is increased.

Key words are generally used as index terms in a situation where the reference itself is filed according to some other method, usually a numeric or hierarchical classification. In general, key words are easier to assign, requiring less training than either hierarchies or subject headings. They are, however, less comprehensive, since more than one key word is usually required to classify an article.

One of the benefits of key word indexing is the ability to use combinations of key words in searching for specific documents. We might, for example, search for all correspondence to Company XYZ in which shipments were discussed.

2.4.2.5 Modifiers

Up to this point, we have considered classification schemes in which there is no grammatical connection between the words used to index items. Using the example in the previous paragraph, it might be better to index letters by "shipment, computers" than by shipments alone. In this example, "computers" serves as a modifier subdividing the category of shipments (there could be many other items shipped as well). The benefit of adding modifiers is reducing the possible volume of inappropriate items retrieved. The cost is in more effort required to index.

2.4.2.6 Phrases

Although modifiers are useful concepts in indexing, they often are not used in personal computer systems. Instead, combinations of words often are grouped together using an extended key word approach, and these "phrases" serve to index some types of documents. Suppose our file cabinet contained documents that were going to support a legal suit against some company for failure to perform. It might be very important to index these documents by specific terms such as "failure to perform," "legal action," or "conditions of acceptance." In fact, some very large class-action lawsuits depend heavily on the ability to retrieve quickly for courtroom use documents by topics such as these in addition to information as to who received the document and when it was sent or received.

2.4.2.7 Natural Language

A phrase is a fragment of a sentence. A natural extension of this approach to indexing would be to allow true sentences to be used in indexing. This approach is rare in personal computer indexing, but for some documents it might apply. If an entire document were itself machine readable (instead of microfilmed, as in our example), we might search for sentences and interpret them. A simple example would be to index the sentence "You're fired," or its equivalents. The difficulty with this approach is the problem of how many ways this sentence could be expressed. There are very few letters with that exact phrase included, but on the other hand, letters of dismissal may be important in certain situations.

There have been major strides made in applying natural language processing and classification to some information systems. To date, however, the techniques are limited in DBMSs to permitting some user flexibility in phrasing queries, with minimal attention given to basic classification. Natural language processors are still rare in the personal computer environment.

2.4.2.8 Performance of Different Indexing Methods

In the previous sections we illustrated several conventional techniques for indexing with an example that might apply to a microcomputer-based indexing scheme. The next question would be, Which one(s) should be selected for a specific problem? The answer of course is always a compromise between the cost of indexing versus the benefits anticipated from doing the indexing. In general, the more detailed and specific the index, the greater the cost in time, training, and modification. Hierarchies are quite expensive by these measures when compared to other forms of indexing. Many of the indexing schemes, including hierarchies, require training, whereas others, such as key words, can be done by less experienced individuals. On the other hand, some forms of indexing are not specific enough to be useful. If a hierarchical search only narrows the potential documents down to a few thousand out of a larger list, it may not serve its purpose, and therefore its value is insufficient.

There are several measures used to evaluate the effectiveness of an indexing system. Some of these measures are summarized in Table 2.1.

Table 2.1. Relative Costs and Benefits of Different Indexing Techniques*

Measures	Hierar-chical	Subject Headings	Key-words	Modi-fiers	Phrases	Natural Languages
Cost to index	10	8	6	6	2	1
Flexibility of definition	3	4	5	6	7	10
Specificity in retrieving	10	9	6	5	3	1
Storage efficiency	10	9	8	8	4	2
Retrieval efficiency	10	8	7	6	3	1
User training required	10	9	8	9	4	2

* Numeric values approximate; 1 = least (costly, flexible, etc.),
10 = most (specific, efficient, etc.).

From this table, we can see that there is no optimal solution to indexing; the tradeoffs are evident, and the decision must be tailored to the individual application.

2.5 FILES AND FILE TYPES

In this section, we deal with file types and the index techniques used to access these files. These concepts are at a more physical level than the classification methods presented in the previous section, but an understanding of the options is important to understanding DBMS design strategies.

There are many different types of file structures that can be used for organizing data. We have selected a few of the most important for further discussion, based on the frequency of their use in DBMSs and on personal computers. They are:

Pile
Sequential
Index sequential
Indexed
Multiring
Hashed
Balanced tree (B-tree)

We will discuss each of these files briefly. In order to compare the relative performance of these file types, one should consider the following performance measures:

Storage space efficiency
Time to fetch a record
Time to fetch next record
Time to insert a new record
Time to change a record
Time to read an entire file
Time to reorganize file
Time to delete a record
Time to process a record (decode data elements in each field)

These measures may not be relevant to some file types, but they will be useful in establishing relative merits of the alternatives. They depend not only on the organization of the file, but also on the nature of the storage medium.

Larger computers generally use two types of on-line auxiliary storage: magnetic tapes and disks. Tapes can store large amounts of data that can be rapidly transferred from tape to the computer's internal memory, but a tape must be read from beginning to end to access all data. On a typical 2,400-ft, 1/2-inch magnetic tape, this process may take several minutes (five or more, depending on various factors). Magnetic tapes were the stock-in-trade of early computers and hence of early DBMSs, and clever techniques were devised to use them efficiently. Despite such tricks, however, search times for data stored on magnetic tapes represent a severe constraint on system performance.

Disk files, on the other hand, can be directly accessed, no matter where they reside on the disk, in a matter of milliseconds. Once accessed, they may be read sequentially (like tapes), and for certain file types, individual records may also be directly accessed, again in a matter of milliseconds.

Files used in DBMSs can be designed to be read sequentially or they may take advantage of direct record access. In the latter case, a special indexing technique must be devised to permit selection of the appropriate record. All of the file types described in the following section can be implemented on auxiliary disk storage of personal computer. These files are defined rigidly, but in common practice, many files are actually hybrid combinations of the types described in the following sections.

2.5.1 Pile

The name pile implies a disorganized heap of something (laundry, football players) that will require some sorting out to use effectively. In DBMS terminology, the term *pile* is used to define a file type that is indeed loosely constructed, but there are a few rules imposed. Data elements in pile structure can occur in any sequence, but each data element will include both the name of the element and the value for that entry. Entries such as AGE = 43 or TITLE = "Shop Foreman" would be examples of such entries. In addition, the computer's operating system keeps track of the location of the end of the file, so that new records can be added as needed.

In this structure, the length of each field and each record is not specified. There is no indexing, other than the implicit sequencing resulting from the order in which new records are added. There is no primary key. In fact, the structure is extremely flexible. This flexibility is both the strength and the weakness of this type of file.

A pile structure is useful when the data to be stored are expected to be highly variable. If, for example, one were to ask a client a great many questions about buying preferences, recording only the positive responses, it probably would not make sense to reserve a field for each answer. Instead, one might give the client's name and then list those fields for which a positive response was given.

Another type of file that often uses a pile structure is a transaction log or *journal*. This is a record of every action that has taken place in some field of activity. In a database, it might represent a list of every addition, modification, or deletion made to each file. For an office receptionist's desk, it might log the telephone or personal contacts for the day. The basic characteristic of such a file is the extreme variability of anticipated entries, making a fixed field file structure inappropriate. Figure 2.1 illustrates a typical transaction file.

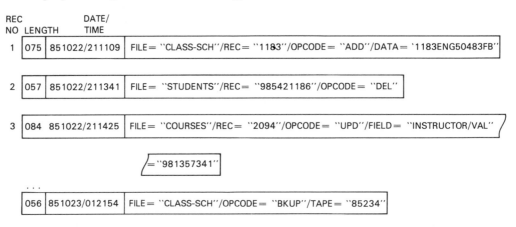

Figure 2.1. Transaction log in pile format. Each record has information on record length, date, time, plus names and values for each field.

Piles have several advantages over other structures. They are easy to update by simply adding a new record at the end of the file. Modifications to existing records are made by writing a new record and (later) marking the old record as invalid. Deleting is done by marking the record to be deleted as invalid.

There are, of course, obvious disadvantages over more highly structured files. The first is in accessing a specific record, which requires reading the file from the start until the particular record is encountered. It does no good to know that the record was a late entry, because the length of each record is variable and a file of this type can only be read sequentially. Getting the "next" record may be easy, but it is uncertain whether the next physical record is the one sought. Space used in storing piles is in one sense inefficient, since the name as well as value of each entry is stored. On the other hand, it may prove more efficient in comparison with a fixed field structure that has many empty fields. Finally, processing time for each record is slower than for fixed field records because it is necessary to decode both name and value instead of relying on position in the file for data interpretation.

Lane Medical Library

Please Return Books and Journals on/before due date Renew by phone: 723-6691

We will be moving every book and journal at least once during our remodelling. As full an inventory as possible will make the shifting easier, faster, and more successful. Also, less time spent on overdue notices, saves staff time and speeds our moving progress.

Thanks for your help.

s personal computer DBMSs. Their use is for
ions such as creating backup files, logs of
ndex and used with the assumption that the
it is accessed. Notice that, although there is
tten in a time-sequential manner, so that it is
ce to the file. This "index" is sometimes
to the record, a feature that may prove help-

butes that distinguish it from a pile. First, it
idual fields and records. Second, it is ordered
structure is fixed, it is not necessary to record
the name is implicit by the location in the
file.

	INSTRUCTOR	UNITS	MAX ENROLLMENT
ry	MacKenzie	3	300
s	MacKenzie	4	35
g	McNamee	3	200
	McNamee	3	50
ı	Newmark	4	100
ın	Newmark	2	20
y	Francis	2	55
ıg	Carswell	5	20
	Goldman	3	300
	Patrick	3	30
	McGrath	3	25
es	McGrath	4	40

re fixed length, sorted in order of course number.

useful in the DBMS environment. In many
en sophisticated indexing and the total disor-
eated and maintained in an ordered fashion,
key can be quite rapid, with the maximum
base 2 of entries, since each access can divide
could contain the key. Search among 30,000
uire no more than fifteen disk accesses (since
ach access and fifteen such subdivisions would
whereas in a pile structure, on the average
and interpreted.
eval speed is inevitably paid in update.
n a sequential file is not difficult since the
value may be substituted for another without
tions can be marked without actual removal.
te of the file, since a new record must be
ding to the primary key, and all subsequent
e room. The easiest way to update such files,
and do them in a merge operation, rewriting

the file with new values added and with deleted records removed. This technique means that on-line searches will continue to be rapid, but the updates may be less frequent, depending on the schedule selected for file updates.

The performance of a sequential file represents a good compromise for many applications. As previously noted, access to an individual record is rapid, and access of the next record by primary key is even more rapid. Reorganization of a sequential file (removing deleted records, inserting new ones) requires sorting the update information according to the primary key and then merging the two files, a fairly rapid operation once the sorting is completed.

Sequential files can be used for many DBMS applications, especially when only one key is to be used in searching for a record. They are relatively efficient in storage space, and they require no separate index maintenance operation. In addition, they function well in the personal computer environment.

2.5.3 Index Sequential

The first two file types already discussed make use of a single file without any external index. The index sequential file represents a departure from this method, in that a separate index file is created to speed searches. The index is much smaller than the data file, which means that it may be possible to load the index into memory and search it rapidly to obtain the specific location of a given entry.

To understand how the index sequential file works, we have to introduce a new concept in file retrieval from disk. When a record is read from a disk, it is brought into a buffer in memory. The buffer is usually defined by the computer's operating system to be large enough to accommodate several typical records. In fact, therefore, a disk read usually results in transferring a physical *block* of data from disk to the buffer in memory. A block usually contains several records, so that when a file is read sequentially, the next record may already be in the buffer, and a physical disk read only occurs when the records in the buffer are exhausted. Blocks are important concepts that affect file performance. They are especially important in the design of an index sequential file.

The data file in an index sequential file structure is a sequential file similar in most respects to the simple sequential file. However, this file makes use of the block structure by keeping track of the first record in each block, and keeping a separate index of the primary key for those records. Figure 2.3 illustrates this concept. In order to avoid having to rewrite the file each time a new record is inserted, a few blocks are initially left empty. These spare blocks are defined as *overflow areas*, and new records are added at the next available position in the overflow area. Second, in order to maintain the sequential search capability, the file itself is also modified by adding a pointer field to each record (including the overflow area records). When a record is added, the preceding record in the primary key sequence is modified by adding a pointer to the next available space in the overflow area, where the new record is written, as shown in Fig. 2.3.

This technique has several important advantages over the sequential file, the most important being the ability to add a new entry on-line without having to rewrite the file. Files updated in this manner will reflect the most current informa-

INDEX

KEY	BLOCK PTR
C624	7
E504	8
G726	9

BLOCK/RECORD	COURSE	DEPT	OVERFLOW PTR.
7.1	C624	CHEM	X
7.2	C655	CHEM	X
7.3	CS520	COMP.SCI.	26.2
7.4	CS781	COMP.SCI.	X
8.1	E504	ENGLISH	25.3
8.2	E821	ENGLISH	X
8.3	E925	ENGLISH	X
8.4	G634	GEOLOGY	X
9.1	G726	GEOLOGY	25.4
9.2	G912	GEOLOGY	26.1
9.3	P709	PHYSICS	26.3
9.4	P811	PHYSICS	X
10.1	. . .		
24.4	. . .		

	BLOCK/RECORD	COURSE	DEPT	OVERFLOW PTR.
OVERFLOW BLOCK 1	25.1	E796	ENGLISH	8.2
	25.2	M853	MATHEMATICS	9.3
	25.3	E690	ENGLISH	25.1
	25.4	G843	GEOLOGY	9.2
OVERFLOW BLOCK 2	26.1	M521	MATHEMATICS	26.4
	26.2	CS543	COMP.SCI.	7.4
	26.3	P721	PHYSICS	9.4
	26.4	M639	MATHEMATICS	25.2
	. . .			

Figure 2.3. Index sequential file. Records are grouped into physical blocks, sorted by course number. A separate file indexes the first record of each block. Overflow areas are used to insert new records in sequence, with pointers indicating chain of insertion.

tion available, rather than being out of date until the next batch update is processed. Searching for a given record will be fast if the search is on a primary key, faster than a sequential file because the index will reduce the number of disk accesses required to get to the correct record. The speed is improved even when overflow records are accessed, unless the ratio of overflow records becomes excessive. Of course, it will be necessary to reorganize the file at intervals depending on the modification activity. This reorganization process will be more difficult than in the sequential file, requiring revision of the index as well as rewriting the basic file itself.

Since the index sequential structure seems to represent a nearly ideal balance between update efficiency and access speed, it is very widely used in large computer file systems. ISAM, an acronym for Index Sequential Access Method is the work-horse of many database systems written for the IBM 370 series of computers. Other large computers have similar index sequential file types. Personal computers do not commonly offer this capability at present, but this situation may change as larger disk storage becomes available.

2.5.4 Indexed

The major difference between the index sequential file and the sequential file is the creation of a separate index, used to speed searches of a file. Once we have started down this path, it is natural to consider other options involving indexing.

An index to a file is valuable only if the key used for indexing is the one that the user needs in a particular application. However, it often is desirable to search a file in more than one way. A mailing list file, for example, may require creating a list that is alphabetical by name, but mailing labels that are sorted according to ZIP code. The need to sort files in more than one way often leads to long computer runs in which a secondary file is sorted according to a *secondary key* (or keys). It has been estimated that sorting occupies at least 25 percent of computer time in large data-processing shops. Computational costs could be reduced if means were found to generate alternate indexes for given files. The indexed file is one such alternative.

The indexed file differs from index sequential in that the basic file need not be sorted in any way. This change means that updates to the main file can be made more rapidly, with no need to use overflow blocks. To make up for this deficiency, one, two, or more indexes are created, one for each key likely to be used in access-ing the file. Since an index record consists only of the key and a pointer to the main file, these files are smaller, easier to update, and faster to search. Further-more, having multiple indexes means that several user viewpoints can be accommo-dated by the same file structure. Figure 2.4 illustrates use of separate indexes to access an address list.

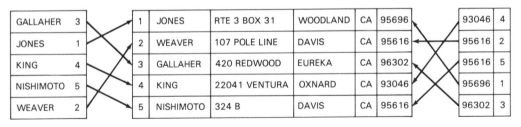

Figure 2.4. Indexed file, indexed by name and ZIP code. Master file is not kept in any specific order.

Since an index is in fact a sorted sequential file pointing to another main data file, it is sometimes called an "inverted file" because it is an inversion of the main file. Inverted files are very efficient tools for searching according to multiple keys. They do require maintenance, however, and the maintenance grows as new keys are added. For this reason, indexed file structures are not used for files that change dynamically on a frequent basis. Instead, they are used when files are more or less static and require multiple key access. An indexed file structure is also efficient for dynamic files in which only nonkey attributes change.

Indexed files, using our strict definition, are not as common as index sequential files. In a personal computer environment, however, the notion of two or more small index files to larger data files is attractive, especially since disk accesses to floppy disks are very slow compared to memory access. Hence, many personal computer DBMSs use this file structure.

Performance of indexed files is comparable to index sequential files in accessing a given record according to the primary key, slightly slower in accessing the next record according to that key (since records are no longer stored in order), but a great deal faster than any method previously described in accessing records according to other keys for which indexes exist. Update is a bit slower than for index sequential files, since more than one index must be updated. On the other hand, manipulation of the main file is easier, since new records can be appended to the end. Deletions can be handled in several ways, such as flagging a record as deleted, without requiring reorganization of the file.

Up to this point, we have not discussed the manner in which an indexed file is created. In fact, we have tacitly assumed that the file is a simple linear set of records with only the index and the pointer available, into which a new entry must be inserted by moving down all subsequent entries. There are other alternatives to this approach, and we will consider them in a separate section.

2.5.5 Multiring Files

So far, we have described two methods for indexing files using external index methods. There is, however, another alternative that can be used even if more than one index is used. Suppose we wished to index a file according to two attributes, each of which is a set of choices, such as job classification or city of residence. We assume that for each job or city there will be multiple occurrences in our data file, and that the total number of job types and cities is not large. One way to index such a file is to create a very small index file for job types and a second one for cities. For each job, we find the first record of an individual who has that job classification, and point to that record from the index. We do the same for each city, so that we now have two files with a single pointer in each to the first occurrence of each unique set member.

In the file itself, we add two new fields, one pointing to the next individual with the same job classification, the other pointing to the next record with the same city. We store these entries in sorted order by primary key at update time by breaking the chain in the appropriate location and inserting the new record pointer. The last record in our "linked list" points back to the first entry, so in effect this structure consists of two "rings." If two or more keys are indexed in this manner, we have a multiring structure, which is the origin of the name for this file type. Figure 2.5 illustrates a file organized in this manner. Notice that the records do not need to be stored in any particular order, but that insertion in each ring, or linked list, is according to a primary key, in this case the name of the employee.

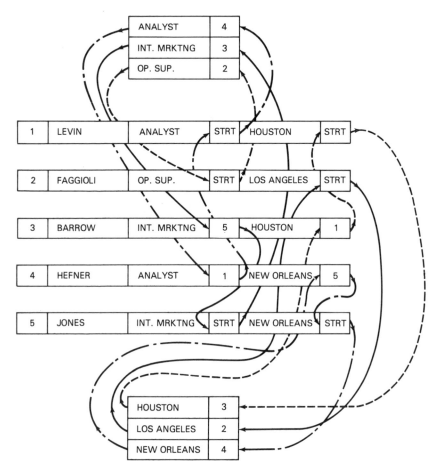

Figure 2.5. Multiring file, indexed on jobs and cities.

The multiring structure sounds complex, and it is indeed somewhat compli-cated to create this structure from scratch. However, once such a file is created, maintenance is roughly comparable to that of indexed files, and the index file itself is a great deal smaller, because no secondary indexes are required. This latter feature is attractive for personal computers, in which main memory is limited.

Searching for first occurrence of multiple keys is very fast in the multiring structure. Searching for all entries matching multiple key requests is usually slower than for indexed files. Reorganization of the file (for example, adding a new key) is an extremely complicated process requiring major modification of the basic file.

2.5.6 Hashed Files

Next, we consider two techniques that can be used to index files in ways that offer major increases in efficiency over the standard binary searching methods. The first of these is "hashing," which is a method for calculating the address of a record based on the primary key. In this method, the primary key is not used directly.

Instead, an address for a group of records is generated from the key, and the search then examines that group to find the correct record. The groups are called "buckets," and each bucket contains several records. When a bucket is filled, overflow areas are used and the search continues in the overflow area much like an indexed sequential file. The physical size of buckets selected for this file structure is usually closely related to the block size available on that system.

Hashing has some very important advantages over other methods. First, no index is maintained at all. Instead, the index is calculated each time a search or update is requested. This approach means that valuable storage space is not wasted, and it also means that searching an index file for a pointer is not required. Although the bucket contains several records, searching a single bucket is usually a fairly rapid process, so overall retrieval time is rapid. Updating is fast, much faster than for indexed or multiring files, because no separate index is maintained.

Although hashing is a very powerful technique, it requires adaptation to each situation. Since hashing depends on calculating addresses for buckets in which groups of data are to be stored, effective use of this technique requires (a) a thorough knowledge of the likely distribution of the primary key in order to generate a hashing function that spreads data more or less evenly; and (b) understanding of the physical medium on which the data will be stored, so that the number and size of buckets is reasonable. Inappropriate hashing functions can seriously degrade performance. A hash function that works well for one set of data may be ineffective for another.

One hashing function that is widely used in DBMSs is the Soundex code, used to store names in situations where spelling errors may cause problems in retrieving the correct name. The Soundex hash function is based on phonetics in English and on distributions of letters in common surnames for the United States. The Soundex code is created as follows:

1. The first letter of the last name is retained.
2. A three- (or four-) digit number is calculated and appended to that letter to give the complete function. The rules used are as follows:
   a. Letters in the name are considered from left to right. Numbers are assigned to each letter. The values are:
      1 if B,F,P, or V
      2 if C,G,J,K,Q,S,X, or Z
      3 if D or T
      4 if L
      5 if M or N
      6 if R
      vowels, H,W, and Y are ignored

   b. If two letters with the same value are next to each other, the second and subsequent duplicates are ignored.
   c. If insufficient numbers are calculated, the number is padded with zeros to the total length. If more numbers are calculated, the number is truncated.

Using this technique, the name Walters would generate a Soundex code of W436 (W4362 if four digits are used). Then, a file is created in which each bucket (usually the size of a buffer block) has an address associated with one (or perhaps a group) of the hashed functions. If 3 digits were used, and each combination was assigned to a unique bucket, there would be 26,000 buckets (1,000 for each letter of the alphabet). In addition, overflow buckets are created in much the same manner as index sequential overflow areas when one bucket becomes filled.

The Soundex function works well for very large collections of names. A major hospital, for example, stores all names of all patients seen in the last twenty years in a Soundex file. Over a million names are in the file, yet access of specific names can be made in a fraction of a second once the name has been typed in. The function was developed so that names that sound alike would be placed in adjoining buckets, even if there were spelling differences. The technique works very well for Western names, although the system has obvious difficulties with many oriental names. Figure 2.6 illustrates a partial hashed file. Retrieval programs could access adjacent blocks to locate individuals whose names sound alike.

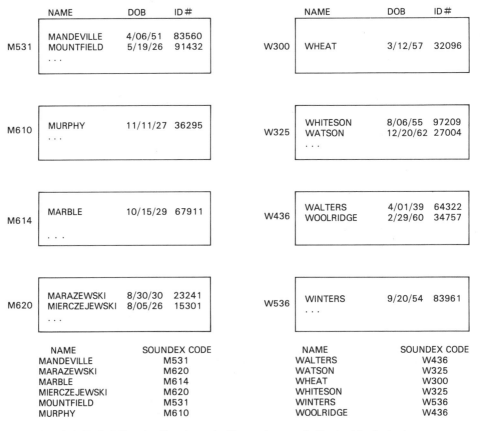

NAME	DOB	ID #
M531	MANDEVILLE 4/06/51 83560	
	MOUNTFIELD 5/19/26 91432	
	. . .	

NAME	DOB	ID #
W300	WHEAT	3/12/57 32096

NAME	DOB	ID #
M610	MURPHY 11/11/27 36295	
	. . .	

NAME	DOB	ID #
W325	WHITESON 8/06/55 97209	
	WATSON 12/20/62 27004	
	. . .	

NAME	DOB	ID #
M614	MARBLE 10/15/29 67911	
	. . .	

NAME	DOB	ID #
W436	WALTERS 4/01/39 64322	
	WOOLRIDGE 2/29/60 34757	

NAME	DOB	ID #
M620	MARAZEWSKI 8/30/30 23241	
	MIERCZEJEWSKI 8/05/26 15301	
	. . .	

NAME	DOB	ID #
W536	WINTERS 9/20/54 83961	
	. . .	

NAME	SOUNDEX CODE	NAME	SOUNDEX CODE
MANDEVILLE	M531	WALTERS	W436
MARAZEWSKI	M620	WATSON	W325
MARBLE	M614	WHEAT	W300
MIERCZEJEWSKI	M620	WHITESON	W325
MOUNTFIELD	M531	WINTERS	W536
MURPHY	M610	WOOLRIDGE	W436

Figure 2.6. Hashed file using Soundex code. Names that sound alike tend to cluster in same or adjacent "buckets" (physical blocks whose address is linked to the hashed Soundex function).

Hashing functions work very well with direct access by a single key. They are not at all suited to "get next" functions, since the next key is unknown to the system. Updates are efficient, but if the distribution created by the function is not appropriate for the data, overflow areas and crowded buckets may be present in some places while other buckets remain virtually empty. Reorganization is usually done only when the physical medium is no longer large enough to accommodate the file or when serious distribution problems are encountered.

Since the technique of hashing is sensitive to the nature of the data being indexed, it is not used in general-purpose DBMS packages. The value of this approach in certain files may warrant writing a special hashing function for that application. Due to its lack of generalizability, hashing often is not available without special programming on personal computers.

2.5.7 Balanced Trees (B-Trees)

In the previous section, we considered hashing as a special technique that works extremely well for accessing large data files, provided that the hashing algorithm is suited to the data. There is another technique that is more flexible, requiring no foreknowledge of the keys (except perhaps their maximum length). This technique, as many of the concepts in this chapter, did not really take hold until the mid-1970s, although the first papers on the subject appeared late in the 1960s.

Earlier in this chapter, we noted that many collections of data lend themselves to organization according to a hierarchy. Figure 2.7 illustrates a typical hierarchical structure listing the academic units in a hypothetical university. Notice that there are several layers in this structure, that the number of descendants from any node may be none, one, or more. Due to this structure, the depth may vary from one category to another (there are no "Divisions" in the College of Liberal Arts, for example). A key that is based on a hierarchy is different from a normal "subscript" as we think of it in many programming languages. Subscripted arrays require reserving a position for each possible integer value of the subscript within a given range. Hierarchies don't fit this classification. They tend to have gaps, to include indexes at several levels, and to cover ranges of keys that may extend not only beyond normal integer ranges, but even to include non-integer information, including alphabetic keys.

We also introduced the notion of pointers, where a value might serve as a pointer to another file. Putting together the concept of hierarchies and pointers leads to the concept of a treelike set of keys, each pointing to a data value in some other location. The idea of a "tree," then, is an important departure from the notion of a linear file of indexes and pointers. Trees enable us to express information at great depth in one field without requiring the same depth of indexing in another.

There is one more notion that will further help in the use of a tree type of structure. Branches on one part of a tree often will have more elements than another, as shown in Fig. 2.7. Ideally, however, a disk file based on a tree structure should be designed so that the total number of disk accesses will not exceed a uni-

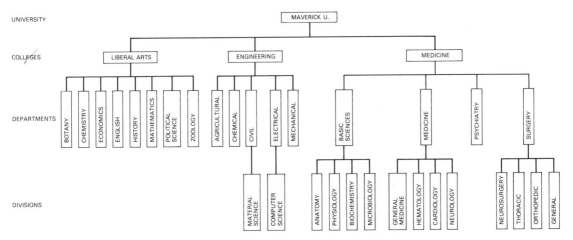

Figure 2.7. An example of the Hierarchical file structure describing academic departments on a campus.

form maximum for the entire file. This goal can be accomplished if the tree is "balanced" so that no single branch is longer (deeper) than any other.

The principal characteristics of a balanced tree (B-tree) file structure are as follows:

1. A tree is defined to be of order n, meaning that a given block in the tree can have at most n keys.

2. Every block, except possibly the root, has at least $n/2$ keys.

3. Every block with m keys has $m+1$ descendants. A pointer within the tree identifies each block at the next lower level.

4. Every path down a tree is of the same maximum depth. Although a key may be found higher in the tree, the worst cases (those at the bottom of the tree) all require the same number of block accesses.

5. Every key also points to a data block containing the record identified by that key. (This definition refers to a specific type of tree called a B+tree, one of the most common forms in use today.)

In most B-tree implementations, two further refinements are introduced. The data elements are stored in blocks separate from the tree itself, and each key points to the start of the data block in which that information resides. The second refinement in this structure is to have forward pointers in the data blocks, so that the next element in a database can be retrieved without the necessity of retraversing the tree. This structure is illustrated in Fig. 2.8.

B-trees behave in interesting ways. They grow and shrink in accordance with the size of the file, always maintaining a balanced structure. To illustrate, we will take an example and show how each new entry in the key structure is accommodated. For this example, we will assume that there can be only four keys in a block (the actual number is usually much larger), and that the actual data is in blocks pointed to by the various keys. Consider first the creation of this type of tree. We will add, one at a time, the following keys (selected at random):

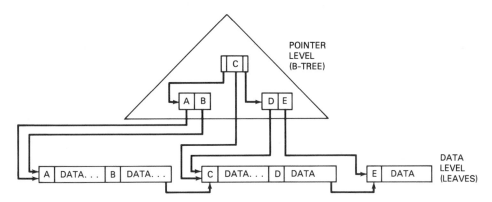

Figure 2.8. Generalized structure of a B+ tree.

N D W K B P R A X G O L V C E T Y U F Z O

Figure 2.9 illustrates the process of creating this file. As the first four keys are inserted, no structural change occurs, since all can be accommodated in one block. When the capacity of the first block is exceeded, however, the block is split, which occurs with the addition of the key B. The lefthand block retains the two lowest value keys (B and D), the newly created righthand block receives the highest key values (N and W), and a new pointer block is created with the middle value.

This principle is maintained throughout the growth of the tree. Notice that the tree grows upwards, and no new higher layer is added until it is required. Notice, too, that no block except the topmost in the tree can have less than 2 keys, since the maximum number is 4 and, according to rule 2, there must be at least $n/2$ keys in each block. Each pointer block, located above the bottom layer of the file, contains one more pointer than keys, for a maximum of five pointers in a block with four keys. When the tree is more or less filled, the lowest entry will be at the leftmost block on the bottom layer, and the pointer at the top will be somewhere near the middle of values for the entire tree.

With a tree constructed in this fashion, access to any element will not exceed the depth of the tree, which is balanced across all entries. In other words, a tree of this structure can access all records with the same degree of efficiency and with a guaranteed consistent worst case that is the same for all entries at the bottom of the tree.

This example illustrates insertion of randomly selected keys. At the end of the insertion process, the blocks are not all full, although one block at the base is completely filled (DEFG) and two others are missing only one entry. The overall efficiency of the final file can be expressed in the number of empty spaces in the blocks allocated to the file. Since there are nine blocks in all, each of which could contain four entries, and since fifteen entries are blank, the overall efficiency is 21/36, or 58 percent. If the entries had been inserted in order, using the same algorithm followed in this example, the maximum efficiency possible would be 50 percent, since each lefthand block would be half full and have no opportunity for subsequent insertions. One of the interesting areas of research using these files deals with finding better techniques for storage efficiency.

BALANCED TREE
INSERTION

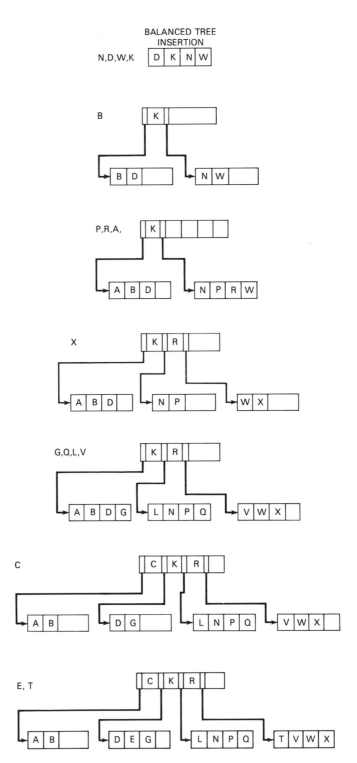

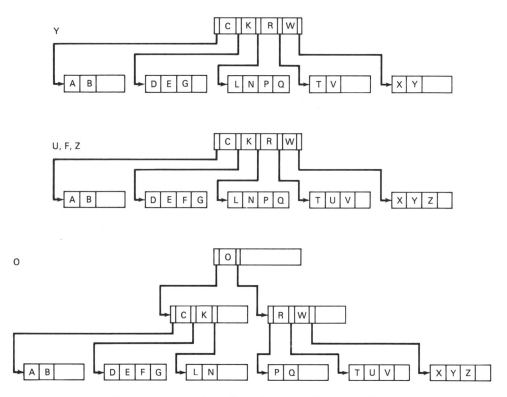

Figure 2.9. Balanced tree (B-tree) Insertion. See text for discussion.

Figure 2.10 illustrates the deletion process. In this example, the same set of keys is deleted, one at a time, in exactly the reverse order from the sequence used to create the structure. Deletion in a B-tree is much more complicated, since it is necessary to retain the balanced structure when "underflow" occurs — i.e., when a block must be deleted because there are too few values available. One paradoxical result is that the structure of the deletion sequence is different from that of the created set. In the first deletion, for example, the value adjacent to the deleted value O at the top of the tree (N) is moved to the top, and blocks lower down are adjusted by borrowing from adjacent blocks so as to retain a balance without pruning one level of the tree until necessary. This approach makes sense in that a file will tend to grow with time, and deleting an entry should not shrink the file structure if possible.

The remainder of Fig. 2.10 illustrates the continued deletion. Notice that the third level of the tree is not deleted until the fifth key (Y) is removed, and that the final three blocks prior to pruning the second index layer are quite different from the blocks created earlier.

Deleting keys from very large index files is sometimes quite complicated, requiring many disk accesses. Despite this drawback, however, B-trees are widely used in commercial DBMSs for personal computer, so it is useful to understand how they are constructed and maintained.

BALANCED TREE DELETION

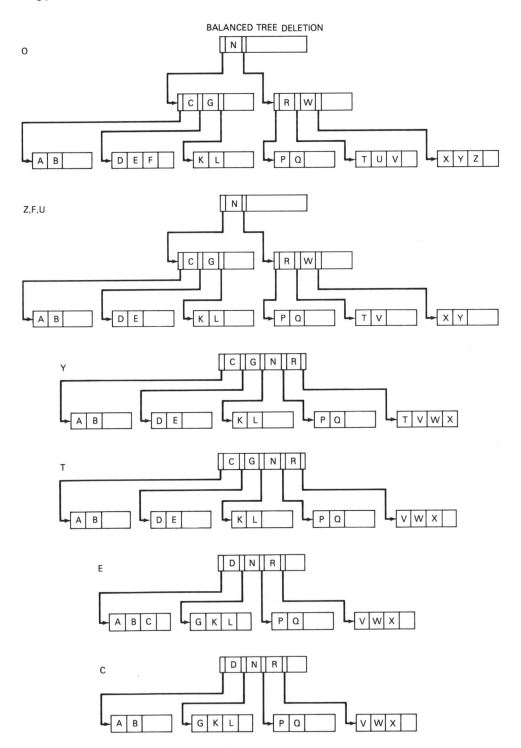

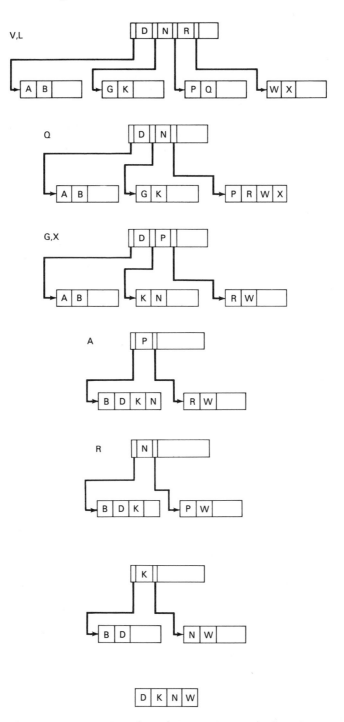

Figure 2.10. Balanced tree (B-tree) deletion. See text for discussion.

2.5.8 Summary of File Types

Table 2.2 summarizes the strengths and weaknesses of the various file types considered in this section.

Table 2.2 Performance Characteristics of File Types

Measure	Pile	Sequential	Index Seq.	Indexed	Multiring	Hashed	B-Tree
Storage efficiency	Poor	Best	Good	Medium	Medium	Medium	Medium
Get record on key	Poor	Medium	Good	Best	Medium	Good	Good
Get next on key	Poor	Best	Best	Good	Good	Poor	Medium
Get nonkey record	Poor	Medium	Medium	Medium	Medium	Medium	Medium
Get record multikey	Poor	Medium	Medium	Best	Good	Poor	Medium
Add new record	Good	Poor	Medium	Good	Good	Good	Medium
Modify record	Poor	Good	Good	Good	Medium	Good	Good
Delete record	Medium	Poor	Medium	Medium	Medium	Good	Medium
Process record	Poor	Good	Good	Good	Good	Good	Good
Read whole file	Medium	Good	Good	Good	Good	Poor	Medium
Reorganize	NA	Medium	Medium	Medium	Poor	Poor	Medium

The foregoing brief overview of file types describes the major types of files that are used in database systems. Some file types are more appropriate than others for personal computers. Others will become appropriate as personal computers are equipped with more main memory. Several DBMSs use combinations of the techniques in order to improve the efficiency of operation. To illustrate one important example used in many systems, Fig. 2.11 shows the use of two B-trees to provide separate indexes to a sequential file. This example shows that the indexed file could be implemented with B-trees for the indexing, and the original file could be maintained as a sequential file.

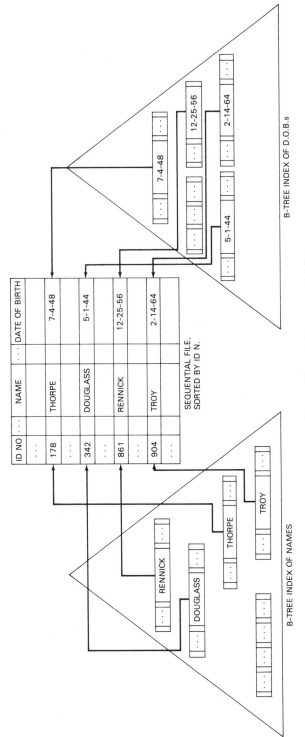

Figure 2.11. Use of B-tree files to index a sequential file.

2.6 USER VIEWPOINTS

Databases are usually created to serve the needs of one or more groups of users. If only one group is involved, the design can be tailored to the specific needs of that group. The collection of their needs in terms of data to be retrieved is sometimes called the *user viewpoint*. Understanding the nature of user viewpoints is a central problem in database design.

One of the key aspects of generalization in database design has to do with its intended use by groups with different viewpoints. A database often is created with only one purpose in mind. A payroll file is created to serve the financial requirements of an institution. Designing a system to meet a single set of needs of this type is much easier than trying to create a database that can meet all possible uses of the data. When multiple viewpoints are to be accommodated, it is no longer as easy to design a structure intended to meet the needs of each with equal efficiency. If a payroll file contains personnel information besides salary, managers may want to analyze that information in terms of length of employment, job distribution, employee assignment to projects, or other viewpoints not anticipated in the original design. Indexing techniques of the types and files designed using options referred to earlier may serve no useful purpose in answering these questions. Indexes will not be available for the (new) keys desired, and the new user may be forced to write special programs to obtain desired information.

The concept of providing for multiple viewpoints raises a problem with respect to system design. To what extent can a given system accommodate a new requested viewpoint? What are the options that make it easier to satisfy more than one viewpoint? What are the penalties in efficiency that result from trying to generalize a system in this direction? These are questions that form the basis of a great deal of research in DBMSs today.

We have already seen that certain file types are more flexible in their ability to accommodate multiple keys. However, given the underlying file types, it is still possible to construct DBMSs in several different conceptual frameworks. Some will be more successful than others in providing flexibility. The price associated with viewpoint flexibility often is decreased efficiency.

In the sections that follow, we will explore the different solutions that have been proposed for DBMS architecture. It is important to bear in mind the concept of user viewpoint in considering these models, since many of the tradeoffs associated with different choices can be best evaluated in this context.

2.7 STRUCTURAL MODELS FOR DATABASES

Structural models fall somewhere between file types and conceptual models (discussed in Section 2.8). They retain a close relation between the structure and the physical mapping of the data, but they permit consideration of the information at a higher level than file type alone. The models can be readily understood on the basis of some of the file types reviewed in previous sections.

Earlier in this chapter, we reviewed the file types that can be used in DBMSs.

Several different file types often will be used in a given database, since different sets of information require different types of processing.

In this section, we will begin to consider database design from a higher level, that of the general model used to structure the information. There are two principal structural models commonly accepted for use in DBMSs: the hierarchical and the network. We will consider each briefly, reviewing pros and cons of each approach.

2.7.1 Hierarchical

A hierarchical structure is most useful when a single viewpoint is to be represented. As we have seen, highly efficient file structures, such as the balanced tree, can readily accommodate hierarchical keys to create database systems that will have good response characteristics for searches based on that viewpoint.

A typical example of a data group that is well suited to hierarchical definition is a record system for patients in a doctor's office. The base key is the patient name or number, and this key forms the top level of the hierarchy. A second hierarchical level is the name of the clinical problem that the patient displays. The third level contains the date for each time that problem was treated; below this would come the tests, medications, physician's findings, plan for further treatment, and instructions to the patient. Table 2.3 and Fig. 2.12 illustrate this type of a database in tabular and graphic form. In order to simplify the illustration, outline headings are added to the table, and these headings are used in Fig. 2.12 to depict the data organization.

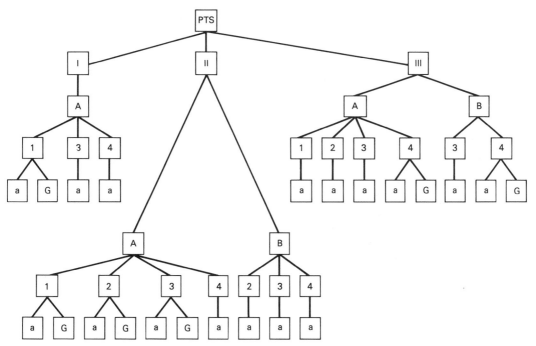

Figure 2.12. Hierarchical file, illustrating diagrammatically data presented in Table 2.3.

Table 2.3 Structure of Patient Data File (PT)

Basic Structure:
   I. Name:
.   A. Problem
.   .   1. Visit Date
.   .   .   a. Tests
.   .   .   .   1). (separate tests)
.   .   .   b. Medications
.   .   .   .   1). (separate medications)
.   .   .   c. Plan
.   .   .   .   1). (separate plans)
.   .   .   d. Patient Instructions
.   .   .   .   1). (separate instructions)

Using this structure, a typical patient database might look like this:

Data File:
   I. Davidson, Todd
      A. Blurred vision
         1. 6/8/85
            a. Tests
               1). tonometry
               2). CAT scan
            c. Plan
               1). rule out neurologic damage
            d. Patient Instructions
               1). rest, recreation
               2). reduce reading load

   II. Range, Jo
      A. infected puncture wound
         1. 9/2/84
            a. Tests
               1). culture exudate
               2). cbc
            b. Medications
               1). ampicillin
               2). cloxacillin
            c. Plan
               1). rule out bone infection
               2). lance and incise wound
            d. Patient Instructions
               1). return in 1 wk
         2. 9/9/84
            b. Medication
               1). ampicillin
            d. Patient Instructions
               1). call if problems

   III. Brian, Leslie
      A. sore knee
         1. 8/16/85
            a. Tests
               1). x-ray knee
            b. Medications
               1). aspirin

c. Plan
   1). obtain physical therapist consult
d. Patient Instruction
   1). rest, no active exercise
   2). whirlpool treatments
B. flu symptoms
  1. 11/12/85
    b. Medications
     1). tetracycline
    d. Patient Instructions
     1). rest
     2). drink fluids

The most important organizational feature of this data set is the unpredictable nature of values for keys. Patients may have few problems, or they may have many. Dates of visits are few and far between. Tests conducted on a patient are specific to the problem and hence variable in type and frequency. The structure is in every sense hierarchical, and a file that is organized conceptually in that form will serve many needs of the doctor's office. In fact, it would be difficult to organize this type of data in a table or matrix. A single table structure would not be suitable for this type of data, since there would inevitably be many fields that are empty for some patients, and the storage efficiency would suffer accordingly. It might be possible, however, to create multiple tables as shown in a later design.

Using a hierarchical file, it will be possible to retrieve any information about a particular patient. Since this is the orientation of the doctor's office, it will serve his or her needs well in this regard. Less frequently asked questions, such as finding all patients who received prescriptions for a particular medication, would require more time, but since this request is less common, the overall cost benefits are favorable.

One point should be made about hierarchical files. Even though a DBMS is organized according to one hierarchical structure, it is still possible, within the hierarchical system, to have an independent hierarchical classification according to a secondary key. Figure 2.11 illustrates this concept. It is not therefore strictly true to say that hierarchical databases only reflect one user viewpoint. However, it is true that searches according to secondary keys will be slower, requiring more accesses to disk.

2.7.2 Networks

For many years, database operations on large computers have relied to a large extent on a database methodology defined by a group called the Conference on Data Systems Languages (CODASYL). This group, which got its start twenty-five years ago, had as its goal the definition of a common Data Description Language (DDL) and in promoting standardization in the definition and support of database systems. In 1967, the Data Base Task Group (DBTG) was formed, extending the work of earlier committees formed under CODASYL. Some of the tasks agreed to were to define more precisely the Data Description Language and its companion, the Data Manipulation Language. This effort was closely related to the evolution of COBOL, the language used most frequently in large mainframe DBMS packages.

Due to this background, DDL is acknowledged to be one of the major models for database systems. It is widely used and widely supported by manufacturers and language standard committees. Although DDL recognizes the possibility of sequential and hierarchical file types, the greatest emphasis is on a network structure. However, DDL incorporates many additional specifications that are more explicit in defining relationships and requirements of this structure. In this review, we will cover only a few basic characteristics. The full description of DDL can be found in the references cited at the end of this chapter.

One of the major differences between networks and hierarchies is that networks permit representation of a "many-to-many" interconnection between data elements, whereas a hierarchy implies a "one-to-many" structure. DDL defines the basic membership in sets as consisting of one "owner" and one or more "members." The many-to-many structure is accomplished by permitting different "owners" to point to the same member records.

To illustrate the network concept, consider a database that contains information about college students enrolled in classes. The information can be considered from the viewpoint of the student, who would like to know which classes he or she is enrolled in, the units he or she will receive and, when complete, the grade assigned for work done. The department represents another viewpoint, with a primary interest in knowing which students and how many students have enrolled for each course. There are many other items that could be included (see Chapter 4 for an expanded description of this database), but this set of items serves to illustrate the network structure.

The network concept is usually illustrated using a multiring structure, as defined previously. Each viewpoint serves to define a ring with pointers through the data records. Since we have two viewpoints, we will require two sets of rings to define our file. In network terminology, the relationship between a viewpoint and the linked list identifying each subgroup in the database is referred to as a *Set*, with an *Owner* and one or more *Members*. This database will contain four different types of records: one defining each department; a second identifying the courses taught by that department; a third listing students and their ID numbers; and the final record type containing the grades assigned to each student.

The formal definition of a relationship of this type is expressed in Table 2.4. This example, based on DDL as defined by CODASYL, illustrates several concepts about data types and specifications described earlier.

The syntax of this schema, or definition, approximates that of the CODASYL Data Definition Language (DDL). It begins with a name (line 1). Lines 3 through 29 define the four record types used in the database. Lines 4 and 5 stipulate that there cannot be two departments with the same name. Similar restrictions apply to course number, student IDNO, and to the combination key of student number and course number in the student-course record type. The data type and size of each element are also defined (e.g., lines 6, 12, and 13).

Once individual records have been defined, they are linked using the SET descriptors, as shown in lines 31 through 53. For each set, an Owner record must

Table 2.4 Schema for Departments, Courses and Students

```
 1 SCHEMA NAME IS COURSES-AND-STUDENTS.
 2
 3 RECORD NAME IS DEPARTMENT;
 4    DUPLICATES ARE NOT ALLOWED
 5         FOR DEPT IN DEPARTMENT.
 6         DEPT     ;TYPE IS CHARACTER 15.
 7
 8 RECORD NAME IS COURSE;
 9    DUPLICATES ARE NOT ALLOWED
10         FOR COURSE-NO IN COURSE.
11         COURSE-NO    ;TYPE IS CHARACTER 6.
12         DEPARTMENT     ;TYPE IS CHARACTER 15.
13         UNITS   ;TYPE IS FIXED DECIMAL 1.
14
15
16 RECORD NAME IS STUDENT;
17    DUPLICATES ARE NOT ALLOWED
18         FOR IDNO IN STUDENT.
19         NAME   ;TYPE IS CHARACTER 15.
20         IDNO     ;TYPE IS FIXED DECIMAL 5.
21
22 RECORD NAME IS STUDENT-COURSE;
23    DUPLICATES ARE NOT ALLOWED
24         FOR IDNO IN STUDENT-COURSE,
25         CRNO IN STUDENT-COURSE.
26         IDNO     ;TYPE IS FIXED DECIMAL 5.
27         CRNO    ;TYPE IS CHARACTER 6.
28         QTR   ;TYPE IS CHARACTER 3.
29         GRADE  ;TYPE IS CHARACTER 1.
30
31 SET NAME IS DEPT-COURSE;
32    OWNER IS DEPARTMENT
33    ORDER IS SORTED BY DEFINED KEYS
34         DUPLICATES ARE NOT ALLOWED.
35    MEMBER IS COURSE;
36         KEY IS ASCENDING COURSE IN COURSE;
37         SET SELECTION IS BY VALUE OF COURSE-NO IN COURSE.
38
39 SET NAME IS COURSE-GRADE;
40    OWNER IS COURSE;
41    ORDER IS SORTED BY DEFINED KEYS
42         DUPLICATES ARE NOT ALLOWED.
43    MEMBER IS STUDENT-COURSE;
44         KEY IS ASCENDING CRNO IN STUDENT-COURSE;
45         SET SELECTION IS BY VALUE OF CRNO IN STUDENT-COURSE.
46
47 SET NAME IS STUDENT-GRADE;
48    OWNER IS STUDENT;
49    ORDER IS SORTED BY DEFINED KEYS
50         DUPLICATES ARE NOT ALLOWED.
51    MEMBER IS STUDENT-COURSE;
52         KEY IS ASCENDING IDNO IN STUDENT-COURSE;
53         SELECTION IS BY VALUE OF IDNO IN STUDENT-COURSE.
```

be defined. In addition, the order in which they are to be sorted is specified; lines 33 and 34 state that the primary key of the Department record is to be used as the key for sorting the sets. In our case, the Department record contains only that data element, but in cases where several data elements exist, other keys can be selected.

In addition to defining the Owner, the Member records must be defined, and once again the sorting key is defined. Line 36 defines the sorting key, and line 37 indicates the field that is to be used in creating the linked list for this set.

The same process is repeated for the other two sets, Course-Grade and Student-Grade. With these definitions, the schema is complete and the CODASYL network structure specified.

Figure 2.13 illustrates a portion of a database following the foregoing structure. Notice that each record type consists of one line on the diagram, and each SET is illustrated by multiring links between these records. Notice, too, that a given record type such as Student-Course can have more than one owner, with different links defined as in Fig. 2.13 and in Table 2.3.

A network file of this type is more responsive to multiple viewpoints than a hierarchy, because of the multiple owners permitted for given records. However, at the physical level, the actual structure used to store the necessary information may be any of several different types, including multiring and even B-tree. What is crucial is that the user can phrase questions from multiple viewpoints and still access the desired information.

Actual support of the network model is sometimes quite complex, requiring, on large mainframe computers, intimate knowledge of the high-level implementation language (usually COBOL) and, in addition, operating system interfaces and many calls to lower-level subroutines are used to complete the conceptual-to-physical links. Personal computer systems have for the most part avoided this overall structure, preferring to have more user-friendly interfaces to the database. Since there will probably be no data-processing professional available to maintain a personal computer database system, it is important to minimize the training required for the personal computer owner to use a DBMS.

2.8 CONCEPTUAL MODELS FOR DATABASES

The structural models described in the previous section can be closely related to file types discussed earlier. The hierarchical model maps nicely into a B-tree type of structure, whereas the network model is usually implemented using the multiring file. In this section, we will consider database organization from a slightly higher level, in which the type of file to be used is not defined or even implied by the model. These models could be implemented in several ways, and in Chapter 4 we will see that several different file types are used to provide the physical implementation of the conceptual model.

If execution efficiency were no problem, the ideal solution for creation of a database would be to provide for any viewpoint of the data that is consistent with the data stored. Research in this field led to publication of several key papers that provided partial solutions to this utopian goal. These papers discussed the concepts

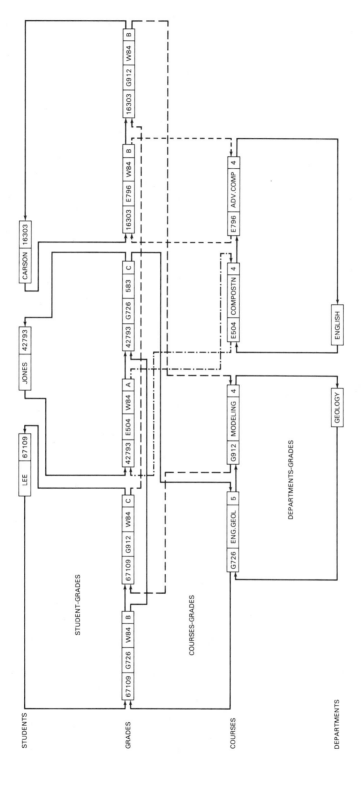

Figure 2.13. Network database structure, showing departments, courses, students, and grades. Viewpoints are departments, courses, and students.

of data definition and storage in a far more general manner than earlier works, and for this reason they are treated in a separate section of this chapter.

2.8.1 Relational Model

One of the chief problems that researchers have wrestled with in databases is the representation of information in a way that is independent of any specific viewpoint. If it is possible to do so, the data can be used in more flexible ways, and the user may be able to do so with less programmer expertise.

In 1970, E. F. Codd of IBM wrote a paper that has since been acknowledged to be a milestone in database systems research. In it, he proposed a radically new model for data storage, and called it the relational model. There were two prime motives that led to this model. The first was to create a system that made data storage independent of any specific user viewpoint, and the second was to find a way to define databases so that they could be treated using formal mathematical methods. We will not consider the latter aspect of relational models in this text, although we will refer to some of the indirect results of his work in this regard.

The cornerstone of the relational approach is the use of tables to represent data. Each table is called a *relation*, and there can be several relations in a given database. Each table or relation is given a name and must follow certain conventions. Records in this database are in the form of rows within these tables. The rows are called *tuples* (pronounced to rhyme with couple). There can be no two identical tuples in a given relation. The sequence of tuples in a table is not important. Tuples consist of sets of data called *attributes*, arranged as columns in the relation. The sequence of attributes is not important, but once it has been established, all tuples must appear in that sequence. In general, the primary key (or keys, if more than one attribute is used) will appear first in the relation.

To illustrate the relational model, let us consider the data used in the network example cited earlier. Figure 2.14 illustrates the way in which these elements would be organized using the relational model structure. Several rules were added to the relational model to eliminate problems that might arise in inserting, updating or deleting records stored in this format. These guidelines, called "normalization rules," are:

1. There can be no duplicate tuples.
2. There can be no tuples with the primary key missing.
3. The attributes in a relation must depend on the primary key.
4. There can be no multiple elements in a single tuple attribute.
5. The nonkey attributes must be independent of each other.

The first three rules are easy to understand. Rule 4 may require explanation. Consider a relation dealing with presidential elections. It would be natural in the Electoral College system to have a column for the winner and another for the loser. However, in 1968, both Humphrey and Wallace received electoral votes, hence they would both have to be placed in the "loser" column. This situation would cause problems in searching for the names of losers. Rule 4 eliminates the possibility of such a problem.

RELATIONS

STUDENTS

ID#	NAME	OTHER ATTRIBUTES
16303	Carson, Jerome	. . .
42793	Jones, Theresa	. . .
67109	Lee, Stephen	. . .

Primary Key   Attributes

COURSES

COURSE NO	DEPT	UNITS	TITLE	OTHER ATTRIB.
E504	ENGLISH	4	COMPOSITION	. . .
E796	ENGLISH	4	ADV. COMP	. . .
G726	GEOLOGY	5	ENGIN. GEOL	. . .
G912	GEOLOGY	4	THEOR. MODELS	. . .

Primary Key

STUDENT-COURSES

ID#	COURSE NO	QTR TAKEN	GRADE
16303	E796	W84	B
16303	G912	W84	B
42793	E504	S84	C
42793	G726	S84	A
67109	G726	F83	B
67109	G912	W84	C

Primary Key   Attributes

Figure 2.14. Relational model representation of data shown in Fig. 2.13.

Rule 5 is also best defined through an example. Suppose we had a demographic file that includes the date of birth and also city and country in which the individual was born. All of these items are dependent on the primary key. In some areas of Europe, however, cities have been a part of many different nations during their existence. If the file is supposed to represent the current status of the city (which might be the case if one were to write for a copy of a birth certificate), the file might contain several different countries for a given city, and updating would be complex.

Without these rules, important information could be lost or the file could become inconsistent. One potential difficulty in applying these rules is that rules 3 and 5 require human judgment (i.e., unless the dependencies between different data elements are explicitly defined, they cannot be reduced to computer programs for verification). However, in general, data can be subdivided into appropriate relations without too much difficulty.

There are some additional observations that can be made with respect to the relational model. As noted above, the sequence of tuples is not necessarily in any order. To state it another way, there is no indexing defined in the relational model. Indexes are considered to lie a level below the conceptual relations. Since no indexes are present, and since no fixed hierarchical structure is required, no specific user viewpoint is addressed, and questions can be asked from any viewpoint with equal retrieval performance.

The user interface in relational models is one of its most attractive features. Since viewpoints are not predetermined, the user can formulate a request using techniques that are designed to make the process as easy as possible. Sometimes, in fact, current literature about database systems refers to "relational" systems whose main claim to that term is their ease and flexibility of data retrieval. True relational models must fit some very specific retrieval functional capabilities, and most relational systems do not meet all these criteria.

Codd's original paper described a new approach to formal definition of the retrieval process from relational models. This approach was called *relational algebra* and was based on an extension of set theory. Figure 2.15 illustrates in graphic form the operators available in this language. Union, Intersection, and Difference are terms taken from set theory. Division in this context involves finding tuples in one relation in which one attribute matches a (limiting) specification. A product of two relations (sometimes called a *Cartesian product*) is the complete set of permutations of tuples contained in each relation. Codd also proposed the terms *Select*, *Project*, and *Join* to describe ways of retrieving different types of data from relations.

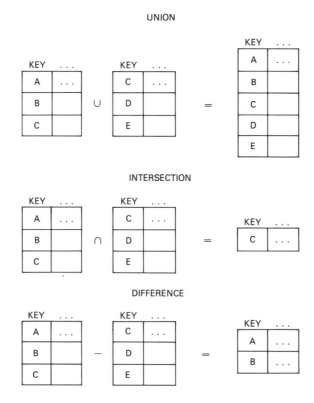

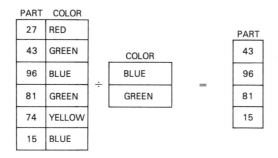

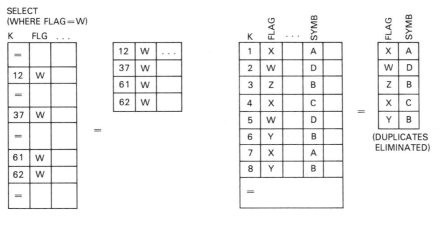

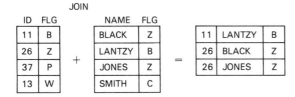

Figure 2.15. Examples of operations in relational algebra language.

The relational algebra operators illustrated in Fig. 2.15 can be modified by various conditions, and together they offer a reasonably complete language for retrieving data from the relational model. The most common retrieval operations from databases involve combinations of select, join and project with various conditions associated with each. Figure 2.16 illustrates the use of these operators on the database described in Fig. 2.14.

OPERATIONS ON RELATIONS

a. 'SELECT' operation on COURSES
   WHERE DEPT = ''ENGLISH''

COURSENO	DEPT	UNITS	TITLE	OTHER ATTRIB.
E504	ENGLISH	4	COMPOSITION	. . .
E796	ENGLISH	4	ADV. COMP	. . .

b. 'JOIN' operation on STUDENTS and STUDENT-COURSES

ID#	NAME	OTHER ATTRIB.	COURSE	QTR TAKEN	GRADE
16303	Carson, Jerome	. . .	E796	W84	B
16303	Carson, Jerome	. . .	G912	W84	B
42793	Jones, Theresa	. . .	E504	S84	C
42793	Jones, Theresa	. . .	G726	S84	B
67109	Lee, Stephen	. . .	G726	F83	B
67109	Lee, Stephen	. . .	G912	W84	C

Data from: both ⏝ Students   ⏝ Courses

c. 'PROJECTION' operation on COURSES:
   DISPLAY COURSENO, UNITS, TITLE

COURSENO	UNITS	TITLE	
E504	4	COMPOSITION	
E796	4	ADV. COMP	(some attributes
G726	5	ENGINEERING GEOLOGY	not retrieved)
G912	4	THEORETICAL MODELS	

Figure 2.16. Relational operations: examples of operations on data shown in Fig. 2.14.

The actual languages used in commercial relational DBMSs are more user-friendly than the pure relational algebra languages. Two main sets of languages have evolved, mapping oriented languages and graphic languages, based on use of CRT terminals to present information in table form. SQL is an example of a mapping oriented language that uses an algebraic-type notation. A typical SQL command line to retrieve all students who received an "A" grade might be

```
SELECT NAME FROM STUDENTS
     WHERE IDNO =
     SELECT IDNO FROM STUDENT-COURSE
        WHERE GRADE = ``A''
```

An example of a graphic language is "Query By Example," an approach that creates a table and allows the user to type "examples" that will be used to define but not limit the search.

Since relational systems are easier to use than many earlier DBMSs, they have become very popular with end users, who would like to have the benefits of database systems without the headaches of learning all about computers, operating systems, or control languages. In the personal computer world, the need for systems that can be used with minimal training has led to development of many database systems that offer aids to the untrained users. The fact that a system has these features does not, however, assure that the underlying system is relational. In fact, because the term *relational* has positive connotations in database environments, it has been used to describe systems whose adherence to the model is minimal.

Although relational models are attractive in terms of user simplicity and independence from predefined viewpoints, they are not designed to solve questions of efficiency in execution. These questions relate to the implementation level, which is not addressed by the relational model. In practice, the implementor of a relational system must face these issues, and over the past decade this subject has been the focus of a major research effort. Much remains to be done, however, and the personal computer user will need to pay close attention to the potential performance characteristics of any relational system to see if it will meet desired performance expectations. For example, most relational model implementations offer indexing as an option to improve access to attributes, and the indexing is usually available for any user-selected attribute.

2.8.2 Entity-Relationship Model

Since the appearance of the relational model, several alternative types of models have been proposed. One of these, the *entity-relationship model*, contains a new concept that may prove to be an important extension of the relational model.

To introduce the key difference between entity-relationship and relational models, let us consider how to store the following two different types of data:

1. A database that describes illnesses, their causes, and the association of multiple causes with known cases as well as the fatality experience for each illness caused by a known factor.
2. A genealogical database, in which it is necessary to record multiple types of family relations between different names in a genealogical tree.

In the first case, we could create a relation associating diseases with causes, and then add attribute columns that contain data on the importance and mortality of those causes. However, we are really dealing with information that is associated both with the illness and a specific cause. This dilemma must be glossed over in the relational model, with the result that certain attributes are dependent on an association between two members of a key rather than being true attributes of known entities.

In the second example, a similar situation arises, since identification of a relationship between two names (father, sister, etc.) depends on both persons, and in a specific sequence (Ralph is the father of Carl; Carl is the brother of Robert). Once again, although relations could be defined, there would be some difficulties in describing these types of associations.

The entity-relationship model expands the concept of relational tables to include (a) entity relations, and (b) relation relations. The semantic benefits come from explicitly stating that, in a relationship relation, there is a functional dependency on two (or more) entities. By defining this semantic dependence, it is possible to avoid many ambiguities resulting from trying to classify information of the type listed above. If we consider the difference between the relational model and the entity relational model from a language viewpoint, we see that the relational model permits description of entities much as adjectives do in a language, whereas the entity relation model makes it possible to convey the meaning of both adjectives (for entities) and adverbs (for relations).

Figures 2.17 and 2.18 illustrate one form of describing the examples of illness and genealogy cited above, using the entity relationship model. Two types of relations are included in the model, one which, like the relational model, describes entities, and a second which describes relationships. From these figures we see that relationships can also have attributes, and that these attributes can be properly associated with the entities they link. Some relationships require no special attributes. More often, however, the list of relationship attributes may form an important part of a database.

Another way of presenting visually the information in an entity relationship model is by use of diagrams as shown in Fig. 2.19. The two examples, Figs. 2.17 and 2.18, are illustrated in the conventions used for entity relationship systems. Rectangles represent entity relations; diamonds represent relationship relations. The letters m - n on these lines indicate whether a relationship could be many to many. In the illness example, one disease may have many causes, and one factor could cause more than one disease (although in some cases there may be a one-to-one relation). Similarly in the genealogical example, a father may have more than one child, an individual more than one sibling, although one-to-one relations (husband) may also exist. Some relationships, such as supervisor-employees, are 1 to many, in which cases the lines connecting entities with relations would be labeled 1 and n.

The entity-relationship model permits operations similar to those of the relational model. This aspect of the model was not expanded as fully in the original paper by Chen in 1976. In this paper, Chen showed that this concept presented a unifying view, placing in a coherent framework both the network and relational models, and he described ways of mapping information using both network and relational methods.

ENTITY RELATION
"ILLNESS"

NAME	SYMPTOMS, ETC.
POLIO	. . .
ANXIETY	
RABIES	
ANEMIA	
. . .	

ENTITY RELATION
"FACTORS"

TYPE	CHARACTERISTICS
VIRUS X	. . .
VIRUS Y	. . .
IRON DEFICIENCY	. . .
JOB STRESS	. . .
. . .	

RELATIONSHIP RELATION
"CAUSE OF ILLNESS"

ENTITY ATTRIBUTES

ILLNESS	FACTOR	RELATIONSHIP ATTRIBUTES	
		% CAUSED BY FACTOR	% FATAL
POLIO	VIRUS X	100	35
ANXIETY	JOB STRESS	23	5
RABIES	VIRUS Y	100	100
. . .			

Figure 2.17. Entity-Relationship Tables, showing difference between entity relations and relationship relations. A hypothetical example of illnesses and factors associated with them.

ENTITY RELATION
"PEOPLE"

NAME	D.O.B	. . .
JILL	4/2/54	. . .
RALPH	7/9/53	
CARL	4/24/85	
ROBERT	4/24/85	
. . .		

Entity Attributes

RELATIONSHIP RELATION
"FAMILY TIES"

Entity Attributes

NAME A	NAME B	REL A OF B
JILL	RALPH	WIFE
JILL	CARL	MOTHER
RALPH	CARL	FATHER
RALPH	ROBERT	FATHER
CARL	ROBERT	BROTHER
. . .		

Relationship Attributes

Figure 2.18. Entity-Relationship Tables, illustrating a genealogy database.

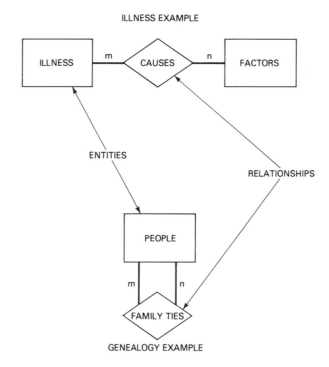

Figure 2.19. Diagrammatic representation of entities and relationships, using examples from Figs. 2.17 and 2.18.

Since the appearance of the original paper on entity-relationships, interest in this concept has grown, and new variations have been proposed. While this work is still at the research stage, it does seem likely that new developments will appear within the next few years, linking findings in database research with basic research in knowledge representation. The ultimate benefit to database systems will be creation of new models representing real world data accompanied by more sophisticated techniques for manipulating these models.

Although there are few examples of existing commercial products using this model, ZIM is one such product, available on IBM PC models. A reference at the end of this chapter provides further information on this package.

2.9 USER INTERFACE

Several preceding sections in this chapter have referred to the need for effective user interfaces. These needs include aids to definition of the database as well as improved methods for updating and retrieving existing data.

Users of personal computers may not even be aware that a revolution in computer interface methods has occurred over the last decade or so as a by-product of the personal computer revolution. For the first twenty-five years of computing, there was relatively little attention given to interactive processing. Database systems required batch operations for all phases of their use. Large mainframes had time-shared operating systems that often left much to be desired. The advent of truly interactive computing was greatly stimulated by the arrival of the personal computer, where all computing was essentially interactive. The changes occurred in many ways. The use of interpretive languages such as BASIC and MUMPS, instead of compiled languages such as FORTRAN and COBOL, permitted users to obtain immediate responses to commands entered by keyboard into a computer. The use of programs that permitted users to enter data directly from a keyboard instead of submitting punch cards revolutionized data-entry techniques. New input methods, including voice and touch screen, further altered images of computing, as did the new output technologies including complex graphic displays.

2.9.1 Computer-Driven Interactions

One technique that evolved in interactive computing is based on a series of questions posed by the computer program and answered by the user. In this approach, the user responds to questions about the design, data-entry, or retrieval process he or she wishes to execute, and the dialogue makes certain that all pertinent questions have been answered before processing the request.

Another computer-controlled approach is to present a menu of choices, ask the user to select the appropriate one, and then branch accordingly. This method is often used in conjunction with other approaches, giving the user the option of choosing the type of action to be taken, then branching into a different mode of interaction once that selection has been made.

2.9.2 Command-Driven Interactions

The third most common form of interaction is to require the user to type one or more commands, each of which is then acted on by the computer program. Since this method does not usually include prompts (or else it may not prompt until an error is made in entering a command), it requires greater sophistication and training on the part of the user. However, it has the advantage of offering a large set of options that the trained professional can use to formulate his or her requests more rapidly than by going through a series of menus or dialogues.

All of these methods (as well as others) are used in various DBMSs available on personal computers. In this text, we have selected examples in part because they demonstrate different user interfaces. Unfortunately, it is not possible at this time to illustrate some relatively new concepts such as touch-screen menu systems or mouse-driven DBMSs, mainly because they have not been widely incorporated in these packages.

2.10 SUMMARY

This chapter has presented a brief overview of a complicated topic. The emphasis has been on those concepts most important for the personal computer database system, but some new ideas were included because they may find their way into DBMSs.

Understanding the fundamentals of database theory is important for any user who wishes to implement an efficient design for a given application. Understanding what options are available, and how those options are used by a given DBMS may make an important difference in obtaining satisfactory results from that system. Usually, the design process will evolve as demands become more complex and the perception of relations between data elements becomes more distinct. As this evolutionary increase in complexity occurs, it is especially important to understand how an existing structure might be modified to accommodate new files and new uses. At the same time, evolution in hardware is going on, improving the options available for handling more sophisticated applications. For this reason, an understanding of hardware concepts is important as a complement to the theory presented in this chapter. Technological principles and evolution are the topics discussed in Chapter 3.

REFERENCES

● Basic Texts on Database Principles

There are many texts that deal with concepts of databases and DBMSs. The ones written before 1970 are obsolete, because new concepts such as the relational model and B-trees did not come along until later. As an instructor of database systems in a computer science major, I have tended to rely on two principal texts, augmenting them with several others. The texts I would recommend are:

Wiederhold, G. *Database Design*, (New York: McGraw-Hill Publishing Co., 1977). 658 pages.

> This text contains an extensive review of tools associated with database systems, starting with hardware and going through file structures and database models. Much of the material in the first part of Chapter 2 is derived from presentations in Wiederhold, which go into much greater depth on storage media, file types and B-tree structures. The coverage of database models is somewhat outdated, and not as complete as the next reference.

> This is truly an excellent reference for the implementation-specific tools associated with DBMSs. If updated to reflect recent developments, if could serve as a single text for an advanced college course in the field.

Date, C.J. *An Introduction to Database Systems, Vols 1 and 2*, (Reading, Massachusetts: Addison Wesley Publishing Co., Fourth Edition of Vol. 1 published 1985. Vol. 2 published 1983). Vol 1: 638 pages; Vol 2: 383 pages.

> This text is the classic database reference for upper-division college courses. C. J. Date worked many years for IBM before he became an independent consultant, and this text contains a large amount of information about IBM versions of the hierarchical and relational models. His coverage of the network model is also good, based on commercial versions running on IBM equipment. This text is weak on the entity relationship model, and it lacks coverage of hardware foundations of DBMSs.

> The combination of Wiederhold and Date together represents a reasonably complete coverage of the principles discussed in this chapter (with the exception of the entity relationship model). So far, I have not found a single text that does a better job.

Korth, H. F. and Silberschatz, A. *Database System Concepts*, (New York: McGraw-Hill Publishing Co., 1986). 546 pages.

> This relatively recent text contains more information on the entity relationship model than the previous texts, and as such complements them well. The remainder of the text is also quite good, though it lacks the hardware fundamentals treated in Wiederhold. The discussion is quite strongly oriented to theoretical presentation, a fact that reduces its appeal to non-computer scientists.

- Practical Design Texts

Atre, S. *Data Base: Structured Techniques for Design, Performance and Management*, (New York: John Wiley & Sons, 1980). 442 pages.

> This text is oriented towards the actual design and implementation of a database in a practical application. It contains coverage of the principal models, but it also has excellent sections on data dictionaries, systems management, and performance evaluation. The section on data dictionaries is especially valuable.

Stonebraker, M. *The INGRES Papers*, (Reading, Massachusetts: Addison Wesley Publishing Co., 1986). 452 pages.

> Professor Stonebraker is responsible for what became the first widely used commercial implementation of a relational system, INGRES. This book contains a collection of papers describing its design and evolution. There are many fascinating accounts of implementation problems and solutions. The text gives insight into problems of implementing the relational model under general-purpose operating systems and has interesting insights into new areas of research, such as query optimization.

- Miscellaneous Books and Articles

Indexing

Meadow, C. T. *The Analysis of Information Systems* (New York: John Wiley & Sons, Inc., 1973). 420 pages.

> Although the majority of this textbook is library-oriented, it contains an excellent discussion of the concept of indexing in Chapter 2, entitled "The Languages of Information Retrieval." This material is not found in conventional database texts, but it is a useful tool in database design.

B-Trees

Comer, D. (1979) "The Ubiquitous B-Tree," *ACM Computing Surveys*, Vol. 11, No. 2, pp. 121-138.

> The Association for Computer Machinery (ACM) is the main professional society for computer programmers. *ACM Computing Surveys* is one of its important journals, intended to provide tutorial information on various topics in computer science. This article, written for people who understand about computers but know nothing about B-trees, traces the history, implementation, and variations of this concept in a readable, informative manner.

Soundex

Perelman, B. and Calmus, L. (1986) "Soundex or S532?," *Aston-Tate Quarterly*, April/May/June, pp. 7-10.

A good review of the concept and its use. This article also relates the concept to dBASE III, one of the two DBMSs discussed in Chapter 4.

Network Model: The CODASYL System

Taylor, R. W. and Frank, R. L. (1976) "CODASYL Data-Base Management Systems," *ACM Computing Surveys*, Vol. 8, No. 1, pp. 67-104.

> Another tutorial in the *Computing Surveys* series, this article is strongly oriented toward the COBOL implementation of the CODASYL system. It contains may graphs that help understand not only the underlying concepts, but the manner in which they are implemented in COBOL-based DBMSs.

Relational Model

Chamberlin, D. D. (1976) "Relational Data-Base Management Systems," *ACM Computing Surveys,* Vol. 8, No. 1, pp. 43-66.

> This issue of *ACM Computing Surveys* has several articles on DBMSs, of which Chamberlin's is perhaps the best. Written clearly, it presents a helpful tutorial on the concepts and some of the difficulties associated with this model.

Entity Relationships

Chen, P. (1976) "The Entity-Relationship Model — Toward a Unified View of Data," *ACM Transactions on Database Systems*, Vol. 1, No. 1, pp. 9-36.

> This is the first article on the entity-relationship model. It has led to expanded research in more effective representation of data, and a growing number of research groups are focusing their interests in this area. The article is quite readable, containing some fundamental concepts in information representation.

Foard, Richard M. (1986) "A Data Manager Using Entity-Relationships," *PC TECH Journal*, Oct., pp. 96-117.

> The only commercial implementation of the entity-relationship model is ZIM, the package described in Foard's article. *PC TECH* is one of the best technical reference journals in the personal computer world, both for its discussion of hardware and its review of various types of software. This article is an excellent description of the concept and its specific features as implemented in ZIM.

3

Personal Computer Environments

3.1 INTRODUCTION

Effective use of database systems on personal computers requires (a) a knowledge of the principles of database systems (given in the previous chapter); and (b) an understanding of the strengths and limitations of personal computers as they are used to support DBMSs. This chapter introduces features of personal computers that most affect the performance of database systems. It is not a comprehensive summary of all that one might want to know about microcomputers, but it does cover certain aspects that are difficult to ferret out from manufacturers' literature or conventional "how-to" texts on database systems. The topics covered include brief discussions of hardware and programming languages, and a review of operating systems.

Readers who are familiar with personal computers may find much of this chapter too elementary for their needs. The sections on operating systems features do, however, provide insights not encountered in normal use of personal computers.

Persons familiar with database systems but not yet experienced in the use of personal computers should find much of the material in this chapter new. Since DBMSs on personal computers often are different from those on large mainframes, it is important to understand the personal computer environment prior to embarking on a database implementation project.

3.2 MICROCOMPUTER HARDWARE

All computers have the following major components: input/output (I/O), central processing unit (CPU), memory, and auxiliary (on-line) storage such as disks, tapes, or bubble memory. Personal computers also have all these features, even though they often are built into a single cabinet. There are abundant references to the functions of these hardware components, and we will not add to them. Instead, we will concentrate on a few features of personal computer hardware that have a direct bearing on database applications.

3.2.1 Microprocessors (CPUs)

The key to the personal computer revolution is the development of silicon wafers containing the equivalent of thousands of transistors linked together to perform various logical functions. In one configuration, such wafers can perform all the functions of a computer's CPU. Such silicon wafers are called *microprocessors.*

Microprocessors are an outgrowth of the Very Large-Scale Integrated (VLSI) circuit technology that evolved in the late 1960s and 1970s. By the mid-1970s, there were four well-known microprocessor chips available for use in personal computers. (It takes a CPU chip plus auxiliary chips, circuit boards, power supplies, keyboard, and displays to make a personal computer.) These early chips were all based on an architecture using 8 bits for internal storage and transfer between hardware components. The following list contains the best-known processors, and some of the better-known personal computers that use them.

Microprocessor	Personal Computer
MOSTEK 6502	Rockwell AIM, Apple
Motorola 6809	SWTP
Intel 8080, 8085	IMSAI, ALTAIR
Zilog Z80 (similar to 8080)	TRS80, Kaypro, Osborne

These chips are all based on an architecture that uses 8 bits for internal storage and transfer between hardware components. The choice of 8 bits was based in part on the use of the 8-bit American National Standard Code for Information Interchange (ASCII), which is the character code used in all personal computers today. The 8-bit microprocessor is a powerful computer, capable of performing database tasks in an effective efficient manner. The computers based on these processors are used for many DBMS packages today. This text deals with more recent processors, but a few of the packages that run on the new systems also are available (at least in earlier versions) for microprocessors.

In the late 1970s and into the 1980s, a new generation of microprocessors was developed, based this time on a 16-bit processor. For reasons discussed in the following paragraphs, the 16-bit architecture made it possible for these computers to transfer information more rapidly between system components and to compute more rapidly. Most of the earlier manufacturers developed chips that were, in part, compatible with the 8-bit processors of the previous generation. The microprocessors that resulted were:

8-bit Processor	16-bit Processor	Typical Microcomputer
6502	65816	None at time of publication

6809	68000	TRS80 Mod 16, Macintosh
8080	8086, 8088	IBM PC, DEC Rainbow
Z80	Z8000	ONYX

Many of the newer versions were similar in general architecture to their 8-bit predecessors. At present, the two most popular microprocessors in the 16-bit family are the 68000 and the 8086 or 8088, the latter being the chip used by IBM in their PC and XT computers.

The computing power of the 16-bit processors is much greater than that of their 8-bit forbears. In the case of the Motorola 68000, this increase in performance is truly spectacular for memory-related functions. For the Intel 8088, performance improvements are not so dramatic. There are, however, several factors noted later in this section that may improve the performance characteristics of the Intel family of processors over the next few years. Since we will be dealing primarily with systems that are based on the Intel 8086 and related microprocessors, it is important to understand some of the factors that can affect the performance of these systems.

The throughput of a computer is based, among other things, on the clock speed of the processor — the rate at which events occur inside the processor. Normal clock cycle times for 8-bit processors have been from 2 mHz (2 million cycles per second) to 4 mHz. The cycle time for typical 8086 and 8088 processors is between 4 and 10 mHz. However, Intel has released newer microprocessors that run at cycle times of up to 20 mHz, giving significant improvements in throughput as a result. Since these newer processors (the 80186 and 80286) are completely "backwards compatible," meaning that they can run 8086 code without modification, they represent easy ways to improve performance. For example, a program running on the Tandy Model 2000 personal computer will run up to three times faster than the same program on an IBM PC, because the Model 2000 uses the improved but compatible Intel APX80186 microprocessor.

The second way in which processing speed can be improved is through use of a personal computer's main memory. The 8086 and 8088 can directly address up to one megabyte (1 million 8-bit locations) of memory. This extended addressing is accomplished on these chips by the use of a 20-bit address, 16 bits in the regular registers and an additional 4 bits obtained from a separate segment register, giving a total of slightly over 1 million accessible bytes. Certain personal computers such as the IBM PC permit maximum memory of slightly less than the addressable maximum (640K bytes), but much more than the 64K limitation of 8-bit processors. Newer processors in the Intel series permit access to more memory (up to 16 megabytes by using a 24-bit addressing scheme), and it is possible that this enhancement will improve performance of code that now runs on the 8086 series of processors. It is interesting to note in passing that the Motorola 68000 permits 16-megabyte addressing without use of special segment registers, a feature that greatly improves its processing of non-numeric tasks.

Another feature of the central processor architecture that can affect throughput is the use of "coprocessors," or auxiliary processing units, to perform some tasks ordinarily executed by the main processor. For example, Digital Equipment's Rainbow personal computer uses a Z80 chip for I/O, even though the main tasks of a program are performed by an 8086 processor. In the Intel series, there are two coprocessors available to assist the 8086 (or 8088) to perform its duties: the 8087, a math coprocessor, and the 8089, an I/O coprocessor. The power of a coprocessor in performing special-purpose tasks is best illustrated by the 8087 chip, which incorporates functions into silicon such as multiplication, division, exponentiation, and trigonometric operations, executing them hundreds of times faster than can be done through software on conventional chips. The Intel family, using math coprocessors, will outperform the Motorola 68000 processor by a factor of 10 or 20 in arithmetic-bound operations. This point illustrates the difficulty in comparing processors, since we previously noted that memory-related operations are much faster on the 68000 chip. (*Note*: Both Motorola and Intel have new chips that resolve some of these shortcomings. Motorola has a coprocessor for the 68020 system, and Intel has enhanced addressing features in their APX80386 processor).

The IBM PC and many systems compatible with the IBM PC provide space on the circuit boards inside their computer for the 8087 coprocessor. In some DBMS applications, availability of the 8087 may improve performance. For many functions, however, the principal improvement will come through addition of an I/O processor such as the 8089. There is at present no space available for the 8089 on the IBM PC or most lookalikes.

Memory access is affected by one other factor that relates to the Intel 8086 and 8088. The 8088, while using a 16-bit processor, still uses an 8-bit architecture for transferring data to and from memory. For this reason, substituting an 8086 processor board with a 16-bit bus will improve performance of any program involving lots of data transfer, such as DBMS packages. Since code written for the 8088 is identical to the 8086 code, packages can run on either chip without modification. As noted earlier, IBM decided to use the 8088 processor, so the IBM PC's performance is slower than compatible systems using the 8086.

The trend toward construction of larger, more powerful systems has affected the personal computer market. IBM began sales of its AT personal computer in 1985, a system based on the Intel 80286 processor that offers important performance improvements over the PC and XT. Other manufacturers have cloned this IBM system, and there are now a large number of AT lookalikes. The result of this competition has led to reduced prices, both for the AT family and also for the PC and XT systems, as the AT prices begin to overlap with the upper end of the earlier systems. This competitive trend will probably extend into the next generation of systems, to be based on the Intel 80386 processor.

With the arrival of the 68020 and Intel 80386 chips, 32-bit processing is available in forms that are backwards compatible with their 16-bit predecessors. These chips will increase the power of personal computers, blurring or rendering less important their performance distinctions. It is likely, however, that the current 16-bit systems, especially the IBM PC, XT, and comparable systems, will remain in use for many years to come, and that they will continue to be supported by manufacturers of DBMSs.

Another new concept in microprocessors has appeared on the scene beginning in 1986, when IBM announced the availability of a new type of personal computer, called the RT, which utilizes an innovative microprocessor design called Reduced Instruction Set Chip (RISC). The RISC design is based on the premise that most of today's microprocessors contain a great many instructions that are rarely needed in most applications, and that these instructions take up space on the processor chip, which could be used for other, better purposes. According to available information, the IBM RT processor chip, a proprietary product not yet cloned in other systems, is designed to serve the needs of database systems far better than conventional processors. Several technical factors contribute to this performance improvement, including the instruction set, the one-clock-cycle execution for each instruction (instructions on conventional processors often require many clock cycles), and the use of buffers on the processor chip to reduce time spent to fetch the next instructions. The net result is a system that may have an important effect on database systems for personal computers. Although the RT is not priced at the same level as the PC or XT, it is possible that the price structure will change as the system becomes better known and supported.

Manufacturers generally provide little information on the processors used in their hardware. The foregoing discussion should serve to remind the reader that this feature is important and should be taken into consideration when selecting hardware for a database application.

In summary, the new 16-bit processors offer important advantages for database management systems. The Motorola family of processors appear at present to be better suited for database applications, whereas the Intel family offers superior numerical computation advantages. Both manufacturers are evolving, however, and the situation may change in future. Other processors, such as the IBM RT chip, may offer serious competition to these two manufacturers. The newly announced 65816, compatible with the 6502 but featuring 16-bit capabilities and extended addressing, may prove suitable for database applications. The evolution of microprocessors is continuing to take place at a rapid rate, and although it may take time for some of the new features to be incorporated into database systems, the possibility for breakthrough impact is real in the next year or two.

3.2.2 Memory

The "main memory" of a personal computer can include read-only memory (ROM), used to store system programs and not available for user modification; and random access memory (RAM), in which the remainder of the system and also user application programs and data are stored.

The 8-bit processors were limited by their addressing schemes to 64K bytes of main memory. This limitation was extended in the Intel 8086 and 8088 to 1 megabyte of memory, a size initially considered more than enough for personal computer applications. Motorola, however, decided to expand available memory to 16 megabytes, and used a very efficient access scheme. As applications on personal computers grew more sophisticated, the need for more main memory grew, and the Intel

80186 and later chips provided addressing space for 16 megabytes. Since many database systems can take advantage of more main memory, this evolution will have a growing effect on DBMS design.

One of the most important factors to bear in mind with respect to memory is the speed of access for use by the CPU. The relative difference in speed between access to memory-based information and the information stored on a floppy disk is so great as to be difficult to comprehend: roughly a million-fold faster for main memory. The actual difference may vary, depending on the indexing information available, but it is still on the order of ten to a hundred thousand times faster in most cases.

Memory in the 8086 family of processors is divided into "segments" of 64K bytes each. Some delays are involved in switching back and forth between these segments; however, compared to disk access times, they are trivial. Mapping of 8086 memory for programs and data requires consideration of the 64K-segment architecture, especially when large data files are stored in memory during program execution. DBMS packages typically use over 256K memory for the programs, and utilize the remaining memory for data buffers, which means that a computer with more memory will execute more efficiently.

The idea of using memory to "simulate" disk access is especially attractive in DBMSs because of the improvements in speed. This concept has led to development of utilities that take over excess memory and create a file system that can be accessed by the same programs used to access disk-based files. This technique is sometimes called "RAM disk" or "solid-state disk" storage. Use of this approach will dramatically improve performance of many DBMS packages. Today it is important even in the IBM PC and XT systems, because vendors now market add-on boards that make it possible for these systems to have additional memory beyond the 1M byte limitation of the 8086 processor.

There is, however, one caution. RAM chips require electric power to maintain the information stored on the chip. When power fails, the information on the chip is lost. A program that relies entirely on RAM disk is therefore susceptible to data loss in the event of power failure or even unplanned program abortion. A few manufacturers have recognized this problem and provide backup support either through battery backup for RAM boards, by providing automatic RAM to disk writes executed periodically without user intervention, or through transaction files. It is important to explore the advantages of utilizing memory fully in any database application.

As a final point with respect to memory, users should be aware that as the price of memory continues to drop, the use of RAM disks or similar techniques will probably continue to grow. New computer systems, such as the IBM AT, offer much larger memory capacities.

3.2.3 Keyboards and Displays

Most individuals assume that all personal computers are more or less identical with respect to the principal I/O devices, keyboards, and displays. There are, however, some differences that can affect DBMS performance.

Data input is the most unjustly ignored aspect of database systems. The use of punch cards has happily given way to other, friendlier, interactive entry techniques, but much remains to be done to further improve data entry. The use of touch-sensitive screens for menu-type selection has not been adequately explored. For many types of database entry, this method could reduce dependence on key strokes and improve the speed and accuracy.

Another innovation that has received inadequate attention to date is the use of keyboards better suited to human dexterity and the frequency distribution of characters in the English language than the "QWERTY" keyboard that comes with most terminals. Two interesting examples are the Dvorak keyboard, which repositions the letters on conventional keyboards, and the Maltron keyboard, which uses a novel configuration that not only repositions keys but places keys in two cup-shaped pods, one for each hand, with multiple keys for each thumb. Both of these keyboards result in demonstrable improvements in speed, but neither has received widespread acceptance. Bar-code readers, available at low cost for personal computers, are efficient devices for certain data-entry tasks. These and other examples only serve to illustrate the wide variety of options generally ignored by available DBMSs.

Video display screens are the most widespread form of display used in personal computers. However, plasma displays, liquid crystal displays, and other chemical technologies are starting to appear. These devices will probably result in different forms of graphic displays, affecting the display aspect of database systems. Mouse pointers and windows (separately programmed areas on a screen representing different functions) may also be used in database systems. High-resolution screens (CRT and other) that provide greater versatility in graphics, the use of different fonts, and more effective displays for all DBMS functions will also affect these systems in the future.

One important difference between terminals, related in part to memory characteristics, has to do with the manner in which displays are generated and maintained. Most terminals use a technique in which the display is maintained via internal storage in the terminal. Some displays, however, are directly linked to a computer's memory, so that changes to memory locations are immediately reflected on the display screen. This approach is many times faster than using serial transfer of data to a terminal screen, one character at a time, which is usually limited to writing approximately 1,000 characters per second, which would require two full seconds to completely fill an 80x25 screen. The IBM PC, for example, uses this form of memory mapping of its video display.

3.2.4 Auxiliary Storage

Database applications require storage of large volumes of data. In most cases, the size of a database will exceed what can be stored in a computer's memory, requiring the use of auxiliary storage devices. There is also a need for data storage on devices that retain information when the computer is turned off. Many storage technologies are available for personal computers. The most important are flexible (floppy) disks and Winchester technology hard disks. Other auxiliary storage systems are appearing, however, and they will be discussed briefly below.

3.2.4.1 Flexible Disks

Most personal computers today use either 8-inch or 5 1/4-inch flexible disks. The new "laptop" computers generally use a smaller size (approximately 3 1/2 inches). An important fact of personal computers is the general incompatibility of disks among manufacturers. Several factors can contribute to the incompatibility problem; these points are discussed later as they relate to the IBM PC.

In order for a disk to be used on a personal computer, it must first be *formatted*. Disks come with a ferric-oxide coating on a mylar substrate that must be prepared so that the read mechanism can recognize the data stored. A newly purchased 5 1/4-inch disk cannot be used until the format function has been performed. Figures 3.1 and 3.2 illustrate the manner in which disks are formatted for use on the IBM PC. Notice first that the information is stored on *tracks* or concentric circles on the disk. Each track is separated into several *sectors*. The size of a sector, the spacing between tracks, and the total number of tracks on a disk are determined at the time the disk is formatted. The "start" of a track (its first sector) is determined by the location of a small hole in the mylar medium. When this hole lines up with a hole in the disk jacket, the disk drive detects the hole with a light beam and photoreceptor and signals the start of a track.

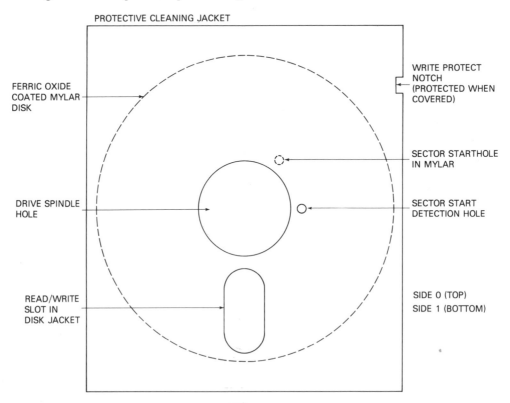

PROTECTIVE CLEANING JACKET

FERRIC OXIDE
COATED MYLAR
DISK

WRITE PROTECT
NOTCH
(PROTECTED WHEN
COVERED)

SECTOR STARTHOLE
IN MYLAR

DRIVE SPINDLE
HOLE

SECTOR START
DETECTION HOLE

READ/WRITE
SLOT IN
DISK JACKET

SIDE 0 (TOP)
SIDE 1 (BOTTOM)

PHYSICAL APPEARANCE OF FLEXIBLE DISK

Figure 3.1. Physical appearance of 5 1/4" flexible disk.

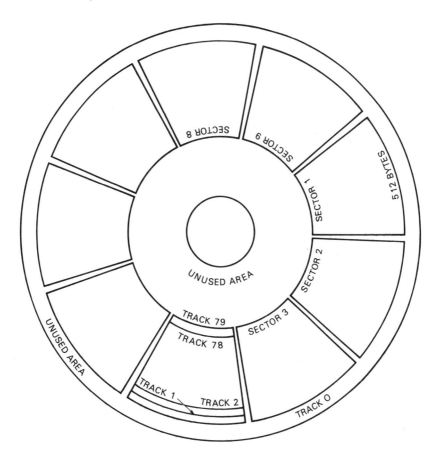

Figure 3.2. Format of IBM PCDOS disk under Version 2.0 and later (one side only shown).
Total data space: 512 bytes/sector; 9 sectors/track; 40 tracks/side; 2 sides = 368,640 bytes.

Formatting is a function controlled by a program. Formats may vary, even on the IBM PC. The format shown in Fig. 3.2 is the one used for double-sided disks under the current operating system used in the IBM PC. (For further discussion on operating systems, see a later section in this chapter.) Since this format is the one most commonly used today, we will use it as our example. However, readers should know that, in addition to this format, there is a single-sided disk format available for the IBM PC under PCDOS 2.0, and that the formats supported under PCDOS 1.0 and 1.1 used 8 sectors (rather than 9) per track and had correspondingly less data on each disk (both single-sided and double-sided versions were also supported on the previous release).

The time required to access information from a disk depends on three factors: head move time, rotation time to get the desired data positioned under the read head (called latency), and transfer rate (which is really a function of the rotational speed).

Double-sided disks require two read/write heads, one for each surface. These heads move in unison, so that information on track 0 of each side is available to the computer without moving the read heads. The PCDOS manual refers to the two tracks with the same number as a *cluster* of tracks, and the operating system tries to fill one cluster with data before moving to a new one, since moving the heads is the slowest step in accessing data on a disk.

Flexible disks rotate at approximately 300 rpm, or 5 revolutions per second. This rotational speed is quite slow compared to hard disks (about 3,600 revolutions per second), and it means that the latency is, on average, 0.1 seconds (one-half revolution). Since it often is necessary to move the head as well as find the correct sector, the average time to start transfer of data will probably be slower still, perhaps closer to 0.3 seconds in many cases. For applications requiring many disk accesses, execution times will be relatively slow on floppy disks, a factor that has an important effect on database operations.

The transfer time is related to the rotational speed of the disk and the maximum amount that can be transferred into a buffer in a single read. Although the transfer rate on a floppy disk is theoretically about 23K bytes/second, the effective transfer rate is slower, depending on buffer size and the physical distribution of data on the disk (see the section on operating systems).

Some IBM PCs only read disks formatted on one side. Although the same disk can be formatted either single or double sided, a disk formatted on both sides cannot be used on a single-sided disk drive. The easiest way to ascertain whether a disk drive is single or double sided is to determine the total storage available on the disk. If an IBM PC disk holds approximately 180K bytes, it is single sided; if 360K bytes are available, both sides have been used. One further note: Disks are sold as being either single sided or double sided, with the latter costing more. The real difference between these disks is the quality control that has gone into checking the mylar surfaces on which data will be written. In practice, many disks guaranteed reliable for one side will also function perfectly well as double-sided disks (the protective jackets are the same). Although it is generally advisable to get disks guaranteed as double sided for critical data, single-sided disks can be used in double-sided mode for many applications.

The way in which the disks are used varies greatly from one manufacturer to another, even with comparable production techniques. The Digital Equipment Corporation Rainbow 100, for example, stores approximately the same amount of information on one side of a 5 1/4-inch disk as is contained on two sides of the IBM PC, and the Data General laptop computer (Model 1), using a 3 1/2-inch disk, has over 780K bytes on one disk.

Most systems that claim IBM compatibility can also read and write disks formatted for the IBM PC. Many use one or more of the IBM PC formats. Others have conversion programs enabling them to read IBM PC formatted disks. However, we have seen in the preceding discussion that there are at least 4 different formats for disks used on the IBM PC. Therefore, "IBM-compatible" does not necessarily mean that the system will be able to read all formats. This statement is particularly true with respect to single- versus double-sided disks, since some systems (e.g., DEC Rainbow) do not provide double-sided drives. In general, however, the compatibility problem with IBM PC compatibles is less severe than with other operating systems, where no *de facto* standard exists and there are scores or hundreds of different formats.

Individuals with more than one type of computer in their working environment should take great care to label disks as to which system they are formatted for. Failure to do so may result in attempting to read a disk on the wrong computer. The user may conclude that the unreadable disk has been damaged or has not been formatted, and may reformat it. Reformatting destroys all information previously stored on disk. Unfortunately, many format programs give no warning that the disk may have been previously formatted.

An important safety feature available on most personal computers, including the IBM PC, is a program that permits partial reconstruction of data on disks that have become corrupted in one way or another. These programs will guide the user through questions that help to identify and string back together sectors of data belonging to a given file. This type of program (there are several commercial systems offering such utilities) are of particular value when an important data set has somehow become unreadable.

Some computer systems are equipped with 8-inch drives. These systems also utilize many different formats, including single density and double density (referring to the number of tracks and the bytes per sector), as well as single versus double sided. In the latter case, double-sided 8-inch disks have the start-of-track locator hole offset in a different place on the disk than single-sided disks. This difference is small but can be recognized if disks of the two different types are examined side by side. Drives designed for single-sided disks cannot read double-sided disks. However, most drives that read double-sided disks are also equipped with sensors to read single-sided disks as well. In general, disks written single sided, single density can be read on many computers. There is virtually no compatibility between different systems for double-density or double-sided 8-inch disks.

The laptop personal computer is another area where incompatibility rules. These systems provide two escape alternatives. Some systems, like the Data General Model 1 offer a separate box containing a 5 1/4-inch drive that is compatible with the IBM PC. Others, such as the IBM lap top, provide a cable and downloading program to transfer programs from PC or XT models to the small disks. A variation of this same approach is to use the communication ports on other systems for transfer through telephone communications.

The volume of information that can be stored on a disk varies as a function of the factors discussed above. The approximate range, however, is from 160K bytes to 1.2M bytes per 5 1/4-inch disk, and 240K to 1.4M bytes on 8-inch disks. The smaller disks vary from 350 to 780K bytes, and higher densities have been projected for the future.

Data files usually cannot extend beyond one disk. This fact is important, because it imposes a physical limitation that may affect database design. Since most personal computers have more than one disk drive, it often is possible to use one drive for data, the other for programs. Although different files can be stored on different disks, it is unusual to find packages that permit simultaneous use of data files on different drives.

The operating system is responsible for manipulating data on disks. In a later section of this chapter, we will discuss the interrelationships between the IBM PC operating system and disks.

3.2.4.2 Winchester Technology (Hard) Disks

In the 1970s, IBM proposed a new type of hard disk, using a sealed environment and theoretically capable of having 30 megabytes of information on 30 tracks of disk space. From this proposed technology of "30-30" came the term Winchester, from the rifle with that nickname. No Winchester drive has achieved precisely this capability, but the ideas embodied in the Winchester concept did take hold, and there are now many Winchester drives available for personal computers.

Winchester drives range in size from 3 to 14 inches and in storage volume from 5M bytes to well over 500M bytes. The increased capacity is due in part to the sealed environment, which permits closer engineering tolerances, and also to the use of hard disk platters with improved surface characteristics. The 5 1/4-inch XT drives, for example, accommodate 305 tracks on each surface.

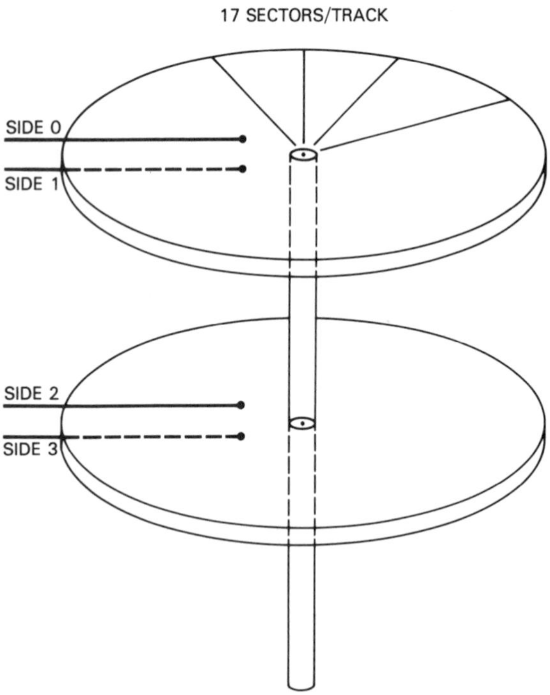

Figure 3.3. Schematic representation of IBM 10M byte Winchester disk. Storage capacity: 512 bytes/sector; 17 sectors/track; 4 sides = 34,816 bytes/cylinder. There are 305 tracks on each surface, giving a total of 10,618,880 bytes/Winchester drive. Note that all read/write heads move in unison on a single arm.

Figure 3.3 illustrates schematically the manner in which IBM XT Winchester drive disks are formatted. The XT disk drive comes with two fixed platters, with read/write heads on top and bottom of each, or four read/write heads. Since these heads move in unison, the data available without moving the heads is four times the data on a single track. This collection of four tracks is referred to as a *cylinder*, a term used in mainframe disks packs with many more platters and read/write heads also moving together. On the IBM XT, a cylinder of data contains 34,816 bytes of data.

The access speed on hard disks is several times faster than on flexible disks, owing to a different technology and the higher rotation speeds. Transfer rates are higher, because of the high rotation speeds. Nevertheless, access speed to information on Winchesters is still slow compared to data in the computer's memory, so that using a combination of memory and a Winchester drive will probably provide the greatest throughput and flexibility.

The size of files that can be stored on Winchesters is significantly greater than on flexible disks. The maximum size a single file can occupy depends on the size of the disk and the limitations of the operating system. If enough disk capacity is available, it is theoretically possible to have up to 30M bytes of storage on a single file on the IBM PC.

One of the most important things to bear in mind with respect to hard disks is the need for backup of the information stored on the disks. Since most Winchester drives are sealed, there is no way to keep a spare copy of the information on that drive without copying it to another device. Some (very few) Winchesters include this backup provision in the box that contains the disk. More often, it is the user's responsibility to find ways to back up the data. Since this requirement is rarely pointed out by vendors, it usually means that the user will have to explore ways to back up data from hard disks.

Using flexible disks for backup is extremely cumbersome. Many flexible disks are required to store the information on one hard disk (28 disks to back up a 10M byte Winchester). Files on hard disks may be larger than can fit on one floppy, meaning that some provision for file overlap must be included in the backup program. The transfer process often is awkward and may have to be repeated from the start if an error (such as a defective flexible disk) occurs during transfer. Reloading the information may also require a long time, multiple disk changes, and possible restarts. The best current technology available for Winchester disk backup is either some form of cartridge tape device, or use of a videocassette recorder with a special board now available for PCs for a cost under $500.

The current price trends in disk drives continues downwards. It would appear that there is little justification at this time for purchasing Winchester drives of less than 10M bytes minimum. The cost differential is small, and it is likely that most applications will quickly outgrow 5M-byte storage capacity.

3.2.4.3 Other Auxiliary Storage Devices

Disks are currently the most common form of auxiliary storage on personal computers. There are, however, several technologies that offer promise of competitive pricing and performance for the near term future.

One storage methodology is called *bubble memory*, chips that store data in the form of magnetic domains that are retained after power is turned off. Bubble memory chips have been available for some years, but despite early promise, they have been slow to gain acceptance in the personal computer market, due to cost/performance ratios that do not yet compare favorably with disks. There are now several companies that have announced auxiliary storage components based on bubble memory, and it appears likely that they may become competitive with disk storage.

The technology of bubble memory involves the sequential retrieval of microscopic magnetic domains that circulate past a read/write mechanism that reads one bit at a time. This technology is slower than RAM, since it is serial, but it is possible to increase the retrieval speed if several chips are used in parallel. If two chips share a byte of data between them, each recording four bits, the two chips can be accessed simultaneously, doubling the data transfer time. Similarly, if eight chips are used, the process is eight times faster. Some bubble memory systems now available for the IBM PC use a single chip; others use a chip for each bit, accessed in parallel, and are accordingly much faster in transferring data.

Speeds of current bubble memory systems range from slightly faster than Winchester disks to marginally faster than floppy drives. Bubble memory systems still cost roughly four times floppy disk systems, but the costs appear to be dropping. Since there are no moving parts, wear on bubble memory system is not a factor. Reliability is very high. Current storage capacities range in the 256K to 512K byte range, but new chips with double the storage capacity are already on the market. Costs should drop as storage capacity rises.

Another technology gaining ground rapidly is that of laser-encoded data stored on optical disks or cards. Credit card storage devices holding 2.5M bytes of data are already being distributed to clients for medical record cards by some Health Insurance companies. Larger optical disks offer huge volumes of data with quite rapid access. Billions of bytes of data are available on many such devices. Laser storage systems are virtually indestructible, using noncontact read/write technologies that eliminate wear.

There are three types of optical storage systems: read-only; write once, read many (WORM); and read-write. The read-only systems use the same technology as compact disks developed for audio markets. The disks are relatively inexpensive, although it costs approximately $20,000 to make a master. These disks are suitable for static information in database applications, such as large dictionaries, census tract data, or texts. One compact disk can hold approximately 2.5 billion bytes (2.5 gigabytes) of data.

The WORM disks are much more versatile, since they can be used to store files that grow with time, such as archival data and transaction logs. Since the volume of data on one WORM disk is also in the gigabyte range, they can be used for very large database applications or to store archival records covering long periods. The cost of WORM system drives is in the $2,000 range today, but these costs are expected to continue to drop as they have in the past few years.

The technology of read-write optical disks is still in the development stage, and it is not certain how soon cost-effective systems will be available.

The foregoing examples serve to indicate that disk storage systems may eventually give way to new technology. However, until new devices can demonstrate improved access times, storage volumes, price performance, reliability, and market acceptance, magnetic disks are likely to remain the chief storage devices of database systems. It is also true, of course, that magnetic disk technology is improving and cost/performance ratios are dropping, so the competition should be intense in the next few years.

3.2.5 Printers

All database applications require printed output in one form or another. There are many devices that can provide this capability, but it is beyond the scope of this text to go into details of each specific type. In general, dot matrix type printers are cheapest and, in the personal computer environment, the fastest. Impact printers, such as daisy wheel devices, produce a higher quality of output, but they usually cost more and are slower. Until recently, ink jet printers, which spray small dots of ink onto paper to create characters, were relatively expensive. Now, however, low-priced ink jet printers are available at prices competitive with dot matrix devices. The advantages of ink jet printers are minimal noise and print quality comparable to dot matrix systems. A disadvantage of the lower-priced ink jet printers is the need to use special paper with different ink absorption characteristics that prevent smearing. Laser printers, devices with exceptional flexibility in fonts, print size, and graphics, are now available for personal computers, with low-end prices starting at about $2,000. The needs of many database applications may be served best by using dot matrix for the majority of output, reserving a daisy wheel, ink jet, or laser printer for special reports and letters.

One fact relating to personal computers and printed output is often overlooked. Most personal computers today can perform only one task at a time. Printing rarely involves intervention (other than inserting new sheets of paper if continuous forms are not used), yet few DBMSs make it possible to use the computer for other purposes while output is being printed. It often takes many minutes or even hours to produce some reports, during which time other activities must cease. This inactivity may prove a serious disruption in some situations.

In general, it is more important to have rapid output than letter quality in DBMS printers. Occasional access to quality graphics or top quality printing is valuable, but the daily medium volume requirements can usually be served better by speed than by appearance. One solution in many environments is to use a cheap printer with a personal computer; transferring files to other systems for high-quality printing is required.

3.2.6 External Communications

Many database applications on personal computers require communication with the outside world, either through direct connection to other computers or through transfer by telephone or network interface. The type of connection greatly influences the communications rate, but options may be limited by many factors, including the type of device and its geographic location.

External communication can take two forms: serial communication, where an 8-bit byte is transferred one bit at a time (with associated start and stop bits), or parallel communication, where all 8 bits are sent simultaneously on a bus containing one line for each bit. Parallel communication is much faster than serial, but it requires close proximity of the two devices. Many systems permit parallel connection through "IEEE 488" communication channels. This standard permits high data transfer rates between nearby personal computers and may also permit connection to minicomputers or mainframes that are close together.

Serial communications are usually measured in terms of "bits per second." We will convert these figures into "characters" per second (one byte = one character), since that is a more understandable measure. Communication at rates of 960 to 1,920 characters per second can be achieved by direct "hard-wired" connections between nearby devices. Serial communication over telephone lines is the slowest form of data transfer available to personal computers. The rate varies from 30 to 240 characters per second on normal telephone lines to a maximum of 960 characters per second on "conditioned" lines (permanent connections between two locations that cost significantly more than dial-up, unconditioned lines).

In the last few years, a new form of communication has evolved to link computers in a local environment. The general term used for these links is local area network (LAN). There are several types of LANs in use today that link personal computers, with transfer rates ranging from approximately 250K to 1.5 million characters per second. The actual data transfer rate may vary depending on the protocol used, but throughput is greatly enhanced over the previously described methods. One widely used protocol for a local area network is *Ethernet*, a technique that uses coaxial cable or fiber optic filaments to connect several minicomputers or personal computers, transferring data at effective rates ranging from 50K characters per second upward to the channel capacity, depending on many factors associated with configuration and usage on the system. Other techniques are under development, and there is a very high interest in standardization of these methodologies.

Establishing adequate external communication capabilities is an important consideration in DBMS design. In general, database applications will eventually require significant volumes of data transfer in one form or another.

3.2.7 Summary of Hardware Considerations

Microcomputer technology is evolving rapidly. Prototypes of new architectures, new input/output peripherals, and new storage devices appear frequently. Some of these devices will become attractive for database applications, but it is difficult to predict which will have the greatest impact. The technologies that augment storage capacity, circumvent disk access delays, and increase storage capacity will probably have the greatest effect on database applications. For this reason, devices such as expanded reliable memory, higher performance special-purpose microprocessors, and optical storage devices are singled out as technologies to watch in the near future.

3.3 PROGRAMMING LANGUAGES FOR DATABASE SYSTEMS

Implementation of a DBMS for a particular computer requires coding its many tasks into a language that will run on that computer under control of an operating system also available on that machine. Selection of an appropriate language in which to execute the database functions is often a trade-off between the benefits and drawbacks of different languages.

There are several functions that are essential to a database environment. Some of them include:

- Ability to manipulate text type data
- Ability to access operating system disk I/O functions
- Ability to operate on several files simultaneously

To these could be added the desirable features of compatibility across machines, ease of use, and specific language features that facilitate database functions. One especially important need is efficient disk I/O.

In selecting a language for a personal computer, it is necessary to know what alternatives are available, and to choose the one that best meets the criteria of the given application. There are hundreds of programming languages. Many of them, like FORTRAN and APL, were designed primarily to perform numeric computation, a task that is unimportant in DBMSs. COBOL was designed for business applications, but COBOL was also designed to run on very large computers and does not run well on personal computers.

Microcomputers offer few languages that meet all the requirements of DBMSs. Commercial database packages are often written in assembly language so as to gain execution speed, but this approach requires rewriting when a new processor with new assembly language is targeted. BASIC is probably the most commonly used language by individuals writing database applications. There are many different dialects of BASIC (70, according to one recent study), with varying degrees of suitability for database functions. PASCAL is another language sometimes used for database development, but this language is generally lacking in random disk I/O, an important requirement of database systems. C, a language now available for the IBM PC has many good features but is less well known, and the C compilers currently available are less refined than those on minicomputers.

One language, relatively unknown to personal computer users, has exceptionally favorable characteristics for database applications. The language is called MUMPS, an acronym for Massachusetts General Hospital's Utility Multi-Programming System. MUMPS was originally designed to serve the needs of medical database processing. It proved so successful that it was adopted by many commercial institutions. MUMPS is one of the few languages approved by the American National Standards Institute as a standard language, and it is available on a wide variety of computers. It offers built-in shared file manipulation capabilities and powerful text manipulation commands. MUMPS is available on many personal computers, including the IBM PC. A general-purpose DBMS package written in MUMPS is also available. (See the references for further information.)

Languages such as COBOL, FORTRAN, and PL/I are generally unsuited to the personal computer environment because of their demand for major resources at compilation time as well as during execution. There are several other languages that offer real promise for database applications, but to date few commercial packages rely on them. It is likely that languages such as C will be used for DBMS development in the future. The dBASE package has been maintained in C since its 1984 release.

Although it is desirable to code in a high-level language for ease of maintenance and portability, it is almost always necessary to incorporate assembly-language utilities for certain functions, especially operating systems interface. Many DBMS packages try to keep these assembly language programs to a minimum in order to gain greater portability to new systems.

In this text, we will consider the need to modify or augment existing DBMS packages. If user modification is to be permitted, it will be necessary to select a system that can interface with a language with which the user is familiar. If the reader is considering learning a new language in order to develop database systems on a personal computer, it might be well to consider either C or MUMPS. Assembly language is considered a poor choice, since new architectures with different assembly languages appear frequently.

3.4 OPERATING SYSTEMS

One of the most important environmental factors affecting database systems performance is the operating system. In the personal computer world, most DBMS vendors do not give the user much information about the interaction between the DBMS package and the operating system. For this reason, and because there are important differences between operating systems for personal computers and those running on larger computers, this section warrants careful reading. The material is presented in enough depth that it may be best to skim it at the first reading, returning to specific paragraphs as practical questions arise.

Operating systems are essential components of all modern computers. They perform the essential functions of I/O management, assist the user in accessing programming languages and application packages, and perform many diagnostic and other utility functions necessary for effective use of the computer. In the minicomputer and mainframe area, very little attention has been paid to standardization of operating systems. The result is that each manufacturer of minicomputers and mainframes offers one or more operating systems unique to their hardware. Operating systems are complex. Months or years of study may be needed to master them. The experienced programmer familiar with one operating system will have to spend almost as much time to learn a new operating system as he or she did to learn the first.

The same situation began to develop in the personal computer market, with incompatible operating systems running on popular equipment such as the APPLE, Radio Shack, and Commodore Pet. However, one operating system, CP/M (Control Program for Microcomputers), gradually gained a preeminent position as a widespread standard, available on literally hundreds of different 8-bit personal computers. CP/M runs on Z80- and 8080-based personal computers. Large libraries of programs were developed that would run under CP/M, including dBASE II, the predecessor of dBASE III PLUS used as an example in this text. The rapid growth in demand for personal computers fueled the trend toward greater standardization, and in time CP/M was acknowledged to be a *de facto* standard.

With the advent of 16-bit microprocessors, decisions had to be made with respect to what standards, if any, would be accepted by the market. IBM entered the personal computer market at this time. They contracted with Microsoft to produce a 16-bit operating system that would function much like CP/M but would contain improvements as well. The product developed through this association was called PCDOS, and because of the dramatic success of the IBM PC, this operating system also began to be accepted as an industry-wide standard. Microsoft developed another operating system, nearly identical to PCDOS, which they marketed under the name MSDOS. In this text, we will use the term PCDOS to include MSDOS. (We will look at differences between these two operating systems later in this section.)

In the meantime, the company that developed CP/M went on to produce a nearly compatible 16-bit version named CP/M86, an operating system that also had enhancements over the 8-bit system, but one that has not gained acceptance as a 16-bit standard, owing to the large share of the 16-bit market captured by IBM and compatible systems. Digital Research Corporation, which developed CP/M and CP/M86, has released new products compatible with the IBM PC, and a new battle for standardization is under way.

As hardware has become more powerful, the original design features of CP/M and PCDOS have become outdated. Originally, these systems were designed to support floppy disks, and later to support Winchester drives with storage capacities of about 10M bytes. They were also designed to support single users. Both of these features are no longer appropriate. Disk capacities are growing so that 30M byte systems are commonplace and 100M byte systems, with very large individual files, are also finding their way into personal computer systems. The new processors can handle more than one task at a time, so multitasking and even multiuser systems are also needed in the personal computer marketplace.

On the other hand, one important design feature of both CP/M and PCDOS remains valid: the goal of creating an operating system that is easy to use, even for beginners.

There is another operating system that deserves attention in this chapter, even though we will not be using packages that run under it. At the time that CP/M was becoming a standard for personal computers, minicomputer manufacturers were also being pressured to develop a standard operating system. UNIX, developed by Bell Laboratories for minicomputers, proved attractive to some commercial vendors and to many universities. As graduates from these computer science departments were employed by industry, there was a growth in demand for increased adoption of UNIX or UNIX-like operating systems. This trend gradually began to affect the 16-bit personal computer world, notably systems using the Motorola 68000 microprocessor. There are now many personal computers using various versions of UNIX, with the result that the current battle for standardization is far from resolved. The IBM personal computers have also been affected by this operating system. XENIX, an operating system very close to UNIX, is now available on the IBM AT, and AIX, an extended version of UNIX, is the principal operating system for the IBM RT.

The UNIX family of operating systems has many features, including multiuser functionality and multitasking (one user starting up more than one job), common to larger, more sophisticated minicomputers. Since it was designed for larger systems, it has virtually no file size limitations of the type described for PCDOS. On the other hand, UNIX is really designed for programmers, and it contains many complex features that are considerably more difficult to learn than the PCDOS commands. It remains to be seen whether the personal computer user will be willing to learn more complex operating system environments in order to gain greater flexibility or will instead settle for a less powerful but more manageable tool. In this text, we will concentrate on PCDOS; however, sometimes we will refer to features found in systems such as UNIX to alert the reader to features that may someday be incorporated into PCDOS. It does seem likely that PCDOS and UNIX will both evolve, the first to add more sophisticated features, the second to provide a more friendly user interface.

Although PCDOS and MSDOS are similar in many respects, there are a few differences that affect database functions. Throughout this text, we will focus our discussion on PCDOS in order to provide a consistent treatment. Section 3.4.8 summarizes some of the differences between PCDOS and MSDOS that affect database operations.

3.4.1 Basic Components of PCDOS

Manufacturers of personal computers must decide whether their product will be specifically designed to run under a single operating system or to permit other operating systems as options. When IBM designed the PC, they elected the latter option. In order to simplify the use of the PC under any operating system, IBM incorporated a certain amount of ROM as a part of the total memory in the system. When power is turned on, the ROM instructions are activated, performing diagnostic checks of the hardware and then checking disk drive A to see if an operating system is available.

Since the IBM PC was designed to run either PCDOS or CP/M86, only a small portion of the operating system, the Basic Input/Output System (BIOS), was placed in ROM, where it can be used by either operating system. The remainder of the operating system must be loaded from auxiliary storage. Every disk that contains the PCDOS operating system programs must be configured in a special way, as shown in Fig. 3.4.

The first information found on track 0, sector 1 of the disk contains the *boot record*, which contains instructions used to read in the remainder of the operating system (the term *boot* comes literally from the analogy of kicking a car to get it started). Following this record are two copies of a special table indicating space used and available on disk. These tables are followed by an area reserved for up to 112 file names (64 on a single-sided PCDOS disk). The next sectors contain three operating system programs: *IBMBIO.COM*, *IBMDOS.COM*, and *COMMAND.COM*. These programs are essential to the function of the operating

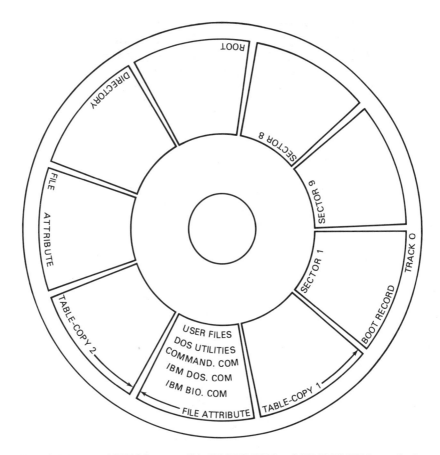

Figure 3.4. Layout of PCDOS system disk. IBMBIO.COM and IBMDOS.COM must be first files on disk.

system. IBMBIO.COM contains the PCDOS-specific information that interfaces with the ROM BIOS code. IBMDOS.COM contains the code used to process function calls to the operating system. COMMAND.COM contains code used to interpret commands typed by the user as described below.

There are two types of commands available under PCDOS, *internal* and *external*. Internal commands are processed directly from instructions located in COMMAND.COM in memory. Commands such as TYPE, COPY, and DIR are available at all times once the system has been loaded. External commands, on the other hand, are processed by programs that reside on a system disk. Each external command is the name of one such file on disk; if the file is not available on the disk, the command cannot be executed. These utility programs perform tasks such as creating and maintaining files on disk.

The remainder of a system disk is available for user files. Additional files can be created until either there is no more space on the disk or there are no further entries available in the file directory. (A method to get around this last limitation is described later.)

Once the operating system has been loaded, the memory available in the IBM PC is configured as shown in Fig. 3.5. Memory between the Resident COMMAND.COM and the reserved memory and ROM at the top of available memory can be overlaid by application programs if necessary. (*Note:* MSDOS has a slightly different memory configuration, described later.)

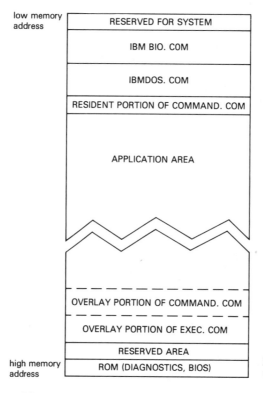

low memory address

| RESERVED FOR SYSTEM |
| IBM BIO. COM |
| IBMDOS. COM |
| RESIDENT PORTION OF COMMAND. COM |
| APPLICATION AREA |
| OVERLAY PORTION OF COMMAND. COM |
| OVERLAY PORTION OF EXEC. COM |
| RESERVED AREA |
| ROM (DIAGNOSTICS, BIOS) |

high memory address

Figure 3.5. Memory map of PCDOS with system loaded.

User application space in memory can be used for programs, data, or user-maintained buffers. In database applications, all three uses are common. In addition, portions of the available memory may be assigned to functions such as disk storage emulators, as described in Section 3.2.2.

3.4.2 Utility Support Functions under PCDOS

One function of an operating system is to manage information stored on auxiliary devices such as disks. In database systems, this function is essential. Creating new files, updating old ones, and accessing data, either through sequential or direct access methods, are typical tasks to be performed. The operating system is responsible for ensuring that all transactions between memory and disk are accurately executed, and that the information stored on disk about its files is consistent with changes made while the disk is in the computer.

Another important function of the operating system is the management of peripheral devices, such as a printer or a serial communications port. Definition of the physical protocols to be used (speed, number of bits per character, etc.) can be changed under PCDOS control. Data transfer to and from these peripherals is also controlled by the operating system, as are the functions used to manage special communication protocols with external devices such as remote computers. For example, the "X-on, X-off" protocol used in some communications permits interruption of transmission when the buffer area is filled, then signals for resumption of data transmission.

Finally, the operating system will invoke language processors and application programs when a user requests this service. The range of languages that can be used depends on the availability of disks that contain the appropriate assemblers, compilers, or interpreters.

3.4.3 File Manipulation Functions

Data on flexible disks are stored in the form of files. A file may contain source statements for an application program, the executable object code for such a program, systems files, or files containing user-generated data. The type of files stored on a PCDOS disk is typically indicated by the "File Extension," a three-letter classification appended to the name of the file. In Section 3.4.1, we mentioned files such as IBMBIO.COM; the designation ".COM" defines that file as an executable program of a systems support type. Other file types are defined by PCDOS: EXE refers to application programs in executable form; BAK is a backup file created by an editor, and so on. A user can, however, define a file with any extent name. If a reserved name is used, the file should agree in type with the extension selected. Database systems usually reserve unique identifiers to designate files that serve special functions. We will note examples of these types of files in reviewing the database packages described in Chapter 4.

One major group of files stored under PCDOS consists entirely of ASCII characters. These files are sequential and can be edited and printed by standard PCDOS commands. Many data files and all program source code files are stored in this format. Sequential files are stored in a packed format, with variable-length records written one right after another, overlapping physical block boundaries on disk. This format makes it possible to read the files rapidly in a sequential format; however, for variable-length records, it usually is not possible to access a specific record within the file without reading all preceding logical records. The operating system keeps track of where the last READ or WRITE was performed and continues accordingly, but no information is maintained as to the location of a specific record.

Sequential files can be updated by inserting or deleting characters, fields, or records, but, since they are packed, the update process must be accomplished by rewriting the entire file. For this reason, editing a sequential file requires writing the revised file to a new area on the disk. Many editors retain the old file as a backup, and automatically change the file extension to "BAK."

Another group of files stored under PCDOS do not necessarily follow the sequential ASCII code format with packed records. Instead, they adhere to fixed record lengths, mapping predictably into specific physical blocks on disk. Such files can be accessed either sequentially or randomly, since it is possible to calculate the address of each record. PCDOS provides users with functions to access random records, and DBMSs take advantage of this capability.

Direct-access files of this type do not require rewriting when updates are performed. New data can be appended to the end of such a file, and old data can be changed without affecting the record size (since records are fixed length). Deleted records can be marked for subsequent removal from the file, so that the size of the file is not immediately affected by a record deletion. Only insertion of new records in the middle of a file requires rewriting the file.

Random files can also be used in other ways, such as for implementing B-tree indexes of data. When such an index is created, pointers to the descendant blocks in such a tree are embedded in the file. These pointers are not stored as ASCII characters. The result is that the file cannot be manipulated by standard editing or printing functions under PCDOS. Attempts to output non-ASCII characters to the screen will result in unpredictable events such as strange characters or setting the screen and keyboard into unworkable states. When such files are created (and they can serve very useful purposes in database systems), the designer must also create separate utilities to maintain them. Editors and error recovery utilities must also be available.

Many DBMS packages create files containing "header" information that is used to define the characteristics of the remainder of the file. Although the data may be stored in ASCII characters, the header usually is not ASCII and cannot be read by system utilities. These DBMS packages usually offer utilities that dump the main file, stripping off the header information so that the files can be processed by other programs.

As users create, edit, and remove files, PCDOS has the responsibility of seeing that the information is stored on disk in a manner that is both efficient and reliable. The basic techniques used by PCDOS to create and maintain disk files are relatively straightforward. First, each disk has a file allocation table and a directory located near the beginning of track 0, as shown in Fig. 3.4. As each new file is created, it is written on the first available sectors, beginning from the first sector after the directory and proceeding toward the center of the disk. Figure 3.6a illustrates such a process, where three files are created and written onto the disk.

When a file is deleted, the directory is changed to reflect deletion and the sectors used for that file are returned to the list of available sectors maintained in the File Allocation Table. Subsequently, when another file is written, PCDOS uses the same logic to assign new program space — the first available sectors, from outside to inside, are used.

After files have been written, modified, and some files deleted, there may be a patchwork of available sectors, with many small, noncontiguous blocks available. Figures 3.6b and c illustrate modification of the disk shown in Fig. 3.6a, with one file removed, and another added as described in the legend. Notice that, at the end of this process, File #4 is no longer located in contiguous sectors on disk. Addition and deletion of files tend to create even more fragmented files, especially large ones. In database applications where new records are added, this problem is quite common, since PCDOS will allocate a new cluster of sectors (or cylinder on an XT) to the file as space is required; it is unlikely that these new sectors will be contiguous to the earlier portions of the data file. One important result of this distribution is slower access speeds, since it is necessary to locate and move to the next physical record in the file before it can be read.

One obvious way to improve disk access performance, therefore, is to rewrite data from frequently used disks to newly formatted disks. If this process is done in such a way as to locate the most used files near the outside of the disk and early in the directory, access times for these files will be minimized. This simple technique may create significant data access improvements in many database applications.

Although we have noted the increased speed of hard disks, the techniques just described are also important on Winchester drives. These disks are rarely purged and completely reorganized, and as a result, files are often badly fragmented, and execution speed is significantly reduced. There are utilities available (advertised in personal computer journals) that will perform disk reorganization for hard disks, thereby improving DBMS performance.

3.4.4 File Limitations

PCDOS imposes several limitations on file size and the number of files that can be accommodated on one disk. The first limitation is the amount of space available on a disk. Since the first tracks of the disk are reserved for the system (boot record, file allocation tables, directory space), the total space available for data or program files is slightly less than the full formatted capacity. It becomes even less if system files are added, since they occupy at least 40K bytes on disk. System files are required to boot the system from disk, but not all disks must have the system if they are used in conjunction with other disks that do have these files. Approximately 360K bytes are available for data files on double-sided, double-density disks formatted under PCDOS version 2.0 and more recent versions if no system files are present.

The directory space reserved near the start of each formatted disk contains the "root directory" of the disk. The root directory can have a maximum of 112 entries, even though there may be space available on the disk for more data.

Each directory entry consists of 32 bytes of information, which includes the file status, name and type, an indication of its attribute (read-only, system, hidden, etc.), the date and time that the file was created, and some systems information about the distribution of the file on disk. This information resides on disk to be used when the system needs to access portions of the files. There is a similar directory entry in the computer's main memory for each active file — the File Control Block (FCB). This block contains the foregoing information as well as information about the size of logical records and the current record number and block number in the file.

The mechanism used to provide random access to data in PCDOS files allows for addressing up to 65,536 sectors, each with 512 bytes. This method places a theoretical limit of roughly 30 million characters to any single file. In fact, the physical limitation of disks currently used with PCDOS is usually much smaller. One vendor of a hard disk system has doubled the maximum file size available by

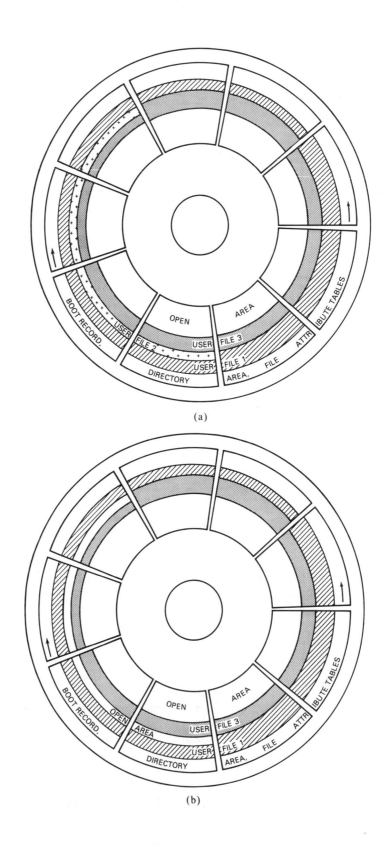

(a)

(b)

(c)

Figure 3.6. Disk file distribution on PCDOS disk. Figure 3.6a: Three files created on newly formatted disk; Figure 3.6b. Disk layout after deletion of User File 2. Note open area between User File 1 and User File 3; Figure 3.6c: Disk file distribution after addition of User File 4. Note that File 4 is not located in contiguous sectors on disk.

using sectors of 1,024 bytes. This modification illustrates the potential of modifying current limitations on file size, even though such changes have not yet become standard.

It is important to remember that a single file cannot overlap from one disk to another. This restriction means it may be necessary to subdivide files into units that will fit on one disk (e.g., creating personnel files for only a portion of the alphabet).

3.4.4.1 Extended File Directories

In the previous section, we described a root directory, capable of accommodating a maximum of 112 files. However, PCDOS provides an escape mechanism that will permit creation of more than 112 files on a single flexible disk. The technique involves creation of subdirectories. In the root directory, one file is designated as a master directory for subfiles (using the attribute byte to designate the file in this manner). Within the regular disk files, one or more directory files are created, each identifying other files within that subdirectory. There is no theoretical limit to the number of subfiles that can be created in this manner. There is, however, a penalty in storage available, since the extended directory is itself a file and the root directory space is not recovered. Further, the fact that the directories and files may be located anywhere on disk invariably slows down execution of these files.

3.4.5 Buffers

In Chapter 2, we noted the benefits of using buffers to reduce the number of disk accesses in database applications. PCDOS offers the user control over the number of buffers available for data transfer. The default number of buffers allocated for disk transfer is two; this number is acceptable for programs that use minimal random disk access. For most database applications, however, it is better to increase the number of buffers to 20 or more through the BUFFERS command to accomplish this task. The maximum number of buffers that can be requested depends on available memory. By increasing the number of buffers, the chances of finding data in memory without having to go to disk is greatly improved and performance is enhanced.

Buffers can be defined through PCDOS, but they can also be incorporated into DBMS packages, separate from the PCDOS function. It is important to check DBMS documentation to see if additional buffers are provided by the system, since database integrity requires that buffers be written out to disk before the system is turned off, and the location of buffers will influence the manner in which the user manages data files.

3.4.6 Backing Up Files

It is extremely important to create backup copies of files on a regular basis in any database system. There are several ways that files can be backed up under PCDOS. First, files can be copied individually, using the COPY command. This technique, when used with a newly formatted disk, will create files that are contiguous and appear in the directory in the order in which they were created. Using the COPY option, therefore, can result in reorganization of files that will improve performance, as described in Section 3.4.3. COPY may not improve file organization if the file is transferred to a disk that has been used before.

Another backup technique available under PCDOS is to use the DISKCOPY command, which will make an identical copy of every track and sector on one disk to another. This technique is faster than COPY if many files on a single disk are to be duplicated. It will, however, take a fixed amount of time whether there are few or many data files, since the process involves simply copying every sector whether or not valid data are present. Remember, too, that DISKCOPY will not improve the efficiency of file organization on a disk.

Since most Winchester disks are not removable, the data on them can only be recovered if the drive is functioning properly. The amount of data on a fixed disk system is far greater than on flexible disks, so it becomes even more important to back up these files regularly . The reliability of Winchester disks is good and continues to improve, but the potential for loss of data due to power failure or other unforeseen calamity remains real. Some hard disk systems have built-in backup cartridge tapes. These systems are useful in copying entire fixed disks, but when only portions of the data have been modified since the last backup, selective backup methods may be preferable.

Backups can be done using hardware devices, as described in Section 3.2.4.2. Sometimes, these devices come with special programs to permit various types of backup. PCDOS also has utilities for file backup. BACKUP.COM permits backing up data from a hard disk to one or more flexible disks, and a companion utility, RESTORE.COM, restores data from backup disks. The potential for data errors is great on multiple disk backups, and this technique should be used with caution.

3.4.7 Retrieving Data from Lost or Damaged Files

Sometimes disaster strikes and a valuable file is corrupted or inadvertently destroyed. It may be worth considerable effort to regain as much of the information as possible. Fortunately, there are some aids to this process under PCDOS, even though the recovery techniques may be complicated.

When the ERASE command is invoked under PCDOS, the file is not actually erased from the disk. Instead, the directory entry for that file is flagged (changing the first character of the file name to a "deleted file" character), and data blocks assigned to that file are returned to the list of available blocks on the disk. Only when a new file is created or new blocks are added to existing files are the obsolete directory entries and data blocks re-used as needed. For this reason, an inadvertent file erasure can sometimes be recovered, either partially or completely, depending on the subsequent activity on that disk.

File recovery can be done in two ways. One involves the use of special PCDOS function calls that can be used to restore the active status of a file previously declared "erased." Use of this function call requires knowledge of assembly-level programming and considerable experience with PCDOS. Fortunately, however, software vendors have developed user-friendly programs that can be used to recover information from erased or corrupted files. Although these programs are not available as utilities distributed with PCDOS, they are extremely useful. All database users should purchase a utility to assist in recovering information when the inevitable calamity occurs.

3.4.8 Differences between PCDOS and MSDOS

Although Microsoft, Inc., wrote both PCDOS and MSDOS, the two operating systems are not identical. Some of the reasons stem from proprietary features incorporated in PCDOS that are not available for duplication on other systems (several lawsuits have upheld the proprietary nature of these distinctive features). Other features reflect evolutionary changes in the operating systems, not all of which have been incorporated into each implementation. Due to the dominance of IBM in this market, the trend to maintain as complete compatibility as possible remains strong.

No operating system is static. PCDOS has experienced two major revisions since its first release. Version 1 has become obsolete with the appearance of version 2. Version 3 retains compatibility with version 2, although new features have been added. The comments in this text refer both to versions 2 and 3, unless specifically stated otherwise.

MSDOS has also evolved, replicating most of the same new features found in later versions of PCDOS. However, as noted in the following section, there remain differences between PCDOS and MSDOS. The key point is that the marketing success of the IBM PC has dictated a strong degree of compatibility between MSDOS and PCDOS, which is likely to continue. Differences will persist, but they are not likely to become more significant in subsequent releases.

3.4.8.1 Memory Mapping

Figure 3.5 depicts the general mapping of memory under PCDOS. MSDOS is slightly different. There is no provision for ROM at the upper part of memory; the COMMAND.COM file remains resident and in one contiguous location before user space, and another file, the EXEC processor, also remains resident and cannot be overlaid by user applications. With these changes, it is possible for the user application area to extend from the end of the COMMAND.COM file to the upper limits of available memory. This difference usually is not noted by the user, but it may affect attempts to utilize more fully augmented memory. It also means that systems with limited memory will have less applications space available under MSDOS, since more space is required for memory-resident systems programs.

3.4.8.2 Use of ROM BIOS

The IBM PC uses ROM for a portion of its BIOS. This ROM is copyrighted and cannot be imitated exactly. It contains many functions that permit more rapid manipulation of the screen and of graphic displays, as well as other features that enhance performance. Other manufacturers would like, on the one hand, to retain complete compatibility with PCDOS programs, and on the other, to exhibit comparable execution speeds. To retain compatibility, it is necessary to simulate the ROM BIOS functions of the IBM PC through some other means, usually at the cost of slower execution. Some "IBM compatible" personal computers have enhanced graphics resolution that may reduce their true compatibility with the IBM PC.

Software developers have the option of fully utilizing the faster ROM BIOS function calls on the PC, thereby potentially limiting use of these programs on other systems, or adhering to standard DOS calls with slight degradation of performance. Some programs such as VisiCalc have a version for the IBM PC and other versions for other systems.

Certain software packages utilize timing and other hardware factors. These packages will almost certainly not run correctly on other hardware without revision of the IBM-specific features. Many of the better-known DBMS packages use varying degrees of direct access to ROM BIOS and hence require special modifications for other systems.

In general, calls utilizing DOS functions will remain compatible between MSDOS and PCDOS, whereas programs that bypass DOS and go directly to the ROM BIOS may not work properly.

3.5 ENVIRONMENTAL PROBLEMS AND SAFEGUARDS

Personal computer users are inevitably more involved with the details of hardware and environmental factors than users of large systems. Using a personal computer is unlike using a terminal. The terminal connects to a remote system "somewhere," where trained professionals are supposed to keep the computer running, mount disks and tapes, and take care of system operation. Personal computers, on the other hand, are in the same room with the user, and there is rarely anyone around to help with operational questions. For this reason, the database user must know more about the operational details of the system and the consequences of any malfunctions that may occur. In this section, we point out some of the common problems that can arise during use of a personal computer for database applications, and we suggest ways in which these problems can be minimized.

3.5.1 Power Failure

If power is turned off or a plug is inadvertently disconnected, all information in main memory is destroyed. In addition, if the disks were active at the time of failure, it is highly likely that errors will be generated on the disk, or even that major portions of the disk will become unusable. This is one of the most frustrating problems that confronts a personal computer user. Related problems such as power surges or voltage drops can also result in data loss or damage to equipment. Lightning storms often create problems with power supply that directly affect operation of personal computers.

When power is interrupted and information in memory is destroyed, data in memory that has not been transferred to disk is lost. Since there is no way of knowing what information was in buffers at the time of failure, it is difficult to determine whether or how the files were damaged.

There are several ways to minimize problems caused by power failure. The first is to establish an operations policy that will limit the magnitude of the loss and provide for its recovery, at least in part. This policy should include frequent backup of data onto files that are stored away from the computer, and also manual or automated methods of recreating transactions that have been completed since the last backup. Maintaining a manual log of all transactions, either as a printout or through notation on input source documents is one way that changes can be identified and, if necessary, repeated.

Another way that data loss problems can be minimized is to copy buffered data to disk frequently during an interactive session. The frequency of this process depends on usage, criticality of the task and data, and optimism of the user. However, almost anyone who has worked with a personal computer will recall times when data have been lost as a result of power problems.

Finally, power failure losses can be minimized by maintaining a steady power supply or providing battery backup. Several inexpensive hardware solutions are available to provide both of these functions. It is therefore surprising that relatively few individuals take the trouble to guarantee the reliability of their systems in this manner.

3.5.2 Hardware Failure

Despite the great reliability of today's personal computers, hardware problems do arise. Symptoms such as an unresponsive keyboard or strange characters on the display usually indicate that something is amiss. System error messages describing inability to read or write to disks occur unpredictably, usually at the worst possible times (Murphy's law). Personal computer users should be prepared for these situations, and they should know how to take whatever corrective steps may be called for. A few examples will illustrate these points.

The most important guideline in the case of hardware failure is to minimize your losses. If a disk cannot be read or written on, the disk itself may be salvaged despite this problem, but in the meantime it is important, if possible, to copy the information in memory to another drive or another disk. Care must be taken not to corrupt other disks by improper copying procedures, but it is often possible to save data in this manner.

If one disk drive goes out, it is sometimes possible to use system utilities to copy information from one disk to another with a single drive. To do so, however, usually requires exiting from an application program in order to access operating system commands.

Other types of failures may require more creativity. Sometimes, when it is impossible to store on disk information still in memory, an alternative solution is to send the data out via a communications port to another system or even to a printer. Another option is to use system utilities to examine the contents of memory, copying the information to a printer or external port.

3.5.3 Problems with Disks

Since most data will be stored on disks, it is important to know what can go wrong with these storage devices. We have already discussed backup provisions for fixed disks. However, there are several ways in which data on flexible disks can be corrupted other than by the physical failures decribed earlier.

Flexible disks can be removed from the disk drive, which is a benefit. However, if a disk is removed from a drive and another inserted while an application program is active, care must be taken that the new disk is recognized by the system as being different from the one just removed. Earlier, we described the contents of the file control block on disk and in memory. The version in memory may reflect changes that took place on the disk. If those changes are not written to disk before the disk is removed, the disk data may be incompatible with its directory information. If a different disk is put into the drive and then directory information from an old disk is written out to the second disk, the directory will be incompatible. PCDOS does not offer adequate protection for this type of human error. It is important, therefore, to practice extreme caution in changing disks during execution of an application program.

Sometimes, disk capacity is exceeded during a database activity. When this occurs, it is important first to retain the validity of the data on disk, then to provide for means to recover the data remaining in memory. Many DBMS packages offer means to examine a disk to see if files can be erased to make room for the remaining data. Some give warning when the disk is nearing capacity. If neither of these options is available, the user should take precautions before starting the operation to ensure that adequate space is available for the anticipated growth of a data file. A common cause of this situation arises when a file is edited, but there is no room for the updated version. This problem often can be corrected by inserting a new disk in another drive and copying the edited file to the new disk.

Data files can be of several types as described earlier. If a file is of a type that can only be read by a particular application package, or on only one type of hardware, it is a good idea to create a backup file of the data in an alternate format so that the file can be recreated on other hardware.

The foregoing examples represent only a small sampling of problems that can occur. In many cases, however, what originally appeared to be a major catastrophe can be minimized through careful analysis and creative problem solving. Remember: The most common causes of serious data destruction are *haste* and *panic*.

3.6 COMMUNICATIONS

Personal computers usually function as standalone devices. However, it is often important to transfer information from one personal computer to another, or to a larger computer. Data transfer can be done by transferring flexible disks between compatible systems. In addition, there are several other ways in which information stored on one computer can be transferred to another. This section covers some of the details associated with file transfer and communication between machines.

3.6.1 Direct Links between Two Computers

Most computers have both serial and parallel output ports that can be used for communication with peripheral devices, and also with other computers. These ports can be reconfigured, using PCDOS calls, to transfer data at different rates and with different character configurations. The MODE command in PCDOS provides this capability.

When two computers are linked through serial auxiliary ports, it is necessary to adjust the wires used to send and receive through those ports. Since the auxiliary port is used to send data to peripheral devices, standard pins on the serial connector are selected to send and receive information. Typically, one of the wires is used to transmit data, another to receive data. When two computers communicate, however, one must transpose these two wires, so that information sent from one will appear on the receiving wire for the other and vice versa. A special connector for this purpose, sometimes called a "null modem," is available at low cost. Individuals who have access to a soldering gun, pliers, and a screw driver can build their own connector at even lower cost.

Once the communication protocol between two personal computers has been established, it is advisable to verify that data are in fact being sent and received as expected. One way to make sure that the transmission process is functioning correctly is to use the COPY command on both computers as follows:

Computer 1	Computer 2
(sending data)	(receiving data)
COPY CON AUX	COPY AUX CON
type some lines of data	data should appear on screen
Ctrl-Z (end of transmission)	normal prompt should appear

If this process works correctly (preferably testing in both directions), the process is established, and it is possible to transfer files.

3.6.2 Modem Communications

It often is desirable to transfer information via telephone lines from one computer to another. This process involves use of the auxiliary serial port and a data conversion device that converts the digital computer signals to forms that can be transmitted over telephone lines. Communication rates by telephone are limited, as described earlier. Moreover, noise often is present on the lines, further degrading performance.

There are two types of telephone data transmission devices used with personal computers. Both devices are called a *modem*, an abbreviation of the words "modulate" and "demodulate," indicating that the digital signal from a computer is first modulated to an analog signal for transmission, then demodulated, or converted back to a digital signal at the receiving end. An acoustic coupler uses the regular headset of a telephone to send and receive the analog impulses representing digital data, with one tone used to mean "0" and another for "1." The second system uses a direct data connection between computer and the telephone jack, transmitting 0 and 1 tones without using the circuitry of the phone headset. This latter system is affected less by noise and is more reliable at communication rates above 30 characters per second. Some direct connect devices permit voice and data to be sent over the same connection, which is particularly helpful when trying to establish an effective computer-to-computer connection at long distances. Since telephone networks are being used increasingly for data communications, many changes can be expected to improve the speed, reliability, and versatility of this communications process.

Modem communication assumes that one such device is "calling" the other. The device that does the calling is called an *originate modem*; the receiving device is called an *answer modem*. Some modems can be switched to serve either in originate or answer mode. An answer modem must be connected to a computer that is prepared to receive external messages.

Software packages are available that make the process of remote communications simple and convenient. These packages offer automatic redialing and login, and they aid in the data transfer process. New features are being added to these packages, and the competitive nature of this market will continue to force new improvements.

3.6.3 Methods for Transferring Files

There are several ways that files can be transferred between computers. One relatively straightforward way is to use the COPY command in PCDOS. With this method, characters are simply transferred from one machine to the other, and the result is stored as specified in the COPY command arguments. This technique has three drawbacks. First, there is no error checking, which means that improper data transfer will not be detected. Serial communications are not infallible; the probability of errors increases with transmission speed, and the errors that occur may be difficult to detect in a standard ASCII file, since invalid or control characters may be embedded in the receiving file. Second, the size of file that can be transferred without loss of data is limited to the buffer space available in memory. When the buffer is full, it must be emptied to disk, during which time no further data are accepted. If the sending computer does not halt transmission, many characters or lines will be lost. The third drawback is that certain types of files such as executable code and files with non-ASCII characters (e.g., B-trees) may not be accurately transmitted because they may contain embedded characters (ctrl-Z) that are interpreted as representing the end of data. Transmission ceases when these characters are encountered; hence, the COPY command will not work to transfer these types of files between computers.

Fortunately, several software packages are available that enable the user to accomplish data transfer more effectively. Some such programs are available without charge, having been developed in universities or other institutions willing to sponsor cooperative program exchange. A number of such programs are available under PCDOS. They have several features in common. Each program must follow certain software protocols, in addition to the hardware conventions previously described, in order for the transfer to take place. The word *protocol* in this context refers to the manner in which the two systems establish a link, inform each other when it is appropriate to send or receive, and package data into units that may also contain error detection and correction features. Several communication protocols are in common use today, and different packages may or may not use the same protocol. Sometimes, two different packages use virtually the same protocol and can be used together; more often it is necessary to have identical programs on each computer.

An important feature common to most communication packages is error detection and correction. The techniques vary, but they often include some sort of check for nonmatching bit patterns sent or received, and they provide for retransmission if the data do not match. This error checking is extremely important, especially at higher data transfer rates or over phone lines. However, the overhead incurred in error detection and correction can amount to 50 percent or more of the actual data throughput. Sometimes it may be advisable to select slower communication rates when excessive errors are reported. Usually, the communication package will include some sort of warning message if too many retries are required to send data accurately.

There are some additional features that are quite valuable in communication packages, though not all packages contain them. It is extremely valuable to provide for interruption of data transmission in one form or another (several protocols are in use). With this interruption, it is possible for the receiving computer to empty buffers, check data for validity, or request retransmission of an invalid block of data before a new block is sent. Likewise, the ability to transfer object code files and other non-ASCII files is valuable because many such files are used in database applications.

Packages that permit transfer of multiple files are useful because it often is desirable to send groups of files. Once the transfer process has been initiated, using a transfer package with multifile options, the user is free to do something else (although the computer will be tied up until the process is complete).

Systems that permit remote initiation of a receiving computer are extremely useful, since it often is necessary for a user to transfer data to an unattended computer. Some packages offer self-correcting transmission features that reduce the need for retransmission.

One communication package available as a public domain product has the name Kermit. This package is unusual in that it permits communication not only between personal computers, but also between large mainframes, minicomputers, and personal computers in any combination. The protocol is suited to file transfers for database systems, with features permitting multiple file transfer, data correction/retransmission, and the use of "wild cards" to specify groups of files with similar names.

3.6.4 Using Network Services

Another way in which data can be transferred between computers is through the use of network services, such as Compuserve or The Source. These networks offer mechanisms for "uploading" files into a database, then "downloading" the same files to other computers. Each network uses one or more special protocols, but they are compatible with several personal computer communication packages. Some packages permit the user to save, on disk, complete dialogues or selected portions of dialogues appearing on the screen, so that a request to list a file from a remote source may be captured in disk form for future reference.

The process of using networks will undoubtedly grow in the future, and database systems will have to be designed to take advantage of the potential these services offer with respect to sharing data with other users.

3.7 SUMMARY

This chapter has presented a brief survey of the personal computer environment, including hardware, operating systems, software, and a general discussion relating these factors to database applications. There are, of course, many more things to be said in conjunction with each of the foregoing topics. The references below offer advice as to places to go for further information on most of the topics covered in this section. The reader may find that some of the material will gain significance as he or she becomes more familiar with the use of personal computers. For that reason, it may be worthwhile to return to selected portions after spending a few weeks or months working with a computer. In the case of database applications, the significance of the hardware will certainly increase as a real application is designed and tested. In the chapters that follow, we will refer to items noted above, and it may also prove beneficial to return to those sections as their significance becomes clearer in the context of this new material.

REFERENCES

The world of personal computers is changing rapidly, perhaps more so than most technologies. Information on the latest in many of the areas discussed in this chapter are likely to appear after this book is published.

Therefore, in an effort to provide the best guide to readers wishing to pursue different areas, this reference section has been designed to offer typical sources of the places most likely to contain updates on specific subject areas.

● Personal Computer Magazines

The dramatic rise in sales of personal computers has led to a large increase in magazines of all types aimed at the personal computer user. Many of these publications have failed; new ones appear, but with decreasing frequency as the market becomes more competitive. The following list contains some of the journals generally considered the best in the field, with brief descriptions of their strengths.

BYTE Magazine

Perhaps the most successful of all general-purpose personal computer magazines, *BYTE* aims to provide information for all types of personal computers, including APPLE, CP/M, MSDOS, XENIX, and others. The technical articles are well researched. *BYTE* attempts to provide a theme for each issue, and the several articles around each theme usually provide in-depth tutorials and reviews on current activities in that area. The magazine has extensive advertisements (average size of each issue is over 500 pages) that provide some insights into new developments. Overall, *BYTE* is one of the best general magazines on personal computers.

PC WORLD

A monthly magazine that focuses on the IBM PC and compatibles, this journal usually contains the most up-to-date information on new developments in this field. It regularly surveys new hardware add-ons and peripherals for PC compatibles, but its main focus is on software applications, and it provides objective reviews of a great many word processors, spreadsheets, and DBMSs during the course of a single year.

PC TECH Journal

This monthly journal, now in its fourth year of publication, focuses on the IBM personal computer family, but ranges into systems that go beyond the PC, XT, and AT, including the desktop 370 and the new RT (RISC Technology PC). The target audience is expected to have a solid background in computer science, and some of the articles are quite advanced, but the result is a reference-level magazine with state-of-the-art reviews on new concepts. A very valuable reference for any serious programmer on PC systems.

Mini-Micro Systems

What *PC TECH* is to the IBM PC world, *Mini-Micro Systems* is to the personal computer world in general. A technical reference magazine, this monthly publication contains extremely valuable articles providing hardware and software insights into systems running under CP/M, MSDOS, UNIX, and other operating systems. It has excellent articles on communications protocols as well as reviewing new technology such as optical disks. This publication is aimed at the experienced computer user, but not necessarily at the professional.

Other Publications of Interest

Other publications also provide valuable update information. *PC Magazine* appears twice monthly, containing articles slightly less polished than *PC World* but still of acceptable technical caliber. *PC News* and *Infoworld* are weekly news magazines that often contain the first announcements of marketing as well as technical significance. *Dr. Dobbs Journal* is the most sophisticated software general-purpose personal computer magazine, aimed at serious programmers and containing useful hints on operating systems, compilers, and new languages. In addition, some magazines dedicated to specific manufacturers, such as *Digital Review* (For DEC users), often contain general reviews of much broader interest.

The scientific journals of the computer era include many publications that go beyond the interests of most personal computer users. However, the *IEEE Computer* magazine is one that often contains superb tutorials and reviews on new technologies and new software concepts, and the *ACM Computing Surveys* is also a good place to find comprehensive tutorials on computer science topics that affect personal computers. These references should be available in any library that contains computer science materials.

● Microprocessors, Memory, and Computer Architectures

The manuals that accompany today's personal computers give minimal information about the microprocessors on which they are based. There are, however, several texts that provide good information on these processors, their structure, and their instruction sets. In addition, magazines such as *Byte, Mini-Micro Systems*, and *PC TECH* frequently carry good introductory summaries of new chips. For readers who are not planning to program in assembly language, the articles in the aforementioned magazines are recommended. For individuals who wish to study the architecture in greater detail, the following texts will contain the technical specifications needed to use and understand these chips.

8-Bit Microprocessors

Osborne, A. *An Introduction to Microcomputers*, (Berkeley, California: Adam Osborne Associates, 1975). 396 pages.

> Although this text appeared near the beginning of the personal computer revolution, it remains one of the best introductions to the whole subject, including a comprehensive review of a number of the early processor chips, including the Intel 8080 and Motorola 6800. For someone interested in learning the fundamentals before studying 16-bit or 32-bit improvements, this remains a very valuable text. In the past, the original IMSAI computer kits each came with a copy of this text (which is where I got mine).

16-Bit Microprocessors

The Intel Family (8086, 80186, 80286)

Gorsline, G. W. *16-Bit Modern Microcomputers: The Intel I8086 Family*, (Englewood Cliffs, New Jersey: Prentice-Hall, Inc., 1985). 516 pages.

> A good reference to architecture, language, and relationships between the 8086, 8087, and 8089 microprocessors, with a brief introduction to the 80186 and 80286 chips. A good review of the 8089 IO processor is included, with examples of programs using this co-processor. The discussion on operating systems is outdated, since it does not mention MSDOS.

Liu, Y. and Gibson, G. *Microcomputer Systems: The 8086/8088 Family Architecture, Programming and Design*, (Englewood Cliffs, New Jersey: Prentice-Hall, Inc., 1984). 550 pages.

> Similar in many ways to the Gorsline text, except that its discussion of the architecture is more comprehensive. However, the coverage of the 80286 is less complete, and there is no discussion of operating systems.

Morse, S. P. and Albert, D. J. *The 80286 Architecture*, (New York: John Wiley & Sons, 1986). 279 pages.

> A better reference for the 80286 than the Gorsline text, Morse and Albert discuss architecture, addressing modes, and the instruction set of the Intel 80286 microprocessor. The text has fairly good coverage on the differences between this chip and the earlier 8086 system. Morse also wrote a primer on the 8086, and he is able to draw on this earlier experience in discussing the innovations of the later chip.

There are as yet no good texts published on the Intel APX 80386 processor. It is likely that texts will appear soon.

The Motorola Family: 68000, 68010, 68020

Harman, T. T. and Lawson, B., *The Motorola MC68000 Microprocessor Family: Assembly Language, Interface Design, and System Design*, (Englewood Cliffs, New Jersey: Prentice-Hall, 1985). 574 pages.

> This is a new textbook that has had good reviews. Its main strength is the review of the instruction set of the 68000 and 68010. Unfortunately, it does not describe the 68020 or its associated math co-processor. There are good chapters on addressing, system operation, and debugging features built into the instruction set.

Kelley-Booth, R. and Fowler, B. *68000, 68010, 68020*, (Indianapolis: Howard W. Sams & Co., 1985). 354 pages.

> This text is mainly a primer on programming the 68000 family, but it contains little about the specifics of the architecture. I would recommend the Harman book for more complete coverage of both, but this text is readable and informative in treating the instruction set.

Bubble Memory

Awalt, D. (1985) "Bubble Boards," *PC TECH Journal*, Vol. 3, No. 5, pp. 123-136.

> An excellent review of the technology and of boards currently available for the IBM PC.

Optical Disks

Laub, L. (1986) "The Evolution of Mass Storage," *BYTE*, Vol. 11, No. 6, pp. 158-249.

The May issue features a review of optical storage systems. There are seven articles in this comprehensive reivew, which includes discussion of principles as well as review of specific products. An excellent tutorial. One article goes into the database problems associated with file maintenance on write-once systems, a feature that is alluded to in this chapter.

Jaworski, J. (1986) "Lasers Anticipate Mass Storage Appeal," *Hardcopy*, Vol. 6, No. 2, pp. 42-49.

Articles appear with increasing frequency describing laser disks of various types. This one is a good review of the three different forms of storage, and the problems associated with read-write optical disks. It also gives projected growth patterns of the technology.

● Programming Languages

From the wealth of languages available on personal computers, I have selected two to include in this reference section. Together with assembly language specific to each microprocessor, they represent the languages most suited to DBMS development.

The C Language

Kernighan, B. W. and Ritchie, D. M. *The C Programming Language*, (Englewood Cliffs, New Jersey: Prentice-Hall, Inc., 1978). 228 pages.

The authors of this book were instrumental in development of the language, and this is the classic reference on C programming.

Kelly, A. and Pohl, I. *A Book on C*, (Menlo Park, California: The Benjamin / Cummings Publishing Co. Inc., 1984). 362 pages.

This book is more tutorial in nature than the Kernighan/Ritchie text, and it emphasizes interactive programming, giving abundant examples. It is both readable and well organized to present the language effectively.

Hunt, W. J. (1986) "The State of C," *PC TECH*, Vol. 4, No. 1, pp. 82-108.

A very thorough review of about a dozen different C compilers for PCDOS systems. This article emphasizes the variety in capabilities offered by these systems. An important article for anyone seriously considering acquisition of a C compiler for the PC.

MUMPS

Walters, R. F., Bowie, J., and Wilcox J. C. *MUMPS Primer*, (College Park, Maryland: MUMPS Users' Group, 1983). 122 pages.

Despite the fact that one author of this text is also the author of this review, the MUMPS Primer is a good reference to a language designed for database applications. It presents the language in a logical sequence and shows some of the unique facilities offered by MUMPS for database manipulation.

● Operating Systems

There are a great many books that supplement the user manuals of the principal operating systems used for personal computers. These books may be found in technical bookstores as well as personal computer outlets. The following books are a few that I found well written and readable.

PCDOS/MSDOS

Sheldon, T. *Introduction to PCDOS and MSDOS (including 3.0)*, (New York: McGraw-Hill Publishing Co., 1985). 374 pages.

> The first half of this book is tutorial, the second somewhat more advanced. Numerous illustrations of screens generated in interacting with the operating system. Quite well written.

Boston Computer Society. *Things the Manual Never Told You (IBM PC Edition)*, (Reading, Massachusetts: Addison Wesley Publishing Co, 1985). 188 pages.

> A good review, not only of MSDOS, but also of peripherals such as printers and of some application packages, including spreadsheets and DBMSs. Contains useful tips for practical operation.

UNIX

Kernighan, B. W. and Pike, R. *The Unix Programming Environment*, (Englewood Cliffs, New Jersey: Prentice-Hall Inc., 1984). 357 pages.

> This is the bible for students and regular UNIX users, written by two people who helped develop this system. A reference manual that will become dog-eared over years of use by people working with UNIX.

Birns, P. M., Brown, P. B., and Muster, J. C. C. *UNIX for People*, (Englewood Cliffs, New Jersey: Prentice-Hall Inc., 1985). 535 pages.

> UNIX is complex, and it takes a long time to learn. This text is written for the novice who may not be a professional programmer, and it is considerably more basic, with more complete examples than the Kernighan book. It aims to teach readers how to go about learning about the system as well as helping them with specific areas. Well written and extensively field tested.

Hansen, A. (1985) "XENIX for the XT," *PC TECH*, Vol. 3, No. 6, pp. 129-140.

> An interesting article that describes the UNIX-like features of XENIX and also gives good reasons why this operating system requires a more powerful microprocessor to run effectively, therefore suggesting that XENIX should not be used on the 8088 processor (although it will run well on the 80286 AT personal computer).

4
Design of a Database Application: A Case Study

4.1 INTRODUCTION

In Chapters 2 and 3, we presented principles of database systems and fundamentals of personal computer operations. The purpose of this chapter is to apply those concepts to the development of a database. To do so, we have selected an example that typifies the decisions that must be made in the design of a system and the selection of a package to use for that application. The chapter describes two approaches to overall design and illustrates one of these methods. Subsequently, two commercial database packages are used to implement the design, using a small data set representative of the type encountered in the real world. Contrasting features of the two packages are discussed. The chapter concludes with general observations on database design, implementation, and selection of DBMS packages.

4.2 A CASE STUDY: STUDENTS, DEPARTMENTS, AND COURSES AT MAVERICK UNIVERSITY

Maverick University is a fictitious institution resembling many universities in the United States. It has several colleges, each with several departments. It is supported in part by state funds, but faculty members conduct research using funds obtained from grants awarded by the federal government, private foundations, and industry. Most of the faculty and students at Maverick University live in the community adjacent to the campus. The campus offers undergraduate degrees in many areas as well as master's and doctoral degrees.

Information is the most important commodity dealt with at Maverick University. Information is a vital commodity required to run the campus: information on courses, students, facilities, budgets, construction, schedules of all types of events, and myriads of other types of facts and figures. In this respect, Maverick is typical of many businesses and government bodies that deal more with services than with the manufacture of real objects. The principal products of Maverick U are the education of its students and the results of research conducted by faculty, students, and staff.

There are four classes of individuals at Maverick University: faculty, students, administration, and staff. If you speak to any one of these groups, you would likely be told that the campus would run a great deal more smoothly if it were not for the presence of two of the other groups (staff is generally considered essential by everyone). Keeping this entire system afloat in a sea of world events, budgetary crises, heightened sensitivity to environment, and a need to adjust the content of instruction on a yearly basis is the challenge faced by these four groups. To a large extent, their success is dependent on the effective flow of information.

It is not possible here to cover all facets of information handling that go into the complex operations of Maverick U. Instead, we will treat a small subset that is representative of the overall information needs of the campus, one that involves students, faculty, and administration (as always, with staff help). We restrict our scope to information needs associated with identification of students and faculty and the courses taken (or taught) at Maverick U. Specifically, we will want to be able to answer questions such as "What classes did student XYZ take, when did (s)he take them, and what grades did (s)he receive?" "Is this student in good standing?" "How can we get registration information to a student?" "What is the latest transcript for student XYZ?" "What faculty are involved in teaching these classes, and what mix of academic ranks are represented by these faculty?" "What can we tell the adjacent communities about the distribution of our faculty and students, so that they can plan appropriate community services?" This set of questions could be expanded indefinitely, but the topics posed are sufficient to illustrate a realistic challenge in the design of a database.

4.2.1 Design Approaches

Given the need to answer such questions, what is the next step? If one asks this question of database professionals, the chances are that the answers will vary widely, but in general, two basic approaches will most likely be proposed for the design of such a database.

One approach is to ask what current methods are being used to handle this information (let us assume that the current methods are largely manual). From this study, it is possible to identify data elements available, group them in files and then, when the data have been entered, design reports based on that information that meet or exceed the current report generation system.

A second approach is to start with the information needs of the campus, such as responses to the foregoing questions, and analyze them in terms of the data required to generate these answers. Analysis of these questions will show that they can be grouped into categories, and that the data required will probably overlap in many cases. From this initial analysis, a set of required data elements is defined, then classified into related groups. The sources of each data element must be defined, as well as responsibility for their validity. As these elements are identified and classified, they will be incorporated into files, each containing a set of related data. The files will then be indexed according to the intended questions to be answered. This process also includes analysis of the users, and the requirements of each group for specific reports are classified in terms of the information needed, security restrictions, and timing of their information needs.

These two approaches offer interesting contrasts. The first represents a bottom-up approach, identifying existing data and current methodologies with a goal of replicating many of these elements in an automated system. The implicit assumptions are that what is being done now is what is needed for the future, and that automation can probably do it better. The second method seeks to perform an information analysis of the entire system, then restricts design to solution of the identified needs of the users, bearing in mind the probable need to provide more flexibility than initially perceived by these users. This approach is in effect a top-down method since it begins with analysis of end use and derives data requirements accordingly.

As described, neither method is perfect. Careful analysis of the current process usually fails to identify adequately shortcomings in that process, and quite often the users themselves are not able to provide the information required for an effective DBMS. On the other hand, strict adherence to current data-handling methods will often limit the potential for introducing significant improvements to an existing system. The ideal approach is to do both a top-down functional analysis and also a careful study of the current situation, then design a system that can meet perceived as well as anticipated needs.

In our text, we cannot illustrate all of the human factors associated with the Maverick University campus. We can, however, analyze the informational needs using a top-down approach, and we can use this method to help us design the database system. In later chapters, we will discuss design factors that might affect this process, but for the moment we will limit our study to the functional requirements of the system.

4.2.2 User Viewpoints

The first step in analyzing the information needs of Maverick University will be to characterize the end users of the information generated by the system. There are three types of users of this system: administrators, faculty, and students. Staff help each of these classes achieve their ends, and they have information needs of their own. For our purposes, we will consider the administrator in our system to be the registrar's office, the faculty representative to be a department chair, and the student to be an individual who is for the moment more interested in what courses he or she has already taken than planning for next year's courses. These restrictions will help us limit the analytical process. By making them explicit, we also document the boundaries of our analysis so that, at a later time, we can return and, if necessary, expand the scope of the analysis.

4.2.2.1 Registrar

The registrar's office is convinced that its function is by far the most important on campus. Without it, none of the results of all the instructional process (some of it highly suspect) would have any long-term significance. In fact, it could not take place without the registrar publishing the availability of courses, accepting student requests to enroll, scheduling classes, recording the grades turned in by faculty and transmitting the collected result to students and others interested in the students' performance. This office can provide you with detailed, sometimes painful anecdotes of the problems encountered in each step of this process: courses changed at the last moment by inconsiderate faculty, students who add and drop courses with abandon, and the constant flow of grade changes for courses long since completed. It becomes clear from this analysis that students and faculty seem to exist to complicate the life of the registrar, and the potential role of automation is viewed as a real benefit in helping to achieve some semblance of order in a chaotic situation.

The information needs of the registrar are fairly easy to identify. First, there must be data on each student, including identifying number, address (updated frequently but still rarely accurate), academic major, and financial status (a large number of Maverick U students receive financial aid). Next, there must be a catalog of courses offered, containing the course number, units, instructor(s), when offered, and a description of the course that can be distributed to students considering which courses to select. Third, the registrar's office must have a clearly defined procedure for entering grades for all classes taken. Finally, the registrar is responsible for producing a student transcript, one that details for each student the courses taken, grades received, units earned, overall current and cumulative performance, and when the time finally arrives, degree(s) received.

4.2.2.2 Department Chair

The faculty at Maverick University is convinced that their role is by far the most important on campus. Students come and go, but who but the faculty is qualified to identify what should be taught, how it should be taught, and how to evaluate the learning process? Department chairs, themselves faculty, are slightly more demanding in their information requirements, so we will concentrate on their needs, which also cover the needs of individual faculty. The chair of any department will be able to relate in detail the difficulties encountered in dealing with obstructive administrators and unpredictable students. He or she will describe the never-ending flow of requests to provide, in revised format, data sent two weeks earlier, the persistence of students wishing to take classes for which they have not completed prerequisites, and their ability to excuse poor performance for reasons that indicate creativity not usually reflected in their homework. Throughout this interview, the chair will remind you that the true function of a faculty member is to generate meaningful research, and the instructional requirements imposed by the administration represent a conflicting demand for time that all but negates the benefits of academia.

Information needs of academic department chairs are straightforward. The chair must have detailed information on each faculty member: name, address, rank, salary, time at the university. In addition, there must be an equitable way to assign teaching duties among these faculty members. The process of instruction must be monitored, to see whether the "grade inflation" described in technical journals is reflected in the individual department, and if so, which faculty members are guilty of awarding too many high grades. The chair also needs to know how many students are majoring in disciplines monitored by the department and how these students are progressing.

4.2.2.3 Students

Students will tell you with great sincerity that they represent by far the most important group on campus. After all, what is a campus for except to educate today's youth? If it weren't for their willingness to attend classes, most of the faculty and staff would find themselves competing for real jobs and learning just how difficult that process may be, especially when one tries to market the education provided by the faculty at Maverick U. Students will tell you horror stories of required courses scheduled at conflicting times, of required courses not offered or else scheduled with enrollment restrictions that prevent students from taking them, and of faculty who use random numbers to assign grades and who are insensitive to well-documented reasons for adjusting obvious errors. They will note with some acerbity the failure of the administration to send timely warning of fees due and the resultant late penalties imposed without regard to financial straits. They will detail multiple instances when important letters from the registrar's office were misdirected to apartments several moves prior to the current address, sometimes resulting in late penalty fees that were both unfair and inflated.

The needs of students for course-related information are quite simple. First, students need to know which courses are to be offered, when, and who the instructor will be. They need to have some idea of the nature of the course, its prerequisites, and the restrictions in enrollment. Finally, they need to find out what grades they received in the previous quarter and their progress to date. Their grades must be retained in a confidential manner (some students are anxious that parents not be informed of their academic progress).

The process of interviewing these three classes of individuals at Maverick University is not an easy one. Obtaining the information summarized above requires time, patience, a willingness to listen to extraneous answers, and a need to interpret inconsistent answers so as to arrive at a clear understanding of the true information requirements that should have been obvious. However, we have attempted to summarize both the flavor of the interviews as well as the information needs articulated by each group. One of the skills of accomplished DBMS designers lies in translating such interviews into coherent statements of information needs and flow.

4.2.3 Information Analysis

From the foregoing material, the reporting requirements can be summarized as follows:

> Student Demographic Information Reports
> Faculty Demographic Information Reports
> Course Description Reports (including a Catalog)
> Course Schedule Reports
> Course Enrollment Reports
> Student Course Lists
> Course Grade Lists
> Student Transcripts
> Department Academic Salary Budget Reports

These reports represent the type of information currently required by the groups interviewed. Once each individual is presented with this list, he or she is likely to think of a few more needs, but we will omit this review cycle in our current example.

Each of these reports requires specific data elements. The next step, therefore, is to list the data elements required to generate the reports and to group them in some logical order.

The information needs generated by this list may be summarized as follows:

> Student Information
> > name
> > identification number
> > date of birth
> > sex
> > street address
> > city
> > state
> > ZIP code
> > telephone number
> > date entered
> > degree sought
> > academic major
> > financial aid
> > courses taken:
> > > number
> > > name (incl dept)
> > > units
> > > grade

gradepoints
year and quarter taken
instructor(s)
total units taken
current and cumulative gradepoint average
Faculty Information
name
identification number
date of birth
sex
department
campus address
campus phone number(s)
home address:
street
city
state
zipcode
telephone number
date employed
academic rank
current salary
courses taught:
course number
course name
date(s) taught
students enrolled
grades given
Course Information
course number
course name
department
instructor(s)
units
maximum number of students
description
for each time offered:
date (quarter, year)
section
instructor(s)
students enrolled
grades received
gradepoints earned

The information presented in this list appears to be nicely outlined, with neat indentations and subgroupings. However, this structure has some serious flaws from a file definition standpoint. Most important is the fact that several items of information appear in several places. For instance, one item implies multiple records that were not clearly defined before: the fact that the same course may be offered twice during the same quarter, perhaps being taught by two different instructors. This item is concealed in the "(s)" after instructors under each course offering. This item is included to illustrate a typical communication problem in information systems analysis. As written, "instructor(s)" could mean multiple instructors for a single class or multiple instructors for different course sections. The interviews reported earlier do not make this item clear, and the results of assuming either interpretation without considering the other could lead to serious problems in the DBMS design. Clearly, the process of file design will require additional study.

4.2.4 File Design

Before an analyst can partition data elements into files, he or she must first decide what overall structure will be used in the application. In Chapter 2, we noted that there are two structural models (hierarchical and network) and two conceptual models (relational and entity relationship). Selection of one of these alternatives may not be the optimal way to proceed from an information analysis viewpoint, but there are no mixed structure DBMS packages available at this time. In our example, any of the four models could do the job. We will select the relational model because it is widely available in current commercial personal computer DBMS packages and because it offers an opportunity for more rigorous analysis of the internal data relationships.

At this point, the reader should review the lists of data elements and try to create a set of files that meet the needs of the users interviewed and also fit the definitions of normalized relations as defined in Chapter 2. This exercise will add greatly to the value of the discussion that follows.

The relational model imposes several rules for file design, as described in Section 2.8.1. The importance of these normalization rules will become evident in applying them to the data elements at hand. It might at first seem that three files would accommodate the information listed above: one for student, a second for faculty, and a third for course-related data elements. If, however, we attempt to apply the rules of normalization to these data elements, we find that many elements fail to satisfy the criteria imposed. First, there is the problem noted earlier that the same data elements occur in many places. Course-related information, for example, is found in both faculty and student records. One potential solution to this problem is to eliminate the course file completely and to assign its data elements to the other two files. To do so, however, could result in potential loss of data. If, for example, course descriptions include the name of the instructor who teaches the class, removal of that faculty member from the database would result in loss of information.

A second problem with assigning course information to other files arises when a new course is proposed. If there is no separate file for course-related data elements, a new course could not be added until a faculty member is assigned to teach it, assuming the number, units, and description were stored in the faculty file. This approach may work in some institutions, but not, we are assured, at Maverick U.

One of the criteria for normalization of a relational file is that there should be no duplicate tuples. Common sense tells us that it is wasteful to include multiple copies of the same data elements. Including course information in the student file requires multiple entries, a tuple for each class. Thus, each entry would contain all the demographic information about the student as well as data on the course. If a student were to get married and change her name, each entry for that student would have to be updated. Changing only the first record would result in inconsistent data, a situation to be avoided. Searching for all records to change would be time-consuming and wasteful.

Some of the other normalization requirements are a bit more difficult to illustrate, but their functional consequences are the same. For example, if course name and number are stored with the record for each student (whether or not it is recorded elsewhere), changing the name of the course (even slightly) results in the need to read the entire student file to find each occurrence of that course name. This type of anomaly is a violation of the rule of functional dependence on the primary key. The course number is required to identify the course taken by each student (course numbers change, and this creates havoc as the registrar will tell you). The course name is functionally dependent on the course number, not on the student; hence data independence of elements from each other as well as functional dependence are violated in this case. The result, of course, is the same: multiple occurrences of the same data element and the possibility of data inconsistency in partial updates.

These examples all point to the need to create several files in addition to the three already defined. The design should take into account the source of data, the normalization rules described in Chapter 2 (especially those relating to dependency of data on the primary key), the minimization of redundancy, and the inclusion of dictionary type files where required. On the basis of these criteria, the individual files are designed as follows:

1. Student Information File
    identification number (primary key)
    name (last, first, mi) [alternate sorting key]
    date of birth
    sex
    street address
    city
    state
    ZIP code
    telephone number
    date entered
    degree sought
    academic major
    financial aid
    total units earned
    cumulative grade point average

2. Faculty Information
   identification number (primary key)
   name (last, first, mi) [alternate sorting key]
   department
   campus address
   campus phone
   home street address
   home city
   home state
   home ZIP code
   academic rank
   salary

3. Course Description
   course number (primary key)
   course name
   department
   units
   maximum number students
   description

4. Course Offerings
   course number (primary key)
   year (primary key)
   quarter (primary key)
   section (primary key)
   instructor

5. Grades
   course number (primary key)
   academic quarter (primary key)
   year (primary key)
   section (primary key)
   student number (primary key)
   grade received

6. Grade Point Conversion Table
   letter grade (primary key)
   equivalent numeric value

This file design illustrates several important points. There are now six files, not three. Each has a primary key identified. In one case, the primary key consists of five fields, which together constitute a unique key. Two of the files have a secondary key designated. The data elements in each file are functionally dependent on the primary key and independent of each other. In other words, this structure meets the criteria of normalization as defined in the relational model.

One example serves to illustrate the need for this file design in order to preserve normalization rules and minimize chances of data inconsistencies. File 4, Course Offerings, might at first glance seem unnecessary on the basis of the information presented, since all the elements in this file with the exception of instructor number are found in the Grades file. However, if one were to include the instructor number in the Grades file, that number would occur on each line of the file for a given class. If an error were made or a change were to occur (and instructors are sometimes switched at the last minute), the update would have to be made on every line for that course offering. This is a good example of violation of second normal form, since the instructor name is not functionally dependent on the entire key (i.e., not really dependent on the student number).

Producing reports from a file structure of this type typically requires using two or more files. For example, producing a summary of grades given in a class requires the Grades, Courses, and Students files. Generating a transcript requires all files except the Faculty Information file. In order to use these files together, it is necessary to define relations between the files. The term *relation* in this context indicates that a field may be used to look a valid entry from another file. For example, entering a student number in the grades file might require that the number correspond to a registered student's identification number. In this example, we have used numeric keys of course number, student number, and faculty number to provide those links. Updating a primary key may still require extensive search through the database to find its occurrences in related files. All other dependent attributes, however, are stored in only one file, reducing the possibility of data inconsistency.

The next element in file design is to specify the characteristics of each data element in the file. This process involves defining the data type, its permissible values, whether the field is to be required, and in some cases the manner in which the field is to be calculated or verified. We will defer illustration of this process until we actually work with the database packages selected, since different approaches are used in each package. The following samples give some idea of the types of specifications required for different fields.

Characteristics	Address	IDNO	Birthdate	Salary	Units	Degree
Data type	string	spec number	date	dollar	numeric	set
Special format	none	nnn-nn-nnnn	mm/dd/yy	nnnnnn.nn	n.n	set
min length	3 chars	11 chars	8 chars	none	1 digit	2 chars
max length	30 chars	11 chars	8 chars	9 chars	3 chars	3 chars
permitted chars	any	num,-	num,/	num,.	num,.	alphabet
required	no	yes	no	no	no	yes
numeric fields:						
min value	n.a.	n.a.	n.a.	0	0	n.a.
max value	n.a.	n.a.	n.a.	150000	4.0	n.a.
date fields:						
starting date	n.a.	n.a.	1900	n.a.	n.a.	n.a.
latest date	n.a.	n.a.	1965	n.a.	n.a.	n.a.
set fields						
permitted set	n.a.	n.a.	n.a.	n.a.	n.a.	BS,BA,etc
relations	n.a.	lookup	n.a.	n.a.	n.a.	n.a.

This sampling of data elements illustrates the manner in which data types must be specified. Some DBMS packages check these specifications completely when data are entered; others restrict error checking to length and data type.

Not all possible data types are illustrated in the foregoing table. There are no calculated fields, and there are many different types of special string formats that might occur, such as different forms for ZIP codes or international telephone numbers in the same field; yet each format is specific and should be checked for validity at entry.

Once the file design process is complete, the actual creation of the database can begin. The way we will go about the implementation of this database is as follows:

1. Define the files to be created (described above)
2. Create each file, defining each data element
3. Enter data in each file
4. Edit data
5. Retrieve information from the database

The next part of the database design process involves adapting steps 2 through 5 to a specific DBMS package. We can best illustrate this activity by going through two DBMS packages completely, from steps 2 through 5, and then comparing the experience gained from each to learn more about optimal solutions to DBMS design and selection.

4.3 SYSTEMS SELECTED AS EXAMPLES

Several criteria were used to select examples for this text. The packages had to run under PCDOS. They had to be commercially available and nationally advertised. It was decided to select packages that used the relational model in file structure and functional capability. They were also selected to contrast with each other in illustrating points about DBMSs. Access to external files, both for export and import, was considered desirable. The packages had to have been thoroughly tested, with published reviews available.

After the initial selection, copies were obtained from the vendors, and work began on developing the examples described. During the writing of this text, several updates were released by the vendors. The most recent releases used in each case were major new releases made available early in 1986. Much of the initial writing was done with earlier versions, but the descriptions have been updated to reflect subsequent releases. Since some of the changes that were introduced themselves illustrate important concepts relating to DBMS design, some of these modifications will be discussed in the following paragraphs.

DATAEASE was selected because it is based on the relational model, using a menu-driven style of presentation. Earlier releases are available under several operating systems, and it interfaces to many well-known auxiliary packages. DATAEASE is a product of Software Solutions, Inc., 12 Cambridge Dr., Trumbull, CT 06611. The versions used in writing this text include version 2.0 as released in August 1984; version 2.1, obtained in late 1984; and version 2.5, released in early 1986.

We chose dBASE III PLUS because it also met most of the foregoing criteria. It is based on the relational model, and it provides the most important relational algebra capabilities implicit in that model. It is presently the most successful commercial DBMS sold in the U.S. (DATAEASE is the leading seller in Great Britain), and there are many articles and texts written on this package, its predecessors, and related programs available from the same vendor. dBASE III PLUS is available from Ashton-Tate, 10150 West Jefferson Blvd., Culver City, CA 90230. Versions used in writing this text included dBASE III released in August 1984, updates obtained several times between that date and mid 1985, and dBASE III PLUS, obtained in May 1986.

Although these packages were selected for the reasons stated above, they have also been favorably reviewed by recent DBMS surveys. The June 1986 issue of *PC Magazine* ranks DATAEASE and dBASE III PLUS as two of the three best products in their survey of sixty-four database packages.

Our final reason for selecting the two particular packages is that they offer interesting contrasts in design philosophy, marketing strategy, and evolution.

The format used to present these two packages is to step through all functions of implementing the design described in the previous section, commenting briefly on the unique features of each package as they arise during the process. Following this review is a general discussion of the points raised in comparing the two implementations.

A reminder: This chapter illustrates concepts rather than demonstrating how to use the packages to their fullest. Any DBMS package is complex, and learning to use it well is beyond the scope of this text. In this chapter, you will see how two manufacturers have implemented the relational approach to data structuring. There are undoubtedly other, perhaps better ways to accomplish some tasks illustrated using these packages, and the serious user will no doubt wish to review current offerings of these and other manufacturers since the field is evolving rapidly.

4.4 BRIEF OVERVIEW OF dBASE III PLUS AND DATAEASE

4.4.1 DATAEASE Overview

DATAEASE was first released in 1983 and was extensively revised in 1984 and again in 1986. The version described in this text was configured to run on IBM PC and compatible systems under PCDOS version 2.0. However, other earlier versions also exist. DATAEASE will run under MSDOS versions 1.1, 2.0, and 3.0, and it has been configured for systems marketed by Wang, Texas Instruments, Vertec, and Victor as well as PC compatibles.

On the IBM PC, DATAEASE requires two double-sided disk drives (320K or 360K bytes each) or one Winchester and one double-sided, double-density disk.

It also requires a minimum of 384K bytes of memory, but it is able to utilize additional available memory (up to 640K bytes) to improve execution efficiency.

There are no inherent restrictions to the total size of a single database, other than the limitations of the hardware and operating system available. A given disk (Winchester or floppy) can have up to 26 different databases on it simultaneously. The total number of files (relations) in a single database is 255, and each file is restricted to 65,535 records or entries. Field size limit is 255 characters, as is the number of fields in a single record. Total record size is restricted to 4,000 characters. Since data-entry is usually done via formatted screens, there is an upper limit of 16 different screens for definition of a single file's fields.

This package is based on the relational model, but it also incorporates indexed files for faster searching and execution. Indexing improves search time performance, but it affects data-entry speed adversely, as might be expected. There is no restriction on the number of different fields that can be indexed.

Several different data types and files are used in the DATAEASE system. All data fields are of fixed length. Texts, strings, numeric strings, date, and time are stored as ASCII characters. Numbers are stored either as binary or floating point values. Choices are represented as binary numbers. Files are stored as sequential files. Since they contain binary and floating-point numbers as well as ASCII characters, they cannot be edited by standard MSDOS editors. The basic file structure is that of an indexed file; B-tree index files are used to provide direct access to the principal data file. Multiple B-trees can be defined, one for each index. Data definitions, screen forms, report forms, and other utility files are stored in special internal format accessible only to the DATAEASE system. The result is a closed system that can be manipulated only through the DATAEASE environment. Data files can be "exported" to other formats and "imported" from other packages.

This DBMS is part of a set of packages marketed by Software Solutions that includes a word processor and a graphic output generator. It also supports several popular personal computer data formats, including DIF, dBASE II, Mail-Merge, and user-defined variable and fixed-length formats. Utilities are available to read and write data from some of these formats without special programming. It is possible to call other programs (spreadsheets, word processors, or other applications) from DATAEASE, and it is also possible to invoke MSDOS functions while in DATAEASE.

The package includes two program disks, a demonstration disk, and a tutorial example disk. Most operations can be run from a single program disk, with data stored on a separate disk. A user's manual with examples, index, and appendices is included as well as a tutorial on the language. A separate summary reference booklet is also included.

4.4.2 dBASE III PLUS Overview

dBASE III PLUS is a relational DBMS currently designed to run on IBM PC, XT, and compatible systems. It requires the PCDOS operating system version 2.0 or more recent, or MSDOS versions 2.1 or higher. Systems named in the documentation as supporting the protected disk feature of this package include personal computers marketed by AT&T, Compaq, IBM, ITT, Leading Edge, Sperry, NCR, Sanyo, and Tandy. It also requires a minimum of 256K bytes of memory, two 360K double-sided, double-density floppy disks or one 360K floppy disk and a Winchester drive, and a printer with minimum 80-column capability. In reality, practical application of dBASE III PLUS virtually requires use of a hard disk.

The copy-protected disk feature of dBASE distributions means either that users must use the original (or backup) system disk in drive A when invoking this product or that an installation on hard disk is done on one of the compatible hardware.

A number of changes have been incorporated into dBASE III PLUS that differ from the previous dBASE II release. One set of changes relates to easing the limitations of size and the operating environment. dBASE III PLUS has essentially unlimited number of records (although PCDOS has a theoretical 30M byte file size limit). The file may consist of up to 1 gigabyte (1 billion bytes) of data, including 128 fields per file. Individual records may be up to 4000 bytes long. During operation, dBASE III PLUS permits up to 15 files to be open at one time. Included in this total may be up to 10 data files, seven index files, and one format file (although not all at once). The PCDOS system uses several files that are also included in the total (usually three, one of which is the printer). The actual number of data files open at one time also depends on the number of index files required to access these files.

dBASE III PLUS supports the relational model, but it also incorporates fast indexing capabilities through auxiliary files, and it is possible to specify that a file be sorted according to a primary key. Both of these features are extensions to the relational model that improve performance in many situations.

The data types and file structures used in dBASE differ slightly from those of DATAEASE. Data is stored in fixed-length fields and fixed-length data. All values are stored in ASCII format. At the start of each data file is a mixed ASCII/binary header record that contains the data definition. Index files to the records are stored in B-trees, so the basic structure of the data files is that of an indexed file. User-defined programs are ASCII files that can be created and edited outside the dBASE environment. Utility files are in mixed form not readily manipulated by non-dBASE programs.

The latest release, dBASE III PLUS, has two principal modes of operation, one using standard commands and the dBASE programming language, the other using a HELP mode referred to as the ASSISTANT. Earlier releases had HELP support screens, but it was not possible to execute database manipulation commands while in HELP mode. In this text, we will illustrate portions of the ASSISTANT mode, but we will concentrate on the programming mode, since it offers the greatest contrast to DATAEASE.

Interface both for import from and export to external data file structures is supported. Some specific formats, such as System Data Format (SDF) or Delimited formats are included as options. Command programs may be created and modified using external editors. Other files generally include elements that are not ASCII-compatible, and hence they cannot be manipulated by external editors.

The documentation provided with the dBASE III PLUS version differs significantly from the previous dBASE III release. The former package included a user manual, two system disks, one demonstration/utilities disk, quick reference guide, and a guide to differences between dBASE II and dBASE III. The manual had an extensive tutorial section supported by examples contained on one of the distribution disks, a reference section, an index, and appendices. A large portion of the manual was devoted to description of the command language provided in dBASE III. In the dBASE III PLUS distribution, there are seven disks: two systems plus a backup for the copy-protected one; a set of sample programs and utilities; a tutorial; and two dBASE ADMINISTRATOR disks. The manuals come in two 3-inch binders and include separate sections for introduction, application, programmer reference, and applications generator. This package also has been extended to provide network links to other computers (see Chapter 6), and a portion of the manual treats these features. Other extensions to the language are discussed elsewhere in this chapter.

4.5 IMPLEMENTATION OF THE MAVERICK
INFORMATION SYSTEM: DATAEASE

Using a DBMS package involves several preliminary steps after the computer and software have been purchased. The introductory process often includes sitting down with the manual, going through the initialization steps, working a few examples or following the tutorial, and then finally starting with the practical application. During this introductory phase, the user becomes familiar with the manual and learns the basic mode of communication expected by the package. This initial experience can be made easier or harder, depending on the quality of the manual and the nature of the user interface. DATAEASE is designed to make this process as easy and comfortable as possible.

The DATAEASE User Manual is organized by functions that must be performed in database operations, with separate sections on forms definition, data entry, and report generation. Additional sections are included that describe functions such as relationships to link files, database maintenance, systems maintenance, and utilities. A tutorial is available to illustrate the package's features. The opening section in the manual describes how to get started, how to copy disks, and how to configure the hardware.

As with most DBMS packages, there is no guidance provided on file design. However, we have already covered that material, so we are ready to begin. To simplify the introduction process, we will skip system configuration and start to implement the files described in our Maverick University example.

DATAEASE interacts with the user through menus augmented by prompts at the top and bottom of the screen. Through selection of different options, the user chooses a function and then performs appropriate tasks for that function. The user is led through menus giving options at each level of interaction. Through these options, he or she defines files, input forms, retrieval queries, and report forms. He or she can also use these forms to enter data or generate reports. As a result, the package is easy to learn and use, even for the novice. The manual is consistent with this philosophy, refraining from use of technical relational terms such as normalization and the operators JOIN, PROJECT, and RESTRICT. These concepts are described, but technical jargon is not used.

The first thing that appears when DATAEASE is invoked is a request to identify the database to be used, using a single letter (A through Z) as shown in Fig. 4.1. If this file has not been used before, DATAEASE will request a name and password. The first user is defined as the master user, capable of defining other user names and passwords. If a master user forgets the entry name and password, it is not easy to regain access to the data. Special knowledge of PCDOS calls are required to examine the contents of the appropriate file containing the user codes. The manufacturer will assist with the recovery, but it is better not to forget.

Figure 4.1 illustrates one additional feature often found on standard DATAEASE screens: the Alt-F1 key, which generates a HELP message related to the next action expected from the user.

```
DATAEASE 2.5
Copyright Software Solutions Inc, USA. 1986
                                              Serial Number    00-0015231


      ┌─────────────────────────────────────────────────────┐
      │          D A T A E A S E  -  S I G N   O N           │
      │                                                       │
      │      Data base Name ( A to Z ) : a                    │
      │                                                       │
      │      What is your name              : rfwalters       │
      │                                                       │
      │      What is your security password :                 │
      │                                                       │
      │                                                       │
      │                                                       │
      └─────────────────────────────────────────────────────┘



   Alt-F1 HELP F4 EXIT DATABASE    PROG. C:  DATA A:  DATE 07/29/86  TIME 16:30:09
```

Figure 4.1. DATAEASE: Sign-On screen.

When DATAEASE is initialized, and the proper user code and password have been entered, the user is presented with a menu that lists all functions available in this package. This screen, and all that appear in this package, follow a general format illustrated in Fig. 4.2. The top and bottom of the screen are reserved for system information. The title of the activity (form name, report name, etc.) is at the upper left. The center of the top line is used to indicate the cursor position on the screen in formatting functions, and to inform the user if the Insert Mode is active. The right side of the top line is used to present system messages such as errors encountered or filing action being taken by the package. The bottom of the screen indicates the current meaning of function keys and gives other information about the status of the particular application. The remainder of the screen is used as a work area in which user and system both can enter information to carry out different DBMS tasks.

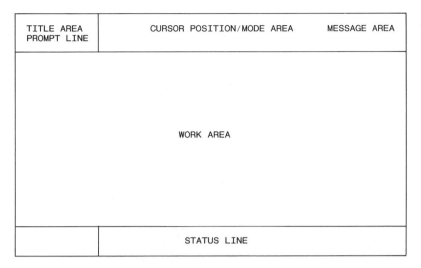

Figure 4.2. Layout of DATAEASE screen formats.

Figure 4.3 illustrates the menu displayed at the completion of the sign-on process. Notice that the database and the disk drives for both programs and data are identified on the status line at the bottom of the display in reverse video. Date and time are also presented, and an option to exit from the current function (the function key, F4). This key is reserved for exit on all menus and at this level returns the user to DOS. The work area in this screen presents a series of options that may be selected either by typing a number or by using the Up and Down keys followed by a return when the correct field is highlighted (END highlights the last field). The user cannot interact with the package except through menus of this type.

At first glance, this approach may seem restrictive. In fact, some additional capabilities are available through options 5, 6, and 7. Option 7 (Menus and Rela-

DATAEASE

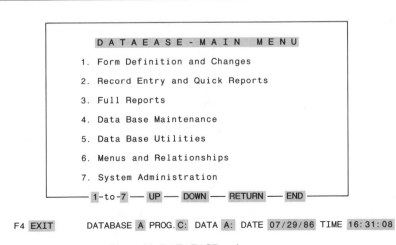

Figure 4.3. DATAEASE main menu.

tionships) provides opportunities to define new menus to be presented to the user and even to access external programs with parameter passing. The controlled menu approach serves the purpose of controlling the database operation. The data files and forms contain non-ASCII characters that make them very difficult to manipulate except through the DATAEASE package.

Because the opening option menu (Fig. 4.3) lists all major options, the user knows from the outset how to proceed with implementation of a database. The next section illustrates the creation of the Maverick University database.

4.5.1 Basic File Definition

In our analysis of Maverick U's data requirements, we defined several files required to run the system. In DATAEASE, file definition is accomplished as a part of input form definition. Therefore, selecting option 1 on Fig. 4.3 leads to display of the forms definition menu (Fig. 4.4), which permits the user to define a new form or modify an existing one. Selecting option 1 from this screen allows the user to name the form, after which the system asks for a name for the new form, as shown in the lower window of the work area in Fig. 4.4. The system then advances into Form Editing mode, used to create the form and at the same time define the data file.

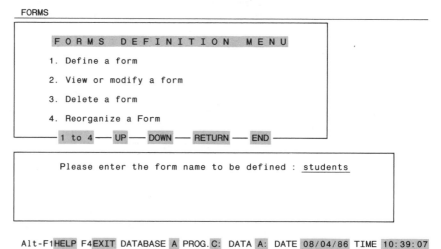

Figure 4.4. DATAEASE forms definition menu.

Form layout is specified by a combination of cursor moves (controlled by keyboard arrows) and function keys, as shown in Fig. 4.5. The user has moved the cursor to row 3 and typed a prompt for the Name field, ending at column 17. At the base of the screen, available options are displayed. When F10 (function key 10) is pressed, indicating that a field is to be defined, the format screen is saved and a new screen appears (Fig. 4.6), used to define the data field identified by the "Name:" prompt. The user should now define the data type, selecting one of the options listed in reverse video just above the data definition section. Since this is a text field, either the number 1 or the letters "te" should be entered to identify this data type as text.

```
FORM students                  R   3  C   17
```

```
        Name:
```

```
F2ENTER F3CUT  F4EXIT  F5COPY  F6PASTE  F7DEL LINE  F8INS LINE  F9PRINT  F10FIELD
```

Figure 4.5. DATAEASE forms definition process.

```
FORM students
1: Text 2: Numeric String 3: Number 4: Date 5: Time 6: Dollar              F1MORE
        Field name :                           Name:
        Field type :                           _____
                                               _____
```

```
F6 CLEAR FIELD
```

Figure 4.6. DATAEASE forms definition process.

After defining the data type, the user is asked for the length of the text field (30 characters in this case), whether the field is required, and whether it is to be indexed (i.e., if a B-tree index is to be created). At this point, the user can skip further questions by typing the F2 (ENTER) key (Fig. 4.7). Doing so returns the screen format created up to that point, with the Name field and the length for its value defined on the screen. The user then moves to a new location, types in a prompt "I.D.No:," and types F10 to define this second field (the screen position of this field is shown in Fig. 4.12). In this case, the data type is a Numeric String format (Social Security number). Figure 4.8 illustrates this selection process. This field is also defined as a unique field, meaning that it is the primary key of this table, and no duplicates will be allowed in the file.

```
FORM students
1: no 2: yes
        Field name :                                       Name:_____
        Field type :                                       Text_____
        Maximum length of field :                           30
        Press ENTER, MODIFY or DELETE any time to skip the remaining questions
        Is this field REQUIRED to be entered? :                      yes
        Does this field require fast (INDEXED) access ?:              yes
        Is it one of the UNIQUE fields? :                           _____
```

```
F2 ENTER F7 DELETE F8 MODIFY
```

Figure 4.7. DATAEASE forms definition process.

```
FORM students
1: no 2: yes 3: yes, and do not save (virtual)
        Field name :                                       IDN_____
        Field type :                                       Numeric String___
        Is it a formatted string ?                         soc.sec.no.
        Press ENTER, MODIFY or DELETE any time to skip the remaining questions
        Is this field REQUIRED to be entered? :                      yes
        Does this field require fast (INDEXED) access ?:             yes
        Is it one of the UNIQUE fields? :                           yes
        Does the field require a RANGE CHECK? :                      no
        Is the field DERIVED (calculate/lookup/sequence/default)? : no
        PREVENT data-entry in the field? : _____    no_____
```

```
F2 ENTER F7 DELETE F8 MODIFY
```

Figure 4.8. DATAEASE forms definition process.

The form definition process continues with the addition of each field. For different data types, appropriate choices must be made, after which the current status of the entry form is once again displayed. A few special situations are shown to illustrate portions of this process. For example, we wish to enter the student's sex, allowing either M or F. In our previous example, Fig. 4.6, six data types are listed on the prompt line, but at the far right, F1(MORE) also appears. Pressing the F1 key opens a window, shown in Fig. 4.9, giving all options (more than can be displayed on the prompt line). The selection process in this window is similar to that of other windows. Selecting the Choice option (8) allows the user to complete the specification of M and F as two choices allowed for this field. A more

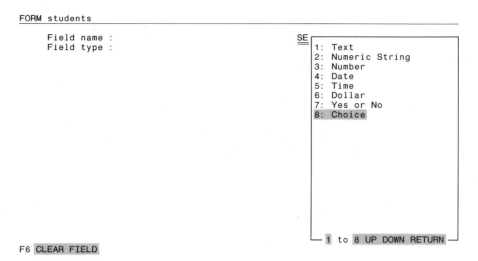

```
FORM students

    Field name :                              SE
    Field type :                                ┌──────────────────────────────┐
                                                │ 1: Text                      │
                                                │ 2: Numeric String            │
                                                │ 3: Number                    │
                                                │ 4: Date                      │
                                                │ 5: Time                      │
                                                │ 6: Dollar                    │
                                                │ 7: Yes or No                 │
                                                │ 8: Choice                    │
                                                │                              │
                                                │                              │
                                                │                              │
                                                │                              │
                                                │                              │
                                                │                              │
                                                │                              │
                                                │                              │
                                                │                              │
                                                │                              │
                                                │                              │
                                                │                              │
                                                └─ 1 to 8 UP DOWN RETURN ──────┘
F6 CLEAR FIELD
```

Figure 4.9. DATAEASE forms definition process.

comprehensive Choice field is the one for degree (the degree for which the student is enrolled). Figure 4.10 illustrates the manner in which a closed set of choices for the degree field are specified. The bottom of this screen illustrates two additional features: a security level definition (typing a null response automatically places security High, as shown), and a help prompt field that the user has defined. Figure 4.11 shows the options used to define a number with decimal fractions. The user has selected a fixed decimal format with one digit to the left and three to the right of the decimal point. In addition, since this field (GPA) will be updated periodically by report generations, it is not necessary to have the data-entry person enter a number in this field. Hence, the question "PREVENT data-entry in the field?" is answered "yes" as shown.

```
FORM students

    Field name :                                DEGREE
    Field type :                                Choice
    Optional choice field type name :           Degree
    Choice 1 : BA
    Choice 2 : BS
    Choice 3 : MA
    Choice 4 : MS
    Choice 5 : PHD
    Choice 6 :
    Press ENTER, MODIFY or DELETE any time to skip the remaining questions
    Is this field REQUIRED to be entered? :                no
    Does this field require fast (INDEXED) access ?:        no
    Is it one of the UNIQUE fieldS? :                       no
    Does the field require a RANGE CHECK? :                 no
    Is the field DERIVED (calculate/lookup/sequence/default)? : no
    PREVENT data-entry in the field? :          no
    Minimum Security Level to View the Field:   High
    Minimum Security Level to Write the Field:  High
    Field Help                                  Please select from: BA, BS, MA,
MS or PHD

F2 ENTER F7 DELETE F8 MODIFY
```

Figure 4.10. DATAEASE forms definition process.

```
FORM students
1: High 2: Medium1 3: Medium2 4: Medium3 5: Low1 6: Low2 7: Low3
          Field name :                              GPA
          Field type :                              Number
          Number Type :                             Fixed point
          Maximum digits to the left of decimal? :   1
          Digits to the right of decimal :           3
          Press ENTER, MODIFY or DELETE any time to skip the remaining questions
          Is this field REQUIRED to be entered? :             no
          Does this field require fast (INDEXED) access ?:     no
          Is it one of the UNIQUE fields? :                    no
          Does the field require a RANGE CHECK? :              no
          Is the field DERIVED (calculate/lookup/sequence/default)? :no
          PREVENT data-entry in the field? :        yes
          Minimum Security Level to View the Field:
```

F2 ENTER F7 DELETE F8 MODIFY

Figure 4.11. DATAEASE forms definition process.

```
FORM students                   R 11 C   43


          Name:                              I.D. No:
          Date of Birth (mm/dd/yy):          SEX:

          Address:
          City:                State:    ZIP:

          Date Entered:        Degree Sought:      MAJOR:

          Units Completed:    Current GPA:          Financial Aid:
```

F2ENTER F3CUT F4EXIT F5COPY F6PASTE F7DEL LINE F8INS LINE F9PRINT F10FIELD

Figure 4.12. DATAEASE Student File Entry Form, completed.

The remaining field definitions are similar to options already displayed. Figure 4.12 presents the final format of the screen to be used in entering data for this file. At this point, it is useful to obtain a printed copy of the result. Pressing the F9 (PRINT) key will cause the complete definition of the form to be printed (Fig. 4.13). This printout (it does not appear on the screen) displays the file name, its format on the screen, and then gives a detailed summary of the file definition, including answers to all questions about data type and other questions associated with each field. The size of the records defined and the form, including data definition, is given at the bottom of this output.

```
      FORM    students
      ---------------------------


1      10      20      30      40      50      60      70      80
----+----+----+----+----+----+----+----+----+----+----+----+----+----+----+----+

          Name:_____    I.D. No:_____
          Date of Birth (mm/dd/yy):_____    SEX:____

          Address:_____
          City:_____  State:_____ ZIP:_____

          Date Entered:_____ Degree Sought:_____ MAJOR:_____

          Units Completed:____Current GPA:_____ Financial Aid:_____
----+----+----+----+----+----+----+----+----+----+----+----+----+----+----+----+
1      10      20      30      40      50      60      70      80
```

```
      FIELD DESCRIPTIONS
      ------------------
```

No.	Name	Type	Long	Reqd	In-dex	Uni-que	Der-ived	Rng Chk	Pre-vent	Record size	offset
1	Name: *	Text	30	Yes	Yes	No	No	No	No	30	4
2	IDN	Num.String	11	Yes	Yes	Yes	No	No	No	9	34
3	DOB	Date	8	No	No	No	No	No	No	6	43
4	SEX	Choice	1	No	No	No	No	No	No	1	49

```
      Choice field type name : sex
          Choice  1: m
          Choice  2: f
```

No.	Name	Type	Long	Reqd	In-dex	Uni-que	Der-ived	Rng Chk	Pre-vent	Record size	offset
5	ADDR	Text	35	No	No	No	No	No	No	35	50
6	City	Text	15	No	No	No	No	No	No	15	85
7	State	Text	2	No	No	No	No	No	No	2	100
8	ZIP	Num.String	5	No	No	No	No	No	No	5	102
9	DAT-ENT	Date	8	No	No	No	No	No	No	6	107
10	DEGREE	Choice	3	No	No	No	No	No	No	1	113

```
      Choice field type name : Degree
          Choice  1: BA
          Choice  2: BS
          Choice  3: MA
          Choice  4: MS
          Choice  5: PHD
      View Security Required: High,  Write Security Required: High
      Field Help: Please select from: BA, BS, MA, MS or PHD
```

No.	Name	Type	Long	Reqd	In-dex	Uni-que	Der-ived	Rng Chk	Pre-vent	Record size	offset
11	MAJOR	Text	12	No	No	No	No	No	No	12	114
12	UNITS	Number	3	No	No	No	No	No	Yes	2	126

```
      Number Type : Integer
```

No.	Name	Type	Long	Reqd	In-dex	Uni-que	Der-ived	Rng Chk	Pre-vent	Record size	offset
13	GPA	Number	5	No	No	No	No	No	Yes	4	128

```
      Number Type : Fixed point
      Digits to left of decimal = 1
```

No.	Name	Type	Long	Reqd	In-dex	Uni-que	Der-ived	Rng Chk	Pre-vent	Record size	offset
14	FINANC	Choice	3	No	No	No	No	No	No	1	132

```
      Choice  1: no
      Choice  2: yes
```

Record size 133

Memory required for form: Text 280, Fields 405, Total 685 bytes.

Figure 4.13. Printed summary: DATAEASE Students File Definition and Entry Form.

After the entry format screen has been completely defined and printed, the F2 (ENTER) key is pressed and both the format and data definition associated with that file are stored. This completes the definition process for one of the files in our database.

Using the same technique, two more forms are created, one for faculty, the other for courses. Figures 4.14 and 4.15 illustrate the entry form and data definitions for these two files. These examples are similar, with the exception that an integer data type is defined in the courses file (items 4 and 5 in field descriptions).

```
FORM    faculty
---------------------------
```

```
1       10        20        30        40        50        60        70        80
----+----+----+----+----+----+----+----+----+----+----+----+----+----+----+----+
       Name:_____     Soc.Sec.No:_____
       Date of Birth:_____             Sex:_____

       Campus Address:_____  Campus Phone:_____
       Department:_____

       Home Address:_____
       City:_____  State:_____  ZIP:_____
       Home Phone:_____

       Date Hired:_____  Current Academic Title:_____
       Current Salary:_____
----+----+----+----+----+----+----+----+----+----+----+----+----+----+----+----+
1       10        20        30        40        50        60        70        80
```

```
FIELD DESCRIPTIONS
------------------
```

No.	Name	Type	Long	Reqd	Index	Unique	Derived	Rng Chk	Prevent	Record size	offset
1	NAME	Text	30	Yes	Yes	No	No	No	No	30	4
2	Soc.Sec.No	Num.String	11	Yes	Yes	Yes	No	No	No	9	34
3	DOB	Date	8	No	No	No	No	No	No	6	43
4	SEX	Choice	1	No	No	No	No	No	No	1	49

     Choice field type name : sex
       Choice 1: M
       Choice 2: F

No.	Name	Type	Long	Reqd	Index	Unique	Derived	Rng Chk	Prevent	Record size	offset
5	CAMP-ADDR	Text	30	No	No	No	No	No	No	30	50
6	CAMP-PH	Num.String	6	No	No	No	No	No	No	5	80
7	DEPT	Text	15	No	No	No	No	No	No	15	85
8	HOM-ADDR	Text	30	No	No	No	No	No	No	30	100
9	CITY	Text	15	No	No	No	No	No	No	15	130
10	STATE	Text	2	No	No	No	No	No	No	2	145
11	ZIP	Num.String	5	No	No	No	No	No	No	5	147
12	HOM-PH	Num.String	14	No	No	No	No	No	No	10	152
13	DAT-EMP	Date	8	No	No	No	No	No	No	6	162
14	TITLE	Text	20	No	No	No	No	No	No	20	168
15	SALARY	Number	10	No	No	No	No	No	No	8	188

     Number Type : Fixed point
     Digits to left of decimal = 7

```
Record size 196
```

```
Memory required for form: Text  342, Fields 384, Total 726 bytes.
```

Figure 4.14. Printed summary: DATAEASE Faculty File Definition and Entry Form.

Forms may be modified, adding, deleting, or redefining fields. The effect on existing data entered using the previous form will vary depending on the nature of changes made. The manual describes the result of each type of change and offers appropriate warnings about possible adverse effects. For example, if the field name or type are changed, previous data are lost. Reducing field size results in truncation

```
    FORM    Courses
    ---------------------------


1       10      20      30      40      50      60      70      80
----+----+----+----+----+----+----+----+----+----+----+----+----+----+----+----+
        Department:_____
        Course Number:_____ Course TITLE:_____


        Units:____          Maximum Enrollment:_____

        Brief Description:_____
                          _____
                          _____
----+----+----+----+----+----+----+----+----+----+----+----+----+----+----+----+
1       10      20      30      40      50      60      70      80


        FIELD DESCRIPTIONS
        ------------------
```

No.	Name	Type	Long	Reqd	In-dex	Uni-que	Der-ived	Rng Chk	Pre-vent	Record size	offset
1	DEPT	Text	15	Yes	Yes	No	No	No	No	15	3
2	COURSENO	Text	6	Yes	Yes	Yes	No	No	No	6	18
3	COURSE-NAM	Text	30	Yes	No	No	No	No	No	30	24
4	UNITS	Number	1	Yes	No	No	No	No	No	1	54
	Number Type : Integer										
5	MAX-STUD	Number	3	No	No	No	No	No	No	2	55
	Number Type : Integer										
6	DESCRIP	Text	200	No	No	No	No	No	No	200	57

```
Record size 257

Memory required for form: Text  284, Fields 161, Total 445 bytes.
```

Figure 4.15. Printed summary: DATAEASE Courses File Definition and Entry Form.

of existing fields to the new size. Changing a field from "not required" to "required" will not check previous records for adherence to the new specification.

In the previous examples, we covered most options of file definition. However, in our case study, we need to create an additional file, used to store grades received at Maverick U. This file illustrates the use of relations between files not shown in the previous examples. Course number should match an entry from the Courses file, and the student and faculty numbers listed should find their counterparts in Students and Faculty files, respectively. At data-entry time, these keys are checked against the appropriate files, and invalid keys are not accepted.

The mechanism used to define linkages between two files is illustrated in the next three figures. Figure 4.16 shows the printout of the entire Grades form and field descriptions. The first item, COURSENO, is shown to be a derived field. This definition is explained by the detailed field description, Fig. 4.17, in which the field derivation formula is given as "lookup Courses 'COURSENO'." "Lookup" is a reserved word in the DATAEASE system that invokes a check of a separate file for the field named. If a value in that file matches the user entry, the entry is accepted. Otherwise, the field must be corrected. This process is described further in the section on data entry. Similar relations must be specified for the identification numbers of students and faculty.

```
        FORM    grades
        --------------------------

1       10       20       30       40       50       60       70       80
---+----+----+----+----+----+----+----+----+----+----+----+----+----+----+----+

        Course No:_____Year Taken:____Quarter:_____Seq:____

        Student ID number:_____ Grade Received:____

        Units:_____Gradepts:____
---+----+----+----+----+----+----+----+----+----+----+----+----+----+----+----+
1       10       20       30       40       50       60       70       80
```

```
        FIELD DESCRIPTIONS
        ------------------
```

No. Name	Type	Long	Reqd	In-dex	Uni-que	Der-ived	Rng Chk	Pre-vent	Record size	offset
1 COURSENO	Text	6	Yes	Yes	No	Yes	No	No	6	3
Field calculation formula : lookup Courses ''COURSENO''										
2 YEAR	Number	2	No	No	No	No	No	No	1	9
Number Type : Integer										
3 OTR	Choice	4	Yes	No	No	No	No	No	1	10
Choice 1: Fall										
Choice 2: Wntr										
Choice 3: Spr										
Choice 4: Sum										
4 Seq	Number	1	No	No	No	Yes	No	Yes	1	11
Number Type : Integer										
Field calculation formula : lookup qtrseq sequence										
5 IDN	Num.String	11	Yes	No	No	Yes	No	No	9	12
Field calculation formula : lookup students idn										
6 Grade	Text	2	Yes	No	No	No	No	No	2	21
7 Units	Number	3	No	No	No	Yes	No	Yes	4	23
Number Type: Fixed point										
Digits to left of decimal = 1										
Field calculation formula : lookup gradepoint value										
8 Gradepts	Number	5	No	No	No	Yes	No	Yes	4	27
Number Type : Fixed point										
Digits to left of decimal = 2										
Field calculation formula : units * lookup courses units										

```
Record size 31

Memory required for form: Text  156, Fields 482, Total 638 bytes.
```

Figure 4.16. Printed summary: DATAEASE Grades File Definition and Entry Form.

In addition to defining a file linkage through the lookup function, it is also necessary to define a relation between the two files invoked. This definition is done through the Menus and Relationships option of the master menu (item 6 on the menu shown in Fig. 4.3), as illustrated in Fig. 4.18. The definition form shown identifies the two files to be linked and the fields that will be used to provide that link. Similar relationships are described separately for each pair of files as required in our example.

Returning to Fig. 4.16, items 7 and 8 illustrate other options in the field description process. Each of these fields is defined as "prevent data entry," which means that the field will not be completed at entry time by the data clerk. Instead, a derived formula is used to generate each value automatically. In the case of the

```
FORM Grades
1: no  2: yes  3: yes, and do not save (virtual)
          Field name :                              COURSENO
          Field type :                              Text
          Maximum length of field:                     6
          Press ENTER, MODIFY or DELETE any time to skip the remaining questions
          Is this field REQUIRED to be entered? :                    yes
          Does this field require fast (INDEXED) access ?:           yes
          Is it one of the UNIQUE fields? :                          no
          Does the field require a RANGE CHECK? :                    no
          Is the field DERIVED (calculate/lookup/sequence/default) ? :yes
          Field derivation formula :              lookup Courses ''COURSENO''


          PREVENT data-entry in the field? :
```

F2 ENTER F7 DELETE F8 MODIFY

Figure 4.17. DATEASE Grades File: File linkage through LOOKUP Command.

```
relationships                          To skip the menu, press Esc
1: COURSENO  2: Section  3: YEAR  4: QUARTER  5: SEQ  6: IDN  7: GRADE  8: Gradepts

                          FORM RELATIONSHIP
                          -----------------
BETWEEN:
        Form   1:Grades                And 2:Courses

BASED ON
        THE FOLLOWING FIELDS BEING EQUAL:  (Define at least one set of fields.)

        Field    COURSENO              =     COURSENO

   And Field     _____      =     _____

   And Field     _____      =     _____


OPTIONAL RELATIONSHIP NAMES:
        (Form names are used as a default.)

   for  form 1:_____        form 2:_____
```

F2ENTER F3VIEW F4EXIT F5FORM CLR F6FLD CLR F7DELETE F8MODIFY F9REPORT F10MULTI

Figure 4.18. DATAEASE form relationship definition menu.

Units field, it is derived by looking up the value of a letter grade in the Gradepoint file, a dictionary containing those equivalent values. The calculation of the grade point field, on the other hand, illustrates a more complex calculation, multiplying the Units field by the number of units in the course, a value obtained from the Courses file. This example illustrates the ability of this package to perform calculations involving data derived from several different files.

We have now completed the basic files required for our example (the other files illustrate no new concepts). Review of the illustrations associated with this section will show several DATAEASE options not used in this database. Space does not permit inclusion of all possible variations, but our case study illustrates the basic concepts needed in most applications.

4.5.2 Data Entry: DATAEASE

The next major function in implementing the Maverick University database is to enter data into the files defined in the previous section. The principal method used for data entry in DATAEASE is through the formatted screens created in the previous section. Once a file has been defined, the entry process is also defined. An input screen has been created, error checks have been established for data type, range, and other criteria, and the position of the field is defined on the screen.

RECORDS

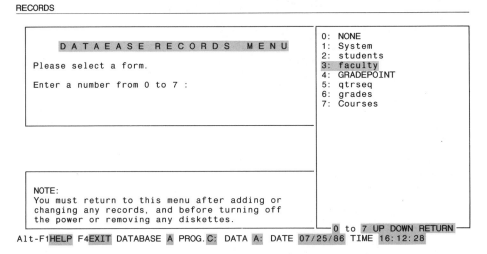

Figure 4.19. DATAEASE records menu.

To enter the Data entry mode, the user selects option 2 (Record Entry and Changes) on the main DATAEASE menu (Fig. 4.3). The package responds by displaying a form from which the files to be edited can be selected (Fig. 4.19). Notice that a warning message instructs the user to be sure to exit normally, since newly entered data are buffered in memory which is not dumped to disk until the entry session is terminated. A window on the right side of the workspace lists the files that are available. Selecting option 3 (faculty) retrieves a blank copy of the form for that file as shown in Fig. 4.20. In this package, the data fields are indicated by underlines representing the maximum length of each field.

During the data entry process, the values for each field are typed in. If an entry is shorter than the prescribed length typing the Return key moves the cursor to the next field. Invalid data types or unrealistic values are noted as soon as the field is typed (Fig. 4.21), with an error message appearing in the message area on the top line. Mistakes can be corrected by backspacing and retyping, or by using cursor move keys to reposition the cursor in the correct location and typing over the incorrect values. The user can insert or delete by using the Insert or Delete keys.

The function keys at the bottom of the screen are used to control actions to be taken with data once typed on the screen. F2 (ENTER) stores the data as a record in the designated file. F10 is used if multiple screens are required for a sin-

```
faculty
No record on screen
_____

        Name:_____      Soc.Sec.No:____-__-_____
        Date of Birth:__/__/____               Sex:____

        Campus Address:_____  Campus Phone: -_____
        Department:_____

        Home Address:_____
        City:_____   State:_____  ZIP:_____
        Home Phone: (    )-   -_____

        Date Hired:__/__/___    Current Academic Title:_____
        Current Salary:_____.__
```

F2ENTER F3VIEW F4EXIT F5FORM CLR F6FLD CLR F7DELETE F8MODIFY F9REPORT F10MULTI

Figure 4.20. DATAEASE data entry: Faculty file.

```
faculty                            Invalid Date
No record on screen
_____

        Name:Carswell, Brett_____      Soc.Sec.No:981-35-7211
        Date of Birth:13/29/29                 Sex:____

        Campus Address:_____  Campus Phone: -_____
        Department:_____

        Home Address:_____
        City:_____   State:_____  ZIP:_____
        Home Phone: (    )-   -_____

        Date Hired:__/__/___    Current Academic Title:_____
        Current Salary:_____.__
```

F2ENTER F3VIEW F4EXIT F5FORM CLR F6FLD CLR F7DELETE F8MODIFY F9REPORT F10MULTI

Figure 4.21. DATAEASE data entry: Error in Date field.

gle record. Function keys F3, F7, and F8 relate to editing, described in the next section. F9, report generation, is also described later. Function keys F5 or F6 can be used when several records are to be entered during a single session. F6 (FIELD CLEAR) is used if only one or two fields will be changed from one record to the next; F5 is useful if totally new information is to be entered and a clean form is desired.

The error checks involving multiple file references are automatically invoked during entry process. In the Courses file, the course number and student numbers must correspond to values in their respective files. If, at entry time, an invalid number is typed for either field, the system immediately blanks the field and proceeds to the next, leaving the field blank. Since both fields are required, any attempt to enter the data into the file generates an error message indicating failure to complete a required field (Fig. 4.22).

```
grades                                    This field must be filled


       Course No:            Year Taken: 86   Quarter: Fall  Seq: 4

       Student ID number: 981-87-9274   Grade Received: b+

       Units: 3.3   Gradepts:  0.00
```

```
F2ENTER F3VIEW F4EXIT F5FORM CLR F6FLD CLR F7DELETE F8MODIFY F9REPORT F10MULTI
```

Figure 4.22. DATAEASE data entry: Error: Required field left empty.

These features provide for a convenient means of data entry closely associated with the process of file definition. Error checking is reasonably complete and can be tailored to each data field. The ability to transfer a machine readable file from some other format into the DATAEASE environment is provided through the Utilities section of the package. Selecting this option makes it possible to import files from several standard formats used for other personal computer application packages such as spreadsheets. Special-purpose formats can also be defined in this manner. With the added capability of file transfer into the DATAEASE format, the package offers a comprehensive entry facility for on-line as well as batch data entry. The process is well suited to entry clerks, who require rapid response and appreciate screens that match the paper forms from which data are transcribed.

4.5.3 Editing

Once a database has been created, it may be reviewed and updated. Updating often merges indistinctly with the process of input, since the three functions of Add, Modify, and Delete can include the function of adding new records. Editing individual records is provided through the same menu that is used for data entry (option 2 on the main menu: Record Entry and Changes). The editing process begins just as though one were to perform data entry; the form to be edited is selected and the blank form appears on the screen. Typing the F3 (VIEW) key will bring to the screen the first record in the file. At this point, the record displayed can be modified on the screen, but the data are not changed in the file unless F8 (MODIFY) is pressed. New records can also be added, as in normal entry, by pressing the F2 (ENTER) key.

Successive records in the file can be reviewed using the F3 (VIEW) function key. When the end of the file is reached, the VIEW function returns to the top of the file. This function is useful when one wishes to browse through the file, reviewing the contents of all records. Sometimes, however, it is more efficient to search for records that match specific criteria. It might be valuable, for example, to examine the records for all male students. To do so, one should use F5 (FORM CLEAR) function key to remove previous entry information, then position the cursor at the Sex field, type M (or m), then once again press the F3 key to obtain the first record matching that condition.

To continue through the file, reviewing all records of male students, it is necessary to hold down the Alternate key and press the F3 (VIEW) function key. This option will find the next record matching the initial search criterion, and successive repetitions will search the entire file for matching records.

Another search feature is to use a partial match search capability. This feature is illustrated in Fig. 4.23. If the user wishes to search for names starting with the letter R, he or she can type r* in the name field, and then press the F3 (VIEW) function key to locate the first name. Notice that either "r" or "R" will locate the appropriate entries, since matches do not distinguish between upper- and lowercase alpha. Typing Alternate VIEW will locate each subsequent record matching the original search criteria, even though the original specification is no longer on the screen.

```
students
No record on screen _____


        Name: r*_____    I.D. No:____  -  -_____
        Date of Birth (mm/dd/yy):   /   /        SEX:____

        Address: _____
        City:_____ State:_____ ZIP:_____

        Date Entered:   /   /    Degree Sought:_____  MAJOR:_____

        UNITS Completed:___Current GPA:_____ Financial Aid:____
```

F2ENTER F3VIEW F4EXIT F5FORM CLR F6FLD CLR F7DELETE F8MODIFY F9REPORT F10MULTI

Figure 4.23. DATAEASE Editing: Search for name with partial match.

Deletions and changes to the file are done by using specific function keys illustrated on the bottom of the screen (Fig. 4.23). Pressing the F8 key deletes an entire record from the database. To change a field, one types in the new value, then presses F8 (MODIFY) function key. The record is not changed until this key is pressed. Sometimes it is useful to make repetitive changes for every record with a particular entry, such as a new pay scale, consistent misspelling, or change in department name. DATAEASE provides for such changes, but it does so in a fashion that is separate from the editing processes. The multiple modification process is handled by the DATAEASE Query Language (DQL), which is done through the Reports and Questions option on the main menu. This approach is inconsistent with the remainder of the package in that an update, single or batch, is still a record change. The choice to place this function in the Report generation section was made to allow the user to formulate complex change statements, an action that requires the use of DQL in this package. Figure 4.24 illustrates an application of DQL to modify the FACULTY file, changing every record with the City field reading "Davis" to "Davisville." The DQL language will be discussed in greater detail in the next section.

```
faccitychange                R  1 C  12
```

```
for faculty with city ='davis';
modify records
  city :=''Davisville''.
```

F1 INTERACTIVE F2 ENTER F3 CUT F4 EXIT F5 COPY F6 PASTE F7 DEL LINE F8 INS LINE F9 LEVEL

Figure 4.24. DATAEASE Editing: Block edit of entire file.

4.5.4 Report Generation

In the previous section, we noted that editing includes the ability to browse through a file, using selective search criteria. The browsing function is actually a form of data retrieval, though it is much simpler than generating actual reports.

The latest release of DATAEASE has an intermediate form of report generation that is available under option 2 of the main menu (Record Entry and Quick Reports) or as a function key (F9) in the Reports section. The intent of this option is to provide printed reports with minimal requirement for query specification. Although limited in its ability to process complex reports, this option serves well for many purposes.

Report generation usually requires four steps: (a) definition of the records to be selected; (b) specification of fields to be listed from those records; (c) definition of the output format; and (d) direction of the output to screen, printer or disk. In many situations, default values for one or more of these options are satisfactory. The Quick Report feature provides default options for each step: all records, all fields for those records, a columnar output, and output to the screen will be selected unless the user overrides one of these defaults.

Reports

```
┌──────────────────────────────────────────────────────────────────────┐
│                 Q U I C K   R E P O R T S   M E N U                    │
│                                                                        │
│        1.  Run Report                                                  │
│        2.  Start New Report                                            │
│        3.  Define Record Selection                                     │
│        4.  Define List Fields                                          │
│        5.  Define Format                                               │
│        6.  Define Print Style                                          │
│        7.  Save Report                                                 │
│        8.  Load Report                                                 │
│        9.  Delete Report                                               │
│        10. Print Report Definition                                     │
│                                                                        │
│                                                                        │
│      1-to-10 ─── UP ─── DOWN ─── RETURN ─── END                        │
└──────────────────────────────────────────────────────────────────────┘
```

F9 FULL   F4 EXIT DATABASE A PROG. C DATA A DATE 08/04/86 TIME 11:03:24

Figure 4.25. DATAEASE Quick Reports Menu.

Figure 4.25 illustrates the manner in which Quick Reports are created and executed. The user can define a new report using option 2, giving it a unique name, then adjust default criteria for any of the options 3 through 6 on that menu. The report can be saved, or an old report can be loaded or deleted. Finally, the full definition can be printed.

```
Select Fields
Press Space to mark field.   Then specify Order Reverse Group Sum Mean Max or Min

            Name: 2 order_____  Soc. Sec. No: _____
            Date of Birth: _____            Sex: ____

            Campus Address: _____  Campus Phone: _____
            Department: 1 group_____

            Home Address: _____
            City: _____ State: _____ ZIP: _____
            Home Phone: _____

            Date Hired: 3_____    Current Academic Title: _____
            Current Salary: 4 sum_____
```

F2ENTER F4EXIT F5FORM CLR F6FLD CLR F10MULTI

Figure 4.26. DATAEASE Quick Report: Field Selection.

To illustrate the use of the Quick Report, we create a report in which faculty are listed alphabetically with their departmental affiliations and current salaries. This report uses the Faculty file, but it will be necessary to select only certain fields in each record. The user therefore selects option 2. In order to select fields, he or she selects option 4 (Define List fields), and the data-entry form is presented with a modified prompt line, as shown in Fig. 4.26. As noted, the user moves the cursor to a field to be selected and presses the space bar, which defines this field as one to appear in the report. The order in which the fields are selected determines their appearance on the report. Optionally, the user can indicate if the field is to be sorted or, in the case of numbers, summarized with the options displayed on the prompt line. In this case, Department, Name, Date Hired, and Salary are the only fields selected. Names are to be listed in order, and the salary total is to be given. No other specifications are required. The criteria are filed using the F2 (ENTER) function, and the report is first saved, giving it a name "facsalaries," then run using option 1, producing a report as shown in Fig. 4.27. In this case, since the report filled more than one line, the Option 6 was also used to output the report to the printer. Notice that, by specifying "group" for Department, "order" for name, and "sum" for salary, the report groups faculty alphabetically by each department, summarizing salaries for each department as well as for the total faculty listed.

```
============================================================================
     DEPT                 NAME                 DAT-EMP        SALARY
----------------------------------------------------------------------------
  Chemistry         MacKenzie, Mark           01/03/71      49,000.00
----------------------------------------------------------------------------
  sum                                                       49,000.00
============================================================================
  English           Newmark, Mary             09/01/74      34,000.00
                    Palmer, Peter             07/01/69      53,000.00
                    Williams, John            09/01/74      44,000.00
----------------------------------------------------------------------------
  sum                                                      131,000.00
============================================================================
  Geology           Carswell, Brett           07/04/81      37,000.00
                    Francis, Richard          07/04/67      46,000.00
----------------------------------------------------------------------------
  sum                                                       83,000.00
============================================================================
  Mathematics       Goldman, Susan            05/10/73      41,000.00
                    McNamee, Cora             09/10/80      31,000.00
                    Patrick, Robert           07/01/67      53,000.00
----------------------------------------------------------------------------
  sum                                                      125,000.00
============================================================================
  Physics           McGrath, Ian              09/10/78      44,000.00
----------------------------------------------------------------------------
  sum                                                       44,000.00
============================================================================
----------------------------------------------------------------------------
  sum                                                      432,000.00
============================================================================
```

Figure 4.27. DATAEASE Quick Report: Faculty Salaries by Department.

It is also possible to use the same approach to select certain records, in which case the entry screen is once again displayed, but the prompt line offers selective conditions to be used to restrict the retrieval.

This type of report is sufficient for a great many purposes, and the ease with which it can be generated makes this approach an attractive option. In some cases, however, it is necessary to specify more complex features in a report. In the remainder of this section, we will deal with more complex data retrieval. Selecting option 3 (Reports and Questions) on the master menu in DATAEASE produces a menu that lists several different functions associated with data retrieval (Fig. 4.28). The options are slightly different from those of the Quick Report, in that the user can use an extended query language and also define run-time data-entry forms that will limit the scope of the report generated.

Reports

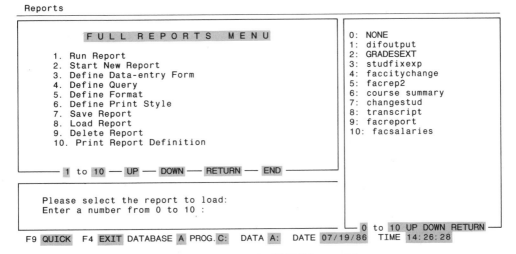

Figure 4.28. DATAEASE Full Reports Menu.

In Fig. 4.28, the user has opted to load an existing report, at which point a window listing available reports appears on the right side of the work space, and a second window in which the user is asked to select the desired report appears below the original menu.

As noted, report generation is a process that consists of several steps. DATAEASE treats these functions separately, completing each step before the next phase is invoked.

The DATAEASE Query Language (DQL) is a comprehensive relational query system that accommodates standard relational functions and permits, in addition, grouping of data and statistical information. In the interactive mode, each step in defining a query is answered through selection from multiple-choice screens. This approach is helpful to the novice user, since no knowledge of the query language is required to complete this process. As one becomes more familiar with the query specifications, it often is preferable to type the commands without prompts, using the Edit mode. Figure 4.29 illustrates the DQL specification of the Quick Report used to create Fig. 4.27. The syntax of the language is readily understood from the example shown. The file from which data are to be retrieved is identified, and in this case no conditional retrieval is specified. The individual data fields that are to appear are selected, with additional specification for grouping and sorting in the report. In addition, subtotals and total for salary are requested, the former by the

```
facsalaries                 R   1  C    1
```

```
for faculty
;
list records
  DEPT in groups with group-totals ;
  NAME in order ;
  DAT-EMP ;
  SALARY :  item sum .
```

F1INTERACTIVE F2ENTER F3CUT F4EXIT F5COPY F6PASTE F7DEL LINE F8INS LINE F9LEVEL

Figure 4.29. DATAEASE Report Specification: Faculty Salaries.

phrase "with group-totals," the latter by the phrase "item sum" after SALARY. In the Edit mode, when a period is typed the query is checked. If errors were made a bell rings and the cursor is moved to the incorrect line in Interactive mode. If the syntax is correct, the program moves on the the next phase of report generation: selecting the output format.

In order to demonstrate the complete process of Full Report generation, we will select a slightly more complex example. To fulfill one request made by the registrar, we wish to produce course reports for all grades given students in a specific course, listing the course number, quarter given, student ID number and name, grade, and grade point units earned by each student. In addition, the report should list the mean numeric grade for that class. This report form should be available to run for individual courses on request, with the course selection to be done when the report is executed.

This report differs from the first example in two important respects: first, the report is to be used to generate single course summaries, based on selection of the specific course, year, and quarter at run time; second, the information required comes from more than one file, since the students' names are not recorded in the Grades file. To satisfy the run-time data selection criterion, a run-time data-entry form must be created that allows the person running the program to identify the course to be summarized. Figure 4.30 illustrates the form created for this purpose.

The report generation process steps in sequence through the options shown in Fig. 4.28, moving next to Query Definition. Figure 4.31 shows the result of this process. Notice that the retrieval is limited to the single course specified by the data-entry form by the statements on the second and third lines of the query. The second new feature in this report is the specification of a relation. The query language allows for related files to be accessed, using a special syntax shown in the last two lines of the output portion of the query. The term "any students name"

```
FORM course summary          R  1 C   1
```

```
          enter course number to be summarized:_____
          Year:_____     Qtr: _____
```

2ENTER F3CUT F4EXIT F5COPY F6PASTE F7DEL LINE F8INS LINE F9PRINT F10FIELD

Figure 4.30. DATAEASE Report Entry Form: Course Summary Report.

```
course summary               R  1 C   1
```

```
for grades
with COURSENO = data-entry courseno and YEAR = data-entry Year
   and QTR=data-entry Qtr;
  list records
 COURSENO ;
  QTR ;
  YEAR ;
  IDN in order ;
Grade ;
any students name;
  Units :  item mean .
```

F1INTERACTIVE F2ENTER F3CUT F4EXIT F5COPY F6PASTE F7DEL LINE F8INS LINE F9LEVEL

Figure 4.31. DATAEASE Full Report with Run-Time Data Entry: Course Summary Report.

implicitly references the file linked through the previously defined relation to locate the first matching ID number. There are three components to this phrase. The term "students" directs the query to search in the Students file, using the defined relation. The query language word "any" will stop at the first matching reference (i.e., where the ID number in the Courses file is the same as the ID number in the Students file). Finally, the term "name" refers to the field called "name" in the Students file, reproducing it in the output report.

```
course summary                    R   3  C    60
==================================================================================
 COURSENO QTR  YEAR       IDN     Grade          Student Name        Units
----------------------------------------------------------------------------------
 .items

 .end
----------------------------------------------------------------------------------
 mean
==================================================================================
```

F2ENTER F3CUT F4EXIT F5COPY F6PASTE F7DEL LINE F8INS LINE F9PRINT F10FIELD

Figure 4.32. DATAEASE Full Report: Output Specification Format.

The remainder of the query is similar to the previous example (Fig. 4.29), except that different statistics (mean) have been specified in order to obtain grade point average.

After completing the Query, the user next defines the output format. The most common form is a columnar report, and selection of this option generates output as shown in Fig. 4.32. The user may modify headings or even customize the report in this phase.

The final definition phase relates to output. Figure 4.33 illustrates the choices available for output medium. In the case of the printer, the user may accept default

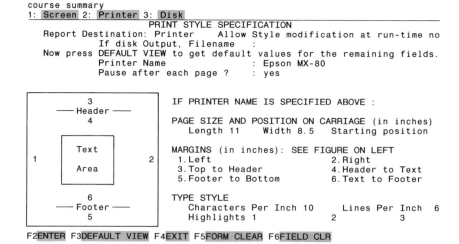

```
course summary
1: Screen 2: Printer 3: Disk
                    PRINT STYLE SPECIFICATION
     Report Destination: Printer     Allow Style modification at run-time no
               If disk Output, Filename   :
     Now press DEFAULT VIEW to get default values for the remaining fields.
               Printer Name                : Epson MX-80
               Pause after each page ?      : yes
```

```
          3            IF PRINTER NAME IS SPECIFIED ABOVE :
     ---- Header ----
          4            PAGE SIZE AND POSITION ON CARRIAGE (in inches)
                          Length 11     Width 8.5    Starting position
       Text
  1           2         MARGINS (in inches): SEE FIGURE ON LEFT
       Area                1.Left                    2.Right
                          3.Top to Header           4.Header to Text
                          5.Footer to Bottom        6.Text to Footer
          6            TYPE STYLE
     ---- Footer ----      Characters Per Inch 10     Lines Per Inch  6
          5               Highlights 1          2            3
```

F2ENTER F3DEFAULT VIEW F4EXIT F5FORM CLEAR F6FIELD CLR

Figure 4.33. DATAEASE Full Report: Print Style Specification Screen.

```
REPORT course summary
----------------------------

DATA-ENTRY FORM
---------------
1      10       20       30       40       50       60       70       80
----+----+----+----+----+----+----+----+----+----+----+----+----+----+----+


        enter course number to be summarized:_____

        Year:____        Qtr:____
----+----+----+----+----+----+----+----+----+----+----+----+----+----+----+
1      10       20       30       40       50       60       70       80


        FIELD DESCRIPTIONS
        ------------------
```

No.	Name	Type	Long	Reqd	In-dex	Uni-que	Der-ived	Rng Chk	Pre-vent	Record size	offset
1	courseno	Text	6	Yes	No	No	No	No	No	6	3
2	Year	Number	2	Yes	No	No	No	No	No	1	9
	Number Type : Integer										
3	Qtr	Choice	4	Yes	No	No	No	No	No	1	10

```
        Choice field type name : qtr
            Choice  1: Fall
            Choice  2: Wntr
            Choice  3: Spr
            Choice  4: Sum
--- -------------------- ---------- ---- ---- --- ---- ---- --- ---- ---- ------
Record size 11

Memory required for form: Text  82, Fields 112, Total 194 bytes.

        REPORT QUERY
        ------------
for grades
with COURSENO = data-entry courseno and YEAR = data-entry Year
   and QTR=data-entry Qtr;
  list records
 COURSENO ;
  QTR ;
  YEAR ;
  IDN in order ;
Grade ;
any students name;
  Units :  item mean

        REPORT FORMAT
        -------------
1      10       20       30       40       50       60       70       80
----+----+----+----+----+----+----+----+----+----+----+----+----+----+----+
=================================================================================
 COURSENO QTR  YEAR      IDN     Grade           Student Name        Units
---------------------------------------------------------------------------------
.items
_____  ___  _____  _____    _____
.end
---------------------------------------------------------------------------------
mean
=================================================================================
----+----+----+----+----+----+----+----+----+----+----+----+----+----+----+
1      10       20       30       40       50       60       70       80


        FIELD DESCRIPTIONS
        ------------------
```

No.	Name	Type	Length	Remove Spaces?
1	COURSENO	Text	6	No
2	QTR	Choice	4	No
	Choice 1: Fall			
	Choice 2: Wntr			
	Choice 3: Spr			
	Choice 4: Sum			
3	YEAR	Number	2	No
	Number Type : Integer			
4	IDN	Numeric String	11	No
5	Grade	Text	2	No
6	any students name	Text	30	No
7	Units	Number	3	No
	Number Type : Fixed point			
	Digits to left of decimal = 1			
8	Units	Number	3	No
	Number Type : Fixed point			
	Digits to left of decimal = 1			

```
Memory required:
  Report Definition:      1604
  Data-entry Form:         194
```

Figure 4.34. DATAEASE Printout of complete specifications for Course Summary Report.

options or override with specific changes as indicated.

Once the report has been completely defined, it can be saved for future use. The report specifications are summarized in Fig. 4.34, which was obtained by selecting option 10 on the Reports menu. An example of the final report is shown in Fig. 4.35, which resulted after the user selected the indicated course, year, and quarter.

Our final example is one needed both by students as well as the registrar: a student transcript. Students have a habit of requesting these forms only in a crisis situation; the transcript is needed immediately, or else the student's job or graduate

```
===============================================================================
COURSENO QTR  YEAR     IDN        Grade          Student Name        Units
-------------------------------------------------------------------------------
  geo843 Fall  82 981-42-5729 C      Reid, Jane              2.0
  geo843 Fall  82 981-87-9274 B+     Lee, Steven             3.3
  geo843 Fall  82 984-66-9523 B      Horton, James           3.0
  geo843 Fall  82 986-33-1233 B-     Rojas, Julie            2.7
-------------------------------------------------------------------------------
mean                                                         2.75
===============================================================================
```

Figure 4.35. DATAEASE Report: Example of course summary output.

```
transcrpt
_____


This report generates transcripts for individual students.
You may specify the range of students for whom transcripts
are to be produced by typing lower and upper ranges, using the
following syntax:

        A*          any name starting with A

For example, to print transcripts for all students named Jones,
use Jones* as starting point, and Jonet as ending point.

        starting point:reid*          ending point:reida
```

`F2`ENTER `F4`EXIT `F5`FORM CLEAR `F6`FIELD CLR

Figure 4.36. DATAEASE Printout of transcript report specifications.

school application deadline will be missed. Consequently, this report must be capable of generating an up-to-date transcript on short order. There must be a data-entry form that allows specification of a single student or, if need be, a larger group of students. Since this report is often run by clerical staff unfamiliar with the program (regrettably, turnover is high in the registrar's office), the entry form must have instructions that will aid the novice in specifying the correct selection information. Figure 4.36 illustrates the input form used by the clerk to select a single stu-

```
REPORT transcrpt
--------------------------

DATA-ENTRY FORM
----------------
1      10       20       30       40       50       60       70       80
----+----+----+----+----+----+----+----+----+----+----+----+----+----+----+
```

```
This report generates transcripts for individual students.
You may specify the range of students for whom transcripts
are to be produced by typing lower and upper ranges, using the
following syntax:

      A*             any name starting with A

For example, to print transcripts for all students named Jones,
use Jones* as starting point, and Jonet as ending point.

      starting point:_____  ending point:_____
----+----+----+----+----+----+----+----+----+----+----+----+----+----+----+
1      10       20       30       40       50       60       70       80
```

```
          FIELD DESCRIPTIONS
          ------------------
```

No.	Name	Type	Long	Reqd	In-dex	Uni-que	Der-ived	Rng Chk	Pre-vent	Record size	offset
1	start	Text	10	No	No	No	No	No	No	10	3
2	end	Text	10	No	No	No	No	No	No	10	13

```
Record size 23

Memory required for form:  Text  415, Fields 59, Total 474 bytes.
```

```
          REPORT FORMAT
          -------------

1      10       20       30       40       50       60       70       80
----+----+----+----+----+----+----+----+----+----+----+----+----+----+----+
.group header
.page
                         Maverick University      _____
Official Transcript for:

Student name:_____
      Address:_____
               _____, __ _____
.group header
.group header
Quarter:_____

  Course no  Course name                  Units Grade Gradepts
.items
  _____   _____  __   __  _____
.group trailer
                                            ----------------------
                         Quarter Totals: _____  _____
                         Quarter GPA: _____

                      Cumulative Totals: _____      _____GPA:_____
=============================================================================
.gorup trailer

.group trailer
.end
----+----+----+----+----+----+----+----+----+----+----+----+----+----+----+
1      10       20       30       40       50       60       70       80
```

```
                      FIELD DESCRIPTIONS
                      ------------------
```

No.	Name	Type	Length	Remove Spaces?
1	current date	Date	8	No
2	name	Text	30	No
3	ADDR	Text	35	No
4	CITY	Text	15	Yes
5	STATE	Text	2	No
6	ZIP	Numeric String	5	No
7	seq	Number	1	No
	Number Type : Integer			
8	YEAR	Number	2	No
	Number Type : Integer			
9	courseno	Text	6·	No
10	any courses course-n	Text	30	No
11	any courses units	Number	1	No
	Number Type : Integer			
12	grade	Text	2	No
13	gradepts	Number	5	No
	Number Type : Fixed point			
	Digits to left of decimal = 2			
14	any courses units	Number	5	No
	Number Type : Integer			
15	gradepts	Number	9	No
	Number Type : Fixed point			
	Digits to left of decimal = 6			
16	sum of grades named	Number	5	No
	Number Type : Fixed point			
	Digits to left of decimal = 2			
17	temp cum units	Number	5	No
	Number Type : Fixed point			
	Digits to left of decimal = 2			
18	temp cum points	Number	5	No
	Number Type : Fixed point			
	Digits to left of decimal = 2			
19	temp cum points / te	Number	5	No
	Number Type : Fixed point			
	Digits to left of decimal = 2			
20	gradepts	Number	5	No
	Number Type : Fixed point			
	Digits to left of decimal = 2			

```
Memory required:
  Report Definition:        4673
  Data-entry Form:          474
```

Figure 4.37. DATAEASE Printout of Transcript Run-Time Entry Form.

dent or groups of students for whom transcripts are needed. The use of "wild card" letters in the form obviates having to type the name exactly.

Figure 4.37 is a composite listing of the program used to generate one or more transcripts. Figure 4.37a defines the data-entry form described above. Figure 4.37b contains the description of the report query. This program is more complicated than previous examples and merits some study. The first two lines:

```
define ``cum units'' number .
define ``cum points'' number .
```

set up two temporary variables that will be used in keeping track of units and grade points earned by the student for each quarter. The availability of temporary variables of this type is important in many reports that require intermediate results.

The next two lines define the file used to search for student names, limiting the search to those specified by the data-entry form. Immediately following these two lines, the temporary variables previously defined are given an initial value of 0. This step is necessary because the report can generate several transcripts, and each student record should begin with a clean slate before course units and grade points are added.

The following section selects fields from the student file to be displayed on the report. The name, current date when the transcript is generated, and address information are included in this section.

The next section summarizes the student's performance for each academic quarter. The section that begins with "for grades" through the first "end" statement accomplishes this task. Initially, for each grade, the temporary variables "cum units" and "cum points" are updated by adding the values for the current grade. Next, beginning with each calendar year, quarters are grouped by sequence number (a number assigned with Winter = 1, Spring = 2, Summer = 3, and Fall = 4), course number, name (from the Courses file), grade, and units (again from the Courses file), with units totaled for each quarter.

The next two lines define a retrieval condition that selects courses for one academic quarter at a time. The "alias" assigned to this definition is "this," which is defined as the year and sequence (taken from the Grades file) and the student IDN (taken from the Students file). For that group of courses with identical values in each of these three fields (i.e., the grades posted for a single student for a single quarter), the statement calculates the total units. Next, the report outputs cumulative grade points, units, and gpa (grade points divided by units) to the end of that quarter.

The final line of the quarter report totals grade points. This statement completes the report generation. A final section of the report specifies the manner in which master file records are to be updated, storing the current cumulative units earned and grade point average in the student's file.

The final section of this report listing (Fig. 4.37c) illustrates the format designed to present this report. The first portion depicts the printed format of the report, followed by a listing of each item, from top to bottom and left to right, that appears in the transcript. The report summary concludes with a notation of the space required by the report and the data entry form.

This example indicates that the DATAEASE query language is flexible enough to generate a complex report, using a special format. Some training would be required to enable a user to take advantage of the features of this language (this report was generated for the author by experts in the language).

A sample of the output from this report is shown in Fig. 4.38.

4.5.5 System Integration: DATAEASE

Our database is now operational in DATAEASE. The files have been defined, the data entered, and we have created at least some of the reports stipulated by our interviews at Maverick U. The next step is to create an environment in which each user group is only exposed to those choices that affect its operations. Put in another way, we want to simplify use of the database for each group, and we also want to protect some data from access by unauthorized individuals. These functions can

```
                          Maverick University
Official Transcript for:                              08/21/86
Student name: Reid, Jane
     Address:  2003 La Brea Terrace
               Davis, CA  95616

Quarter:4  82

    Course no Course name                 Units Grade Gradepts
    geo843    Plate Tectonics               4    C      8.00
                                           --------------------
                           Quarter Totals:  4           8.00
                           Quarter GPA: 2.00

                         Cumulative Totals: 4.00        8.00 GPA: 2.00
======================================================================
Quarter:1  83

    Course no Course name                 Units Grade Gradepts
    CS520     Introduction to Computing     3    B-     8.10
    E504      Basic Composition             4    A-    14.80
                                           --------------------
                           Quarter Totals:  7          22.90
                           Quarter GPA: 3.27

                         Cumulative Totals:11.00       30.90 GPA: 2.81
======================================================================
Quarter:4  83

    Course no Course name                 Units Grade Gradepts
    E79643    Advanced composition          4    C+     9.20
                                           --------------------
                           Quarter Totals:  4           9.20
                           Quarter GPA: 2.30

                         Cumulative Totals:15.00       40.10 GPA: 2.67
======================================================================
Quarter:1  84

    Course no Course name                 Units Grade Gradepts
    M639      Automotata Theory             3    A-    11.10
                                           --------------------
                           Quarter Totals:  3          11.10
                           Quarter GPA: 3.70

                         Cumulative Totals:18.00       51.20 GPA: 2.84
======================================================================
Quarter:2  84

    Course no Course name                 Units Grade Gradepts
    E9250     Computational Linguistics     2    B      6.10
    P709      Optics                        3    B      9.00
                                           --------------------
                           Quarter Totals:  5          15.00
                           Quarter GPA: 3.00

                         Cumulative Totals:23.00       66.20 GPA: 2.88
======================================================================
Quarter:4  84

    Course no Course name                 Units Grade Gradepts
    CS781     Compilers                     4    A-    14.80
    E821      Shakespeare                   4    A-    14.80
                                           --------------------
                           Quarter Totals:  8          29.60
                           Quarter GPA: 3.70

                         Cumulative Totals:31.00       95.80 GPA: 3.09
======================================================================
```

Figure 4.38. DATAEASE Report: Example of output for Transcript Report.

both be accomplished in DATAEASE, using utilities provided by that package. The operational supervisor of a database (who is the first person to create it unless otherwise specified) can assign different levels of security access to users, giving some protection to the database. However, a more important way to control the environment is through user-defined menus. By choosing the Menus and Relationships option of the master menu (option 6, Fig. 4.3), the operations supervisor can define new menus and restrict user access to the system through those menus. Figure 4.39 illustrates the form used to create a new menu, intended for the use of the registrar. The menu is named "registrar," and individuals entering the system through this menu will be given medium security level (which allows them to read and modify data, but not to access system maintenance functions such as the options demonstrated in this section). The lower half of this specification form allows the supervisor to define the options available to this group of users. The first function that the registrar should be able to perform has to do with entering student data. A prompt line is defined, and the system inquires as to what function type is to be allowed, allowing the user to select from the options given on the prompt line on that screen. The choice to be made in this case is record entry. Figure 4.40 shows the completed form defining the registrar's options. Once defined, the screen generated for his use will appear as the initial screen once the registrar has signed on. By defining the options available, the supervisor is also preventing access to any other functions.

In order to link this screen to the registrar, the supervisor must also identify the registrar to the system for log-on purposes. This is done by selecting option 7, System Administration, in the main DATAEASE menu, Fig. 4.3. This option allows the supervisor to define users, as shown as option 1 in Fig. 4.41. The registrar's name, password, security, and security level are defined. In addition, the Start-up menu is identified as the one just created, named registrar. When this user

```
menus
1: MAIN menu 2: user menu 3: record entry 4: query 5: run report              F1MORE
                              MENU DEFINITION
          MENU NAME  registrar              SECURITY LEVEL Medium2

You can define upto 9 choices per menu, selected by digits 1 to 9.
Choice 0 always returns to the previous menu.

For each choice, provide the Choice Description and the Function Type.
Function Name is required for ''user menu'', ''record entry'', and ''run report''
functions, and optional for ''Data Import'' and ''Program Call'' functions.
For ''Program Call'', Function Name may be continued into the next Description.

     MENU  TITLE  REGISTRAR  OPTIONS
NO.          CHOICE DESCRIPTION              FUNCTION TYPE   FUNCTION  NAME
1.enter/edit student information ____        _____   _____
2._____               _____   _____
3._____               _____   _____
4._____               _____   _____
5._____               _____   _____
6._____               _____   _____
7._____               _____   _____
8._____               _____   _____
9._____               _____   _____

F2ENTER F3VIEW F4EXIT F5FORM CLR F6FLD CLR F7DELETE F8MODIFY F9REPORT F10MULTI
```

Figure 4.39. DATAEASE User-Defined Menu.

```
menus                                    Record 1 updated
Record 1 on screen
                         MENU DEFINITION
     MENU NAME  registrar          SECURITY LEVEL  Medium2
```

You can define upto 9 choices per menu, selected by digits 1 to 9.
Choice 0 always returns to the previous menu.

For each choice, provide the Choice Description and the Function Type.
Function Name is required for ''user menu'', ''record entry'', and ''run report''
functions, and optional for ''Data Import'' and ''Program Call'' functions.
For ''Program Call'', Function Name may be continued into the next Description.

```
    MENU  TITLE  REGISTRAR  OPTIONS
NO.            CHOICE DESCRIPTION           FUNCTION TYPE    FUNCTION NAME
1. enter/edit   student information         record entry  students
2. enter course  grade information          record entry  grades
3. run official  transcript                 run report    transcript
4. run course summary                       run report    course summary
5. query data base for Quick Reports        query
6. _____         _____   _____
7. _____         _____   _____
8. _____         _____   _____
9. _____         _____   _____
```

F2ENTER F3VIEW F4EXIT F5FORM CLR F6FLD CLR F7DELETE F8MODIFY F9REPORT F10MULTI

Figure 4.40. DATAEASE User-Defined Menu.

signs on, he or she will be asked for name and password, and then immediately
presented with the menu shown in Fig. 4.42, which was generated by the foregoing
definition When the registrar signs on, the initial display will appear as shown in
Fig. 4.43.

By creating similar menus for other groups (faculty, students, etc.), the
operations supervisor can accomplish the dual tasks of simplifying user interaction
and restricting access to unauthorized data. We have therefore completed our initial implementation of the Maverick University Information System, and we are
ready to demonstrate it.

DATAEASE

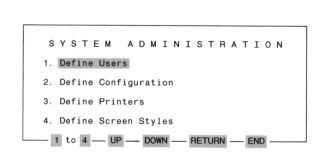

Figure 4.41. DATAEASE System Definition Menu.

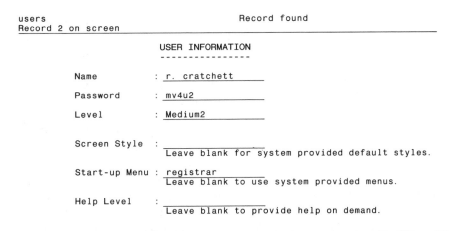

```
users                                    Record found
Record 2 on screen
                        USER INFORMATION
                        - - - - - - - - - - - - - - - -

          Name            : r. cratchett

          Password        : mv4u2

          Level           : Medium2


          Screen Style  :
                            Leave blank for system provided default styles.

          Start-up Menu : registrar
                            Leave blank to use system provided menus.

          Help Level    :
                            Leave blank to provide help on demand.
```

F2ENTER F3VIEW F4EXIT F5FORM CLR F6FLD CLR F7DELETE F8MODIFY F9REPORT F10MULTI

Figure 4.42. DATAEASE User Definition Menu.

DATAEASE

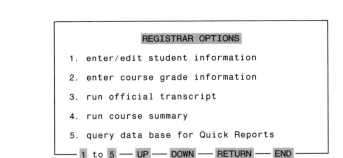

```
                    REGISTRAR OPTIONS

          1. enter/edit student information

          2. enter course grade information

          3. run official transcript

          4. run course summary

          5. query data base for Quick Reports
          1 to 5 — UP — DOWN — RETURN — END
```

F4 EXIT   DATABASE A PROG. C: DATA A: DATE 07/21/86 TIME 13:37:02

Figure 4.43. DATAEASE Example of screen defined in Fig. 4.40.

4.6 IMPLEMENTATION OF THE MAVERICK INFORMATION SYSTEM: dBASE III PLUS

Having stepped through the implementation of the Maverick University Information System using DATAEASE, we will next go through many of the same steps using a different package, dBASE III PLUS. It will not be necessary to go through the detailed specifications of all the examples. Instead, we will concentrate on some of the differences in the way the same examples are implemented using this package.

The dBASE package was designed using a significantly different philosophy. Earlier versions (dBASE II, dBASE III) were written for programmers. A command language controlled all functions in the package. Although HELP screens were available, they did not link directly to the active functions, which had to be performed either interactively, using the command language, or by use of stored programs.

The latest version, dBASE III PLUS, has added an Assist mode that permits naive users to take advantage of menu-driven screens that enable the user to accomplish many tasks associated with database manipulation. We will illustrate some portions of this mode, pointing out some differences between the dBASE and DATAEASE approaches. However, since the principal emphasis in this package remains command oriented, we will concentrate on that aspect.

The manual for dBASE III PLUS reflects the different approach to the user. The latest release consists of a two-volume manual, divided into five sections: Learning dBASE III Plus; Using dBASE III PLUS; Programming with dBASE III PLUS; Networking with dBASE III PLUS; and an Applications Generator. The first of these sections is a tutorial, reorganized from earlier releases to allow a naive user to proceed through a comprehensive set of examples illustrating dBASE features. It assumes that the Assist (prompted) mode is in operation. The remainder of the manual is aimed at individuals who have programmed in one or more languages and have some familiarity with databases.

```
              dBASE III PLUS  version 1.0 IBM/MSDOS
      Copyright (c) Ashton-Tate 1984, 1985, 1986. All Rights Reserved.
          dBASE, dBASE III, dBASE III PLUS, and Ashton-Tate
             are trademarks of Ashtn-Tate


      You may use the dBASE III PLUS software and  printed materials in
      the dBASE III PLUS software package under the terms  of the dBASE
      III PLUS Software License Agreement.      In summary, Ashton-Tate
      grants you a paid-up, non-transferable,  personal license to use
      dBASE III PLUS on one microcomputer or workstation.   You do not
      become the owner of the package,  nor do  you have   the right to
      copy or alter the software or printed materials. You  are legally
      accountable  for any violation of  the License  Agreement   or of
      copyright, trademark, or trade secret laws.
```

Command Line |<C:>|
Press ⏎ to assent to the License Agreement and begin dBASE III PLUS.

Figure 4.44. dBASE III PLUS. Sign-on message.

To illustrate the package, we will begin by starting the system on a hard disk computer. When we type "DBASE" and press the Enter key, the package returns with the screen shown in Fig. 4.44. Once the user has read the cautionary remarks and pressed the Return key, the Assist mode is invoked, and an opening screen appears. The general format of the Assist screens is shown in Fig. 4.45. Figure 4.46 is one example of this format. The Set-Up function is selected (highlighted by reverse video on the top line); a window opens giving options in that function, one of which is highlighted and explained on the bottom line of the screen.

```
┌──────────────────────────────────────┬──────────┐
│ FUNCTION OPTIONS                      │  Time    │
├──────────────────────────────────────┴──────────┤
│ WINDOW - ORIENTED    WORK SPACE                  │
│                                                  │
│                                                  │
│                                                  │
│                                                  │
│                                                  │
│                                                  │
│                                                  │
│                                                  │
├──────────────────────────────────────────────────┤
│ STATUS      LINE                                  │
├──────────────────────────────────────────────────┤
│ General     Prompt Line                          │
├──────────────────────────────────────────────────┤
│          Description of current option           │
└──────────────────────────────────────────────────┘
```

Figure 4.45. dBASE III PLUS. General format of ASSIST Screens.

```
Set Up   Create  Update Position Retrieve Organize Modify Tools 01:26:51 pm

┌──────────────────────────┐
│ Database file            │
├──────────────────────────┤
│ Format for Screen        │
│ Query                    │
├──────────────────────────┤
│ Catalog                  │
│ View                     │
├──────────────────────────┤
│ Quit dBASE III PLUS      │
└──────────────────────────┘
```

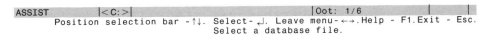

```
ASSIST            |<C:>|                           |Oot: 1/6       |        |
         Position selection bar -↑↓.  Select- ↵.  Leave menu- ←→.Help - F1.Exit - Esc.
                              Select a database file.
```

Figure 4.46. dBASE III PLUS. ASSIST Mode: Initial Menu.

4.6.1 File Definition

To illustrate a portion of this process, we will create one file in the Assist mode. By moving laterally to the Create option, then selecting database file option, we are first asked to name the file (Fig. 4.47). Prompts at the bottom of the screen direct actions at each step of this process. Figure 4.48 illustrates the file creation screen. A window showing options opens above the definition work space. The upper right corner gives the space available for the complete form, and is reduced each time a new field is entered.

Fields are identified by giving a name, then selecting data type from the options Character, Numeric, Date, Logical (true/false), or Memo, a long text form stored separate from the main data file. Character fields may be any length up to

```
Set up  Create  Update  Position  Retrieve  Organize  Modify  Tools    01:34:09 pm
    ┌─────────────────┐
    │ Database file   │
    │ Format          │
    │ View            │
    │ Query           │
    │ Report          │
    │ Label           │
    └─────────────────┘


         ┌────────────────────────────────────────────────────┐
         │  Enter the name of the file:  students             │
         └────────────────────────────────────────────────────┘




Command:  CREATE C:
ASSIST            │<C:>│ TRIAL                    │Rec: 1/2       │          │
                    Enter new value.  Finish with ⏎ .
                         Specify a file name.
```

Figure 4.47. dBASE III PLUS. ASSIST Mode: Creating a new file (Named "Students").

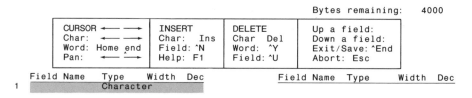

```
                                            Bytes remaining:    4000
   ┌──────────────────┬──────────────┬──────────────┬────────────────┐
   │ CURSOR ←    →     │ INSERT       │ DELETE       │ Up a field:     │
   │ Char:   ←    →    │ Char:   Ins  │ Char  Del    │ Down a field:   │
   │ Word: Home end    │ Field: ^N    │ Word:  ^Y    │ Exit/Save: ^End │
   │ Pan:    ←    →    │ Help: F1     │ Field: ^U    │ Abort: Esc      │
   └──────────────────┴──────────────┴──────────────┴────────────────┘
   Field Name    Type    Width  Dec        Field Name    Type    Width  Dec
 1                Character


CREATE            │<C:>│STUDENTS                 │Field: 1/1     │          │
                      Enter the field name.
Field names begin with a letter and may contain letters, digits and underscores
```

Figure 4.48. dBASE III PLUS. ASSIST Mode: File definition screen.

```
                                            Bytes remaining:    3898
   ┌──────────────────┬──────────────┬──────────────┬────────────────┐
   │ CURSOR ←    →     │ INSERT       │ DELETE       │ Up a field:     │
   │ Char:   ←    →    │ Char:   Ins  │ Char  Del    │ Down a field:   │
   │ Word: Home end    │ Field: ^N    │ Word:  ^Y    │ Exit/Save: ^End │
   │ Pan:    ←    →    │ Help: F1     │ Field: ^U    │ Abort: Esc      │
   └──────────────────┴──────────────┴──────────────┴────────────────┘
     Field Name    Type      Width  Dec      Field Name   Type    Width  Dec
  1  NAME          Character   30
  2  IDN           Character   11
  3  DOB           Date         8
  4  SEX           Character    1
  5  ADDR          Character   35
  6  CITY          Character   15
  7  STATE         Character    2
  8  ZIP           Numeric


CREATE            │<C:>│STUDENTS                 │Field: 8/8     │          │
                      Enter the field width.
Numeric fields are 1 to 19 digits wide, including the decimal point and sign.
```

Figure 4.49. dBASE III PLUS. ASSIST Mode: Prompt for numeric field.

254 bytes. Dates are automatically assigned a length of 8. Numeric fields, as shown in Fig. 4.49, may be up to 19 digits wide. This figure shows the file partially created, with the specifications as provided for in this package. Notice that, except for checking for length, validity of date or numerically valid characters, there is no automatic option for error detection in dBASE III PLUS.

When the file has been completely defined, pressing the Enter key informs the system that the specifications are complete, and the user is asked to confirm by once again pressing Enter (Fig. 4.50). The form is then filed, and the user is asked if he or she wishes to enter data at this time. We will defer data entry until we have created additional files, going through the same process to define Faculty, Courses, and Grades.

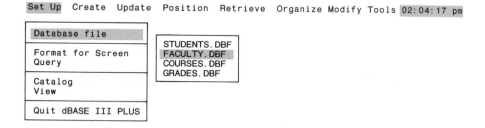

Figure 4.50. dBASE III PLUS. ASSIST Mode: Completed file definition for students file.

4.6.2 Data Entry

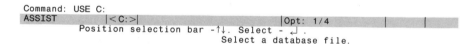

Figure 4.51. dBASE III PLUS. ASSIST Mode: Selecting a data file.

Once a number of files have been created, it is necessary to select a specific file for further actions. Figure 4.51 illustrates the selection options, and this time a window with available files is presented for the user to select from. Notice that, at this time, there is no file name in the Status line near the bottom of the screen. Once the file is selected, the user moves to the Update options, and selects the Append option (Fig. 4.52). A standard entry screen is presented, with each field on a separate line. The user may enter data on each field, observing rules imposed by the data type for each. When the record is complete (the last field has been entered), the record is automatically filed and the screen blanked in preparation for a new record entry. If the user wishes to pause and verify data before proceeding, it is necessary to stop before completion of the last (ZIP code) field.

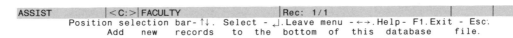

Figure 4.52. dBASE III PLUS. ASSIST Mode: Request to append new records to file.

The data form generated by this process is illustrated in Fig. 4.53.

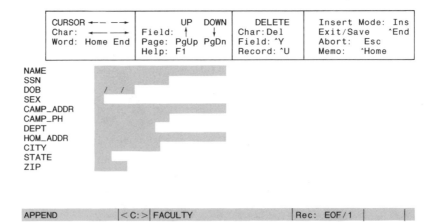

Figure 4.53. dBASE III PLUS. ASSIST Mode: Default Data-entry Form.

We have commented earlier on the desirability of creating input forms that closely match the paper forms used to record data prior to entry into the database. dBASE III PLUS offers an option that permits the user to create screens in which data can be moved to other areas of an entry screen. The next series of figures illustrates this process. First, one must move to the Create Mode and select Format. When this is done, the system asks for a name, as shown in Fig. 4.54. We will use the name FACFORM, and create a new entry form for the Faculty file.

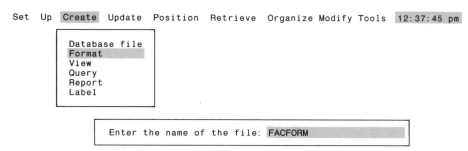

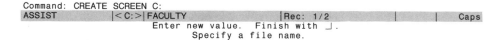

Figure 4.54. dBASE III PLUS. ASSIST Mode: Create special entry screen (to be named "FACFORM").

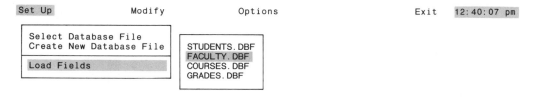

Figure 4.55. dBASE III PLUS. ASSIST Mode: Request to load fields for special data-entry screen FACFORM.

In order to relate this new screen form to an existing database, we follow instructions on the next screen, selecting FACULTY.DBF from the files created and requesting that the fields from this file be loaded (Fig. 4.55). This option displays the fields in the Faculty file in a separate window, and the user can then choose which fields are to be included on the form. For the purposes of illustration, we will eliminate the employment and salary record fields, selecting only demographic information. Figure 4.56 shows that each field to appear on the screen has been identified by highlighting it and pressing the Enter key. The three unselected fields have no arrow to the left of their name.

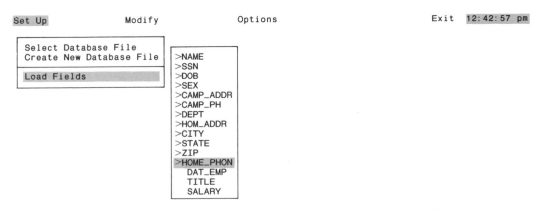

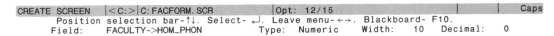

Figure 4.56. dBASE III PLUS. ASSIST Mode: Selection of data fields to appear in data-entry screen.

Once the file and fields have been selected, the original data form appears (Fig. 4.57), much as it did in Fig. 4.53. In this case, however, symbols indicating the data type also appear (XX for character, 99 for numeric, 99/88/99 for date, etc.). This format can now be modified in several ways. First, there is a toggle between Insert and Replace modes. A box near the right end of the Status line indicates which mode is in effect (it can be changed by pressing the Ins key repeatedly). When the Insert mode is in effect, typing a character will add new characters or lines to the screen, moving others appropriately. Figure 4.58 illustrates the use of this feature. Several blank lines were inserted at the top of the form (between the Mode line and Work Space), and a title for the form was entered.

The second major option available is to relocate the fields on the screen. This step is accomplished by moving the cursor to a field, pressing the Enter key once, then moving the cursor to the desired location and pressing the Enter key a second time. The field is repositioned at the new location, although the name of the field remains, and a new prompt must be typed. In Fig. 4.59, the Name field has been moved, a new prompt has been typed, and the old field name has been removed.

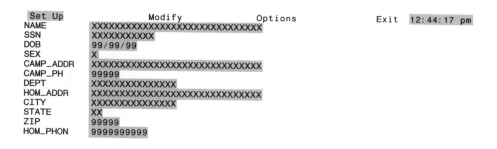

```
   Set Up              Modify              Options          Exit  12:44:17 pm
  NAME      XXXXXXXXXXXXXXXXXXXXXXXXXXXXX
  SSN       XXXXXXXXXXX
  DOB       99/99/99
  SEX       X
  CAMP_ADDR XXXXXXXXXXXXXXXXXXXXXXXXXXXXX
  CAMP_PH   99999
  DEPT      XXXXXXXXXXXXXX
  HOM_ADDR  XXXXXXXXXXXXXXXXXXXXXXXXXXXXX
  CITY      XXXXXXXXXXXXXX
  STATE     XX
  ZIP       99999
  HOM_PHON  9999999999
```

```
CREATE  SCREEN   |<C:>|C: FACFORM. SCR          |Pg 01 Row 00 Col 00  |        | Caps
    Enter text.   Drag field or box under cursor with ↵ .   F10 for menu.
                   Screen field definition blackboard
```

Figure 4.57. dBASE III PLUS. ASSIST Mode: Initial format of data-entry screen.

```
   Set Up              Modify              Options          Exit  12:49:17 pm

                      FACULTY DATA ENTRY FORM

  NAME      XXXXXXXXXXXXXXXXXXXXXXXXXXXXX
  SSN       XXXXXXXXXXX
  DOB       99/99/99
  SEX       X

  CAMP_ADDR XXXXXXXXXXXXXXXXXXXXXXXXXXXXX
  CAMP_PH   99999
  DEPT      XXXXXXXXXXXXXX

  HOM_ADDR  XXXXXXXXXXXXXXXXXXXXXXXXXXXXX
  CITY      XXXXXXXXXXXXXX
  STATE     XX
  ZIP       99999
  HOM_PHON  9999999999
```

```
CREATE  SCREEN   |<C:>|C: FACFORM. SCR          |Pg 01 Row 12 Col 00|Ins  |    Caps
    Enter text.   Drag field or box under cursor with ↵ .   F10 for menu.
                   Screen field definition blackboard
```

Figure 4.58. dBASE III PLUS. ASSIST Mode: Data-entry screen modified by insertion of blank lines.

SSN has also been moved and a new prompt added, but the original name has not yet been deleted. From this example, we see that meaningful prompts that differ from the field names may be used on a format screen of this type. Changing the prompt does not, however, change the field name in the original file definition.

Continuing with this reformatting of the entry screen, the other fields are moved to their final locations as shown in Fig. 4.60. This form now looks quite similar to the DATAEASE form, Fig. 4.14. Notice that the Department field has

```
Set Up              Modify              Options              Exit  12:56:17 pm
                         FACULTY DATA ENTRY FORM

         NAME: XXXXXXXXXXXXXXXXXXXXXXXXXXXX      Soc Sec NO:  XXXXXXXXXX

SSN
DOB          99/99/99
SEX          X

CAMP_ADDR    XXXXXXXXXXXXXXXXXXXXXXXXXXXXXX
CAMP_PH      99999
DEPT         XXXXXXXXXXXXX

HOM_ADDR     XXXXXXXXXXXXXXXXXXXXXXXXXXXXXX
CITY         XXXXXXXXXXXXXX
STATE        XX
ZIP          99999
HOM_PHON     9999999999
```

```
CREATE SCREEN   |<C:>|C: FACFORM. SCR          |Pg 01 Row 03 Col 62|Ins  |     Caps
     Enter text.  Drag field or box under cursor with ⏎.  F10 for menu.
                      Screen field definition blackboard
```

Figure 4.59. dBASE III PLUS. ASSIST Mode: Data-entry screen modified by moving name and SSN field to new position on screen.

```
Set Up              Modify              Options              Exit  01:09:00 pm
                         FACULTY DATA ENTRY FORM

            NAME: XXXXXXXXXXXXXXXXXXXXXXXXXXXX      Soc Sec NO:  XXXXXXXXXX
            Date of Birth: 99/99/99                Sex: X

        Department: XXXXXXXXXXXXX
    Campus address: XXXXXXXXXXXXXXXXXXXXXXXXXXXXXX      Campus phone: 99999

      Home address: XXXXXXXXXXXXXXXXXXXXXXXXXXXXXX
              CITY: XXXXXXXXXXXXXX        State: XX      Zip: 99999

        Home phone: 9999999999
```

```
CREATE SCREEN   |<C:>|C: FACFORM. SCR          |Pg 01 Row 14 Col 07|Ins  |     Caps
     Enter text.  Drag field or box under cursor with ⏎.  F10 for menu.
                      Screen field definition blackboard
```

Figure 4.60. dBASE III PLUS. ASSIST Mode: Data-entry screen with all fields repositioned.

been moved above that of campus address. In the Faculty file, however, this field remains in its original position.

There is a third option available to further enhance the appearance of this entry screen. It is possible to modify fields on the form. For example, the Social Security number is more easily entered if it contains the customary dashes after the third and fifth digits. To modify this field, the user moves to the SSN field, then presses F10 (menu) as indicated on the status line, obtaining the result shown in Fig. 4.61. Using this set of functions, it is possible to modify the actual field definition or to modify its appearance on the screen. In this example, the user

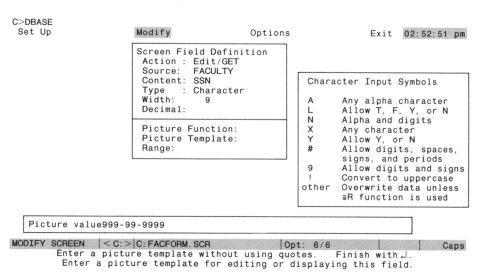

Figure 4.61. dBASE III PLUS. ASSIST Mode: Data-entry screen. Use of window to modify data definition for Social Security number.

selected the Picture Template option, and inserted the dashes as shown. This template will allow any character in the spaces between the dashes. However, the Social Security number in fact consists only of digits (even though these digits are not used for calculation), so a further modification is made to permit digits in a non-numeric mode.

The same type of changes are made for the two telephone numbers, to allow them to conform to the proposed format. The final screen as modified is shown in Fig. 4.62. The results of this definition can then be saved by moving to the Exit mode and selecting the Save option. It is also possible to obtain a printout of the

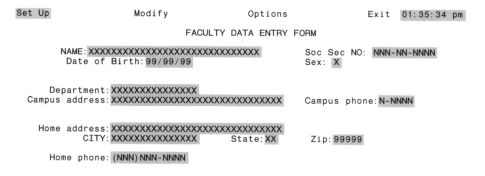

Figure 4.62. dBASE III PLUS. ASSIST Mode: Final format for data-entry screen.

screen format specification, as shown by Fig. 4.63. In this listing, notice that the data types of the three modified fields are retained as alphabetic, but the "PICTURE" for each is different. Notice, too, that the screen image below the columnar description does not differentiate between field types.

```
Field definitions for Screen :  C:FACFORM.scr

Page  Row  Col  Data Base    Field           Type         Width  Dec
   1    3   14   FACULTY     NAME            Character      30
   1    3   63   FACULTY     SSN             Character       9
   PICTURE 999-99-9999
   1    4   24   FACULTY     DOB             Date            8
   1    4   56   FACULTY     SEX             Character       1
   1    8   18   FACULTY     CAMP±ADDR       Character      30
   1    8   64   FACULTY     CAMP±PH         Character       5
   PICTURE 9-9999
   1    7   18   FACULTY     DEPT            Character      17
   1   11   18   FACULTY     HOM±ADDR        Character      30
   1   12   18   FACULTY     CITY            Character      15
   1   12   45   FACULTY     STATE           Character       2
   1   12   56   FACULTY     ZIP             Numeric         5
   1   14   18   FACULTY     HOM±PHON        Character      13     0
   PICTURE (999)999-9999


Content of page :  1

                        FACULTY DATA ENTRY FORM

        Name:XXXXXXXXXXXXXXXXXXXXXXXXXXXXXX      Soc Sec No: XXXXXXXXXXXX
        Date of Birth:XXXXXXX                    Sex: X


        Department:XXXXXXXXXXXXXXXXX
     Campus address:XXXXXXXXXXXXXXXXXXXXXXXXXXXXXX   Campus phone:XXXXX


     Home address:XXXXXXXXXXXXXXXXXXXXXXXXXXXXXX
              City:XXXXXXXXXXXXXX       State:XX      Zip:XXXXX

        Home phone:XXXXXXXXXXXXX
```

Figure 4.63. dBASE III PLUS. ASSIST Mode: Printout of special data-entry screen specifications.

The process illustrated by this series of interactions with dBASE III PLUS in the Assist mode is typical of many other activities that permit nonprogrammers to create applications that take advantage of the programming features of the language. In fact, the screen format defined by the user has led to creation of a dBASE program, FACFORM.FMT, whose extent indicates that it is a screen format program. Figure 4.64 is a listing of this file. Each line beginning with an "@" is a directive to display text at a particular location on the screen. The lines that say "GET ..." are instructions to store data entered in those locations in the Faculty file, using the field specified. The user has, without knowing it, created a dBASE program.

We will use this opportunity to switch from the Assist mode and move into the programming mode, the manner in which this package is most frequently used.

Entry to the command mode is done by pressing the Esc key as noted on the status line, Fig. 4.52. The system responds with a "dot prompt," and the user is invited to enter a dBASE command. In Fig. 4.54, two such commands are used to request a printout of the structure of the Grades file.

Once in the command mode, the user must either know the language or refer to the user manual, using the sections "Using dBASE III PLUS" or "Programming in dBASE III PLUS."

Commands can be invoked directly by typing them on the keyboard, or they can be stored in programs (identified with the file extension ".PRG" in the DBASE data disk file) and invoked using the RUN command. Most operational dBASE functions are accomplished through programs. To illustrate the programming process, we will create a special-purpose program that will provide for special purpose data entry, including error checking, for the Grades file. An important fact to remember, however, is that the user can still use the standard input form to add data to the Grades file, bypassing the error checking provided by the program. It is therefore much more difficult to control the user environment in dBASE.

The problem that we wish to solve using a dBASE program is to create a screen that is similar to the one illustrated in Fig. 4.16, which was designed to facilitate entry from manual grade input forms used at Maverick U. In addition, the course number and student number should be checked to be certain that valid entries exist in the appropriate files.

```
a  1, 30   SAY  ''FACULTY DATA ENTRY FORM''
a  3,  9   SAY  ''Name:''
a  3, 14   GET  ''FACULTY->NAME''
a  3, 51   SAY  ''Soc Sec No:''
a  3, 63   GET   FACULTY->SSN  PICTURE  ''999-99-9999''
a  4, 10   SAY  ''Date of Birth:''
a  4, 24   GET   FACULTY->DOB
a  4, 51   SAY  ''Sex:''
a  4, 56   GET   FACULTY->SEX
a  7,  7   SAY  ''Department:''
a  7, 18   GET   FACULTY->DEPT
a  8,  3   SAY  ''Campus address:''
a  8, 18   GET   FACULTY->CAMP_ADDR
a  8, 51   SAY  ''Campus phone:''
a  8, 64   GET   FACULTY->CAMP_PH  PICTURE   ''9-9999''
a 11,  5   SAY  ''Home address:''
a 11, 18   GET   FACULTY->HOM_ADDR
a 12, 13   SAY  ''City:''
a 12, 18   GET   FACULTY->CITY
a 12, 39   SAY  ''State:''
a 12, 45   GET   FACULTY->STATE
a 12, 52   SAY  ''Zip:''
a 12, 56   GET   FACULTY->ZIP
a 14,  7   SAY  ''Home phone:''
a 14, 18   GET   FACULTY->HOM_PHON  PICTURE  ''(999)999-9999''
```

Figure 4.64. dBASE III PLUS. List of dBASE commands used to generate special data-entry screen.

The first step in creating a special program is to create the file that will be used to store student grades. Figure 4.65 illustrates the structure of this file, which was defined by following steps illustrated in the previous section. This file contains three variables in addition to the course number, quarter, year, student number, and grade. The first, UNITS, is taken from the Courses file and transferred to facilitate reporting at a later date. The second, GRADEPTS, is a calculated value based on the letter grade assigned and the units for the course. The final value, QTRNO, is a number between 1 and 4 representing Winter, Spring, Summer, and Fall academic quarters, respectively. This number will also be used to generate a transcript in sequential order of these time periods. The addition of a group of fields

```
. use grades
. display structure
Structure for database:  C: grades. dbf
Number of data records:        1
Date of last update   : 07/18/86
Field  Field Name  Type        Width
    1  COURSE_NO   Character       6
    2  QTR         Character       6
    3  YEAR        Numeric         2
    4  SEC         Numeric         1
    5  STUD_NO     Character       9
    6  GRADE       Character       2
    7  UNITS       Numeric         3        1
    8  GRADEPTS    Numeric         5        2
    9  QTRNO       Character       1
** Total **                      36
```

```
Command Line    |< C:>|GRADES                    |Rec: 1/1          |          |
                         Enter  a  dBASE  III  PLUS  command.
```

Figure 4.65. dBASE III PLUS. Command Mode: Display structure of Grades file.

not defined by the user at entry time represents an important extension to database systems, which is also available in the DATAEASE package.

Figure 4.66 is a listing of the Grades input program, using the file definition described above. This program is considerably longer and more complex than the program generated in the Assist mode (Fig. 4.64), and it will be described in some detail, so as to illustrate the dBASE III PLUS language. It is not necessary to understand every detail in the program. Instead, the reader should get a general understanding of the dBASE III PLUS language and the versatility that it offers.

The program consists of standard dBASE commands, comment lines (beginning with an asterisk), and blank lines to separate functional units. Indentation is used to identify structural blocks. The program makes use of three data files (Students, Courses, and Grades), a dictionary of grade unit values (GRADEPTS), and a temporary file for short-term data storage (GTEMP). Lines 16 through 28 define these files, assigning each to a separate work area (numbered 1 through 5). The specific index used to establish relations must be referenced as the file is placed in the work area, such as "USE STUDENTS INDEX IDN" (line 19). Line 12 erases the temporary file, in case data remained from a previous entry session.

Lines 14 and 30 use the CLEAR command to clear the screen. The command on line 29 is used to create a blank record in the GTEMP file. This record will be the only record used in the program, retaining previous values until they are overwritten by new data. This approach makes sense when a number of different grades for the same course are being entered.

The remainder of the program consists of an execution loop extending from line 33 through line 130. This loop displays the input form, accepts and checks data, displays error messages if necessary, and files the data in the Grades file when all errors have been corrected. The screen format for data entry is defined in lines 36 through 40. The @ sign signifies the location on the screen of a prompt message (X, Y coordinates), followed by a GET command to provide space for the data element to be entered. dBASE automatically provides the proper number of spaces on the screen from the file definition. Line 40 specifies that GRADE must start with an alpha character (signified by the exclamation point), with the second symbol being any printing character. The READ command on line 41 invokes the data

```
Listing of A:GRADES.PRG          Wednesday, July 23, 1986          Page 1
 1 * Grades.Prg
 2 * modified 12-23-84 by MShulman
 3 * U.C.D. Computer Center, Davis, CA 95616
 4 * (916)752-1667
 5 *
 6 * Interactive entry of course grades
 7 * checks for valid course number, student id number
 8 *
 9 * NOTE: GTEMP erased at start of program. Be sure no data are
10 * in this file before running this program.
11
12 ERASE GTEMP.DBF
13
14 CLEAR
15 ? ''Please Stand By... initializing''
16 SELECT GRADES
17 COPY STRUCTURE TO GTEMP
18 SELECT 2
19 USE STUDENTS INDEX IDN
20 SELECT 3
21 USE COURSES INDEX CRSNO
22 SELECT 4
23 USE GRADES INDEX STUDN
24 SELECT 5
25 USE GRADEPTS INDEX LTRGRD
26
27 SELECT 1
28 USE GTEMP
29 APPEND BLANK
30 CLEAR
31
32 STORE 'Y' TO continue
33 DO WHILE UPPER (continue)= 'Y'
34     STORE .F. TO errs
35
36     a 3,10 SAY 'COURSE NO: ' GET COURSE_NO
37     a 3,30 SAY 'QUARTER: ' GET QTR
38     a 3,50 SAY 'YEAR: ' GET YEAR
39     a 6,10 SAY 'STUDENT NUMBER: ' GET STUDNO
40     a 6,40 SAY 'ENTER GRADE: ' GET GRADE picture ''!x''
41     READ
42
43     REPLACE COURSE NO WITH UPPER(COURSE_NO)
44
45     *check for valid course
46     SELECT COURSES
47     SEEK UPPER(GTEMP->COURSE_NO)
48     IF EOF ()
49       a 19,10 SAY 'Invalid course #. '
50       STORE .T. TO errs
51       SELECT GTEMP
52       REPLACE COURSE_NO WITH ' '
53     ELSE
54       SELECT GTEMP
55       REPLACE UNITS WITH (COURSES->UNITS)
56     ENDIF
57
58     * check for valid student number
59     SELECT STUDENTS
60     SEEK GTEMP->STUDNO
61     IF EOF()
62       a 20,10 SAY 'Invalid stud #. '
63       STORE .T. TO errs
64       SELECT !
65     ENDIF invalid stud #
66
67     * check to see that letter grade is valid, calculate gradepts
68     SELECT GRADEPTS
```

Figure 4.66. dBASE III PLUS: Listing of Grades Data-entry Program written in dBASE language.

```
69       SEEK UPPER(GTEMP->GRADE)
70       IF EOF()
71          a 21,10 SAY 'invalid letter grade.  Please re-enter.'
72          STORE .T. TO errs
73          SELECT GTEMP
74          REPLACE GRADE WITH '  '
75       ELSE
76          SELECT GTEMP
77          SELECT GRADEPTS WITH (GRADEPTS->VALUE) * UNITS
78       ENDIF
79
80       * Add quarter-number for subsequent sorting
81       DO CASE
82          CASE  (AT('W',(UPPER(QTR))) > 0)
83               REPLACE QTRNO WITH ' 1 '
84          CASE (AT('SP',(UPPER(QTR))) > 0)
85               REPLACE QTRNO WITH ' 2 '
86          CASE (AT('SU',(UPPER(QTR))) > 0)
87               REPLACE QTRNO WITH ' 3 '
88          CASE (AT('F',(UPPER(QTR))) > 0)
89               REPLACE ATRNO WITH ' 4 '
90          OTHERWISE
91               REPLACE QTR WITH '     '
92               STORE .T. TO errs
93       ENDCASE
94
95       * check to see if that student already has a grade in that
96       * course, for that quarter.
97       STORE .F. TO found
98       SELECT GTEMP
99       KEY = STUDNO+YEAR+QTRNO
100      SELECT GRADES
101      SEEK KEY
102      DO WHILE .NOT. EOF() .AND. (STUDNO+YEAR+QTRNO = KEY) .AND. .NOT. fou
nd
103         IF (GTEMP->COURSE_NO = COURSE_NO)
104             a 22,10 SAY 'Student already has a grade for that course.'
105             STORE .T. to errs
106             STORE .T. to found
107         ELSE
108             SKIP
109         ENDIF
110      ENDDO
111
112
113      IF .not. errs
114         SELECT GTEMP
115         USE
116         SELECT GRADES
117         APPEND FROM GTEMP
118         a 15,10 SAY  Course added.  Add another course  (Y/N)
119         WAIT TO continue
120         a 15,00 CLEAR
121         IF UPPER(CONTINUE) = ''Y''
122            SELECT 1
123            USE GTEMP
124         ENDIF
125      ELSE
126         a 15,10 SAY 'Try another course (Y/N) '
127         WAIT TO continue
128         a 15,00 CLEAR
129      ENDIF
130 ENDDO continue
131 RETURN
132 * eof GRADES.prg
```

Figure 4.66. Continued.

entry for these fields. In line 43, the user-supplied course number is converted to uppercase, to match the number in the Courses file.

Lines 45 through 56 check for a valid course number. To do so, the Courses file is searched for its indexed field (defined as CRSNO), as specified in line 47. The reference to CRSNO is implicit, defined by the indexing of that file in the USE command (line 21). The literal meaning of this line is "seek the Courses file to see if a match can be found between CRSNO in COURSES and the upper case transformation of COURSE_NO stored in the GTEMP file." If the course number matches, dBASE halts the search, pointing to that record. If the course number is not found (i.e., end-of-file reached), the record is flagged as incorrect (errs is set to .T.), and the field is replaced with blanks (line 52). An error message appears on the lower portion of the screen to inform the user of the problem. If the course number is valid, the Units field associated with that field is stored in the Grades file for future use (lines 67 through 78). A similar check is performed for the student number. The student number is left as is, in case a small correction in the numeric sequence is all that is required to correct the value.

A similar check (lines 58 through 65) is made for valid student number. The next section of the program (lines 67 through 78) checks to make sure that a valid letter grade has been assigned, blanking the field if it is invalid. If it is valid, the numeric value in the GRADEPTS table is multiplied by the units for the course to obtain the appropriate unit credit earned by the student. The remainder of this section (lines 80 through 93) assigns a numeric value to the quarter in which the course was taken, using a CASE construction available in the dBASE III PLUS language. Using CASE, the program checks for the value of QTR, inserting a value of 1 in QTRNO if QTR is W (Winter), 2 for S (Spring), etc.

The final check performed during data entry is to see if a grade for a particular student for a specific course and time period already exists in the file. Lines 95 through 110 accomplish this task, using the permanent GRADES file and comparing its values with the record in GTEMP. Notice that a temporary value, KEY, is created, consisting of the concatenation of the student number, year, and QTRNO fields in GTEMP (line 98). This value is compared against the comparable fields in GRADES. If they match and the course number also matches, the record is rejected (lines 101 through 106).

The remainder of the program files valid data. If no errors were detected, the GTEMP file is closed (USE with no parameters in line 115 closes a file), the record is appended to GRADES, and the user asked if he or she wishes to enter another grade. If so, the GTEMP file is reopened (with the existing data remaining in the record), and the entry continues. The user overrides any field that needs to be changed (usually the student number and grade), and the process continues.

The screen generated by this program is illustrated in Fig. 4.67. Reverse video fields are automatically created for each variable in the field. Error messages will be displayed on the bottom of the screen as specified in the program.

This programming example shows that complex error checks can be performed in dBASE III PLUS, and that calculated values can be generated without the user having to worry about them. It is, of course, necessary to write programs

COURSE NO: ░░░░░   QUARTER: ░░░░░░░   YEAR: ░░░

STUDENT NUMBER: ░░░░░░░   ENTER GRADE: ░░░░░

Command ░░░░░ | < A: > | GTEMP ░░░░░░░░░░ | Rec: 1/1 ░░░░░░░ | ░░ | Caps
                Enter a dBASE III PLUS command.

Figure 4.67. dBASE III PLUS: Data-entry screen generated by program listed in Fig. 4.66.

to accomplish each of these functions, and writing the programs requires experience and practice with the commands available in dBASE III PLUS.

4.6.3 Editing

There are several commands in dBASE III PLUS that can be used interactively to view, modify, delete, or insert records in a file. The USE FACULTY command opens the Faculty file in the workspace, and the editing process starts. In this case, the file will be brought into the workspace and referenced in the sequence in which records occur in the file. By typing a modified command "USE FACULTY INDEX SSN," the file would be accessed by the faculty members' Social Security numbers, beginning with the lowest value.

The dBASE III PLUS editing commands fall into three groups: move, display, and edit. The first set of commands is used to move through the file to a desired location. They include the commands GOTO and SKIP, which access or bypass records by number; LOCATE and CONTINUE, which search conditionally based on match of a search condition of a specified field; and FIND and SEEK, which search only for values in the indexed field in use at the time of the search. GOTO can be modified with the destination TOP, BOTTOM, or RECORD n, where *n* is a specific record within the file. The SKIP command can be used to move up or down in the file <n> records at a time. Figure 4.68 illustrates the use of these commands. Notice that the sequence of record numbers is not in order, because they are being accessed by Social Security number.

FIND is used to get to a specific record based on matching a value in the indexed field, as shown in Fig. 4.69. SEEK works similarly with numeric values. LOCATE is used to search for non-keyed field matches. For instance, to review all records for female faculty members, one would use the LOCATE command to find the first matching record, then use CONTINUE to find subsequent records until the end of file is reached, as shown in Fig. 4.70.

```
. USE FACULTY INDEX SSN
. GOTO TOP
. DISPLAY
Record#  NAME                                              SSN DOB       SEX CAMP_ADDR
                 CAMP_PH DEPT                    HOM_ADDR                        CITY
         STATE    ZIP    HOM_PHNE DAT_EMP    TITLE                    SALARY
      2  Francis, Richard                                    4 08/08/30 M   445 Geology
                 28241 Geology               1211 Wentworth                     Davis
         CA    95616 9167928211 07/04/67 Prof II                      46000
. SKIP 1
Record No.      5
. SKIP 1
Record No.      8
. SKIP 1
Record No.      1
. SKIP 1
Record No.      10
. SKIP 1
Record No.      9
```

| Command Line | < A: > | FACULTY | | Rec: 9/10 | | | Caps |

Enter a dBASE III PLUS command.

Figure 4.68. dBASE III PLUS. Command Mode: Examples of Edit commands.

```
. FIND 983867395
. DISPLAY
Record#  NAME                                              SSN DOB       SEX CAMP_ADDR
   x             CAMP_PH DEPT                    HOM_ADDR                        CITY
         STATE    ZIP    HOM_PHON DAT_EMP    TITLE                    SALARY
      9  Patrick, Robert                          983867395 06/19/27 M   521 Kerr
                 28935 Mathematics           4202 Sacramento Ave.              Davis
         CA    95616 9165265823 07/01/67 Prof V                       53000
```

| Command Line | < A: > | FACULTY | | Rec: 9/10 | | | Caps |

Enter a dBASE III PLUS command.

Figure 4.69. dBASE III PLUS. Command Mode: Examples of Edit commands.

```
. LOCATE FOR SEX=''F''
Record =        3
. CONTINUE
Record =        6
. CONTINUE
Record =        7
. CONTINUE
End of LOCATE scope
```

| Command Line | < A: > | FACULTY | | Rec: EOF/10 | | | Caps |

Enter a dBASE III PLUS command.

Figure 4.70. dBASE III PLUS. Command Mode: Examples of Edit commands.

The second group of commands may be used to view and edit individual records. Earlier, we used the DISPLAY command to illustrate the search process. DISPLAY can also be used to list several records, using the DISPLAY NEXT <n> form (Fig. 4.71), or to view all records by typing DISPLAY ALL.

Another command used to view records is BROWSE, which allows the user to view selected fields rather than entire records. The fields need not be specified in the sequence in which they occur in the record itself. When the fields are displayed, the top record is highlighted and available for editing. Arrow keys and Page-up or Page-down can be used to reposition the cursor. Editing individual fields can be done by typing over existing data or by using the insert and delete keys.

```
. DISPLAY NEXT 3
Record#  NAME                                       SSN DOB       SEX CAMP_ADDR
             CAMP_PH DEPT                 HOM_ADDR
      STATE   ZIP   HOM_PHON DAT-EMP  TITLE                          SALARY
       1  Carswell, Brett                  981357211 10/29/29 M   397 Geology
             28205 Geology               513 Stonewall Ct.                Esparto
      CA    95620 9162722668 07/04/81 Assoc II                    37000
      10  Williams, John                   982538204 02/29/28 M   309 Voorhees
             28451 English               311 N Midland Ave.             Woodland
      CA    95696 9167938675 09/01/74 Assoc IV                    44000
       9  Patrick, Robert                  983867395 06/19/27 M   521 Kerr
             28935 Mathematics           4202 Sacramento Ave.          Davis
      CA    95616 9165265823 07/01/67 Prof V                      53000
```

Command Line	< A: >	FACULTY	Rec: 9/10		Caps

Enter a dBASE III PLUS command.

Figure 4.71. dBASE III PLUS. Command Mode: Examples of Edit commands.

Another editing command is EDIT, which can be modified to address a specific record or used to enter the edit mode when a record has been found by other commands. As in BROWSE, typing EDIT will clear the screen, after which it displays a single record. The options are similar to those in data entry, with the exception that one can move from one record to another. If the cursor is positioned at the last field of a record, typing a down cursor will automatically display the next record. The Page-down key moves to the next record from any cursor position. Conversely, one can move backwards in the file by going up from the first field or typing Page-up. When either end of the file is reached in this manner, the Edit mode is automatically terminated and changes are filed.

The CHANGE command can be used in a manner similar to BROWSE, specifying certain fields to be edited instead of the entire set, as shown in Fig. 4.72. Further restriction on records selected can be specified with conditional FOR or WHILE clauses. For example, one could specify CHANGE FIELDS NAME HOM_ADDR CITY ZIP FOR ZIP > 90000, which would only select records with ZIP codes in the far western portion of the United States.

```
┌─────────────────────┬────────────────────┬──────────────┬──────────────────────┐
│ CURSOR  ←─ ─ ─→      │          UP   DOWN │   DELETE     │ Insert Mode: Ins     │
│ Char:   ←── ──→      │ Field:  ↑     ↓    │ Char: Del    │ Exit/Save    ^End    │
│ Word: Home End       │ Page: PgUp  PgDn   │ Field:  ^Y   │ Abort:   Esc         │
│                      │ Help: F1           │ Record: ^U   │ Memo:    ^Home       │
└─────────────────────┴────────────────────┴──────────────┴──────────────────────┘
NAME          Francis, Richard
HOM_ADDR      1211 Wentworth
CITY          Davis
STATE         CA
ZIP           95616
```

CHANGE	< A: >	FACULTY	Rec: 2/10		Caps

Figure 4.72. dBASE III PLUS. Command Mode: Result of typing dBASE command "CHANGE FIELDS NAME HOM_ADDR CITY STATE ZIP."

Deletion of a record is done with the DELETE command, which can reference the current record or another record by number. In dBASE III PLUS, DELETE does not immediately remove the record from the file. Instead, it flags the record as being no longer valid, but retains the record in the file. This approach is adopted for two reasons. First, deletion of a record in a sequential MSDOS file requires copying the entire file. Second, this approach makes it possible to retrieve records that were inadvertently deleted. The RECALL command is used to cancel delete instructions, whereas the PACK command copies the file, eliminating records flagged for deletion.

A final interactive editing command is REPLACE, which can be used to change several records requiring the same modification. To illustrate the use of this command, we could modify the file by changing the STATE abbreviation in certain records to "ca," using the regular editor. Typing the statement

```
REPLACE STATE WITH ``CA'' FOR STATE = ``ca''
```

results in the response

```
4 records replaced
```

indicating that the entire file has been checked, and four instances of "ca" were located and replaced with "CA."

In addition to interactive editing, dBASE III PLUS permits editing under program control. The options for these types of changes include use of some of the commands previously described, combined with user input through READ and other commands. In addition, an UPDATE command permits editing one dBASE III PLUS file by comparing it with a second and replacing specified fields according to the syntax of the command. In summary, editing in dBASE III PLUS is flexible, with many interactive and batch modifications available.

4.6.4 Report Generation

There are three ways in which data stored in dBASE III PLUS files can be retrieved and viewed. The first is through the editing commands described above, which can be used with conditional searches to find specific records or groups of records. The second approach is through a report generation supported by the Assist mode, and the third option is to write special purpose programs for specific retrievals. Since the first method was described in the previous section, we will only illustrate the report form generator and programming modes.

Using the screen-driven report generator is similar to other Assist menus, in that it offers some, but not all the power of the dBASE language under menu and prompt control. The process is illustrated by Fig. 4.73 through 4.76. Figure 4.73 shows the creation of a report that is given the name FACSALARIES. Note in subsequent screens that the last three letters of this name were truncated. The screen then changes to Fig. 4.74, which provides for specification of the output format. Default values are provided for all except the page title, which is entered in a separate window to the right of the options.

When the format is specified, the user moves to the next Mode option,

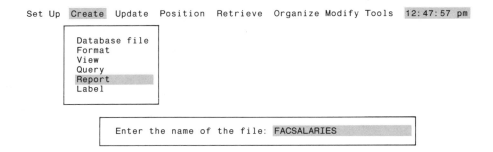

Set Up Create Update Position Retrieve Organize Modify Tools   12:47:57 pm

```
    Database file
    Format
    View
    Query
    Report
    Label
```

        Enter the name of the file: FACSALARIES

Command: CREATE REPORT A:
ASSIST |<A:>|FACULTY |Rec: 9/10 | | Caps
                    Enter new value. Finish with↵.
                      Specify a file name.

Figure 4.73. dBASE III PLUS. ASSIST Mode: Initiating report definition.

Options   Groups   Columns   Locate   Exit   12:52:09 pm

```
 Page title              ,          SU
 Page width (positions)        80
 Left margin                    8
 Right margin                   0
 Lines per page                58
 Double space report           No
 Page eject before printing   Yes
 Page eject after printing     No
 Plain page                    No
```

                                          SUMMARY OF FACULTY
                                            BY DEPARTMENT
                                            WITH SALARIES

```
 CURSOR  ←— —→   Delete char:   Del  Insert column:  ^N  Insert:       Ins
 Char:   ←—  —→  Delete word:    ^T  Report format:  F1  Zoom in:    ^PgDn
 Word:   Home End  Delete column:  ^U  Abandon:       Esc  Zoom out :  ^PgUp
```

CREATE REPORT |<A:>|A: FACSALAR.FRM |Opt: 1/9 | | Caps
                 Enter report title. Exit - Ctrl-End.
Enter up to four lines of text to be displayed at the top of each report page.

Figure 4.74. dBASE III PLUS. ASSIST Mode: Report Definition: Output Report format specification; entering title of report.

definition of Groups. In this case, the salaries are to be grouped by department. One important fact bears on this grouping. The report will be executed correctly *only* if the user specifies that the file is to be indexed on department. If other indexes (such as SSN) are used, the program will not search for non-indexed keys, and a separate group will appear for each record. Figure 4.75 illustrates the selection of DEPT for groupings, with a heading added to improve the output readability. An optional window at the left side of the screen lists available fields. The user then moves to the Columns option and specifies fields to be included in the report (Fig. 4.76), adding titles for each field. Notice that Department is not listed at this level.

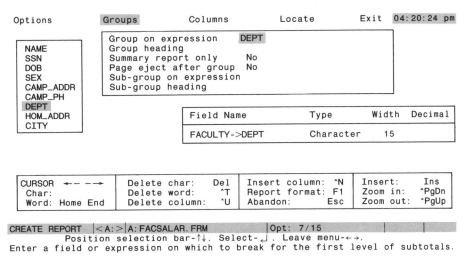

Options   Groups   Columns   Locate   Exit   04:20:24 pm

```
Options          Groups          Columns          Locate          Exit    04:20:24 pm

                 ┌──────────────────────────────────────────────────────┐
  ┌───────────┐  │ Group on expression    DEPT                           │
  │ NAME      │  │ Group heading                                         │
  │ SSN       │  │ Summary report only    No                            │
  │ DOB       │  │ Page eject after group No                            │
  │ SEX       │  │ Sub-group on expression                               │
  │ CAMP_ADDR │  │ Sub-group heading                                     │
  │ CAMP_PH   │  └──────────────────────────────────────────────────────┘
  │ DEPT      │
  │ HOM_ADDR  │     ┌──────────────────────────────────────────────────┐
  │ CITY      │     │ Field Name              Type      Width  Decimal  │
  └───────────┘     │                                                   │
                    │ FACULTY->DEPT           Character   15            │
                    └──────────────────────────────────────────────────┘
```

```
┌─────────────────────┬──────────────────────┬────────────────────────┬─────────────────────┐
│ CURSOR  ←── ──→      │ Delete char:   Del   │ Insert column:  ^N     │ Insert:      Ins    │
│ Char:               │ Delete word:   ^T    │ Report format:  F1     │ Zoom in:     ^PgDn  │
│ Word: Home End      │ Delete column: ^U    │ Abandon:        Esc    │ Zoom out:    ^PgUp  │
└─────────────────────┴──────────────────────┴────────────────────────┴─────────────────────┘
```

CREATE REPORT |<A:>|A:FACSALAR.FRM |Opt: 7/15 | |
      Position selection bar-↑↓. Select-↵. Leave menu-←→.
Enter a field or expression on which to break for the first level of subtotals.

Figure 4.75. dBASE III PLUS. ASSIST Mode: Report Definition: Specification of Groups to be used in Faculty Salary Report.

```
Options          Groups          Columns          Locate          Exit    02:13:58 pm

                 ┌──────────────────────────────────────────────────────┐
                 │ Contents              SALARY                          │
                 │ Heading                 Salary                        │
                 │ Width                   13                            │
                 │ Decimal places          0                            │
                 │ Total this column       Yes                           │
                 └──────────────────────────────────────────────────────┘
```

```
┌─ Report Format ──────────────────────────────────────────────────────────┐
│ Name              Date Hired          Salary        -----                  │
│                                                                            │
│                                                                            │
│ XXXXXXXXXXXXXXXXXXXXX   mm/dd/yy                    ##########             │
└────────────────────────────────────────────────────────────────────────────┘
```

MODIFY REPORT |<A:>|A:FACSALAR.FRM |Column: 3 | | Caps
      Position selection bar-↑↓. Select-↵. Leave menu-←→. Prev/Next Column -PgUp/PgDn.
      Enter up to four lines of text to display above the indicated column.

Figure 4.76. dBASE III PLUS. ASSIST Mode: Report Definition: Selection of Fields to be Included.

This completes the process of form creation, and it can be saved before exiting. The report can then be run using the Retrieve option as shown in Fig. 4.77, producing the report shown in Fig. 4.78. The formatting has been done automatically, and all numeric fields are automatically summed by groups, with a final total at the bottom. The process is fixed in scope, but it provides a simple option for generating straightforward reports. It has inherent limitations with respect to format, file linking, and calculation of output information. To illustrate the programming method of report generation, we will use the course grade report described in the DATAEASE section. Recall that student name and course title are derived from separate files, requiring appropriate links not available in the menu-supported

Set Up Create Update Position Retrieve Organize Modify Tools   02:15:50 pm

```
                              List
                              Display     ┌─────────────────────────────┐
                              Report      │ Execute the command         │
                              Label       │ Specify scope               │
                                          │ Construct a field list      │
                              Sum         │ Build a search condition    │
                              Average     │ Build a scope condition     │
                              Count       └─────────────────────────────┘
```

Command: REPORT FORM A:FACSALAR
ASSIST |< A: >|FACULTY |Rec: 4/10 | | Caps
          Position selection bar-↑↓. Select-↵.
          Perform the command displayed above the status bar.

Figure 4.77. dBASE III PLUS. ASSIST Mode: Running Facsalary Report.

```
Page No.    1
07/23/86
                                    SUMMARY OF FACULTY
                                      BY DEPARTMENT
                                      WITH SALARIES


            Name                       Date Hired                          Salary


** Department Chemistry
   MacKenzie, Mark                      01/03/71                            49000
** Subtotal **
                                                                           49000


** Department English
   Newmark, Mary                        09/01/74                            34000
   Palmer, Peter                        07/01/69                            53000
   Williams, John                       09/01/74                            44000
** Subtotal **
                                                                          131000


** Department Geology
   Carswell, Brett                      07/04/81                            37000
   Francis, Richard                     07/04/67                            46000
** Subtotal **
                                                                           83000


** Department Mathematics
   Goldman, Susan                       05/10/73                            41000
   McNamee, Cora                        09/10/80                            31000
   Patrick, Robert                      07/01/67                            53000
** Subtotal **
                                                                          125000


** Department Physics
   McGrath, Ian                         09/10/78                            44000
** Subtotal **
                                                                           44000


*** Total ***                                                             432000
```

Figure 4.78. dBASE III PLUS. Output from Faculty Salary Report.

report generator described above. Figure 4.79 lists a program to generate this report. Line 1 is the name of the report, with an explanatory description following. Lines 4 and 5 clear the screen and inhibit system messages during execution. The

```
Listing of A:CRSEREPT.PRG          Wednesday, July 23, 1986         Page    1
 1 *CRSEREPT
 2 * generate separate course report for user-specified course, yr, qtr.
 3
 4 CLEAR
 5 SET TALK OFF
 6 SELECT 1
 7 USE GRADES INDEX CRSNO
 8 SELECT 2
 9 USE STUDENTS INDEX IDN
10 SELECT 3
11 USE COURSES INDEX CRSNO
12
13 * read in course number, year, qtrno
14
15 a4,10 SAY 'Program to list all grades for one course at a time'
16 STORE 'Y' TO continue
17 STORE '       ' ctemp
18 STORE '   ' TO yr
19 STORE ' ' TO q
20 DO WHILE UPPER (continue)='Y'
21
22 a6,10 SAY 'Enter course number: ' GET ctemp
23 a8,10 SAY 'Enter (19__): ' GET yr picture ''99''
24 a10,10 SAY 'Enter qtrno (wntr=1,SPR=2,SUM=3,FALL=4): ';
25        GET q picture ''9''
26 READ
27 STORE UPPER (ctemp) TO ctemp
28
29 SELECT GRADES
30 SEEK ctemp
31 IF EOF()
32        a15,10 say 'No course of that number'
33          LOOP
34 ENDIF
35 * loop on individual course
36 DO WHILE (COURSE_NO=ctemp .AND. QTRNO=q .AND. YEAR=val(yr))
37        SELECT COURSES
38        SEEK GRADES->COURSE NO
39        SELECT GRADES
40
41        SET PRINT ON
42        EJECT
43        ?'                    Maverick University                 ',DATE()
44        ?
45        ?'Course Report for ',COURSE_NO,'   ',COURSES->COURSE_NAM
46        ?' ',QTR,'19',YEAR
47        ?
48        ?' Stud #           Student Name           Grade Gradepts'
49
50        DO WHILE (COURSE_NO=ctemp .AND. QTRNO=q .AND. year=VAL(yr))
51              SELECT STUDENTS
52              SEEK GRADES->STUDNO
53              SELECT GRADES
54              ?
55              ? STUDNO,STUDENTS->NAME,GRAD,GRADEPTS
56              SKIP
57        ENDDO for each student
58 ENDDO for one course
59
60 SET PRINT OFF
61
62 a5,10 SAY 'Another course?'
63 WAIT TO continue
64 ENDDO next course
65
66 RETURN
67
68
```

Figure 4.79. dBASE III PLUS. dBASE Program to generate Course Summary Report.

next lines, 6 through 11, identify the files to be used and also specify the fields on which they are to be indexed.

The next section of the program, lines 14 through 19, initializes certain variables and places an opening message on the blank screen. Before a variable is used in this system, it must be defined. The STORE command defines and initializes temporary variables in this language, assigning data type based on the initial value. Line 20 starts a loop to process information for a single course. The name, year, and quarter are to be selected by the user, based on prompts defined by lines 22 through 25. Notice that line 24 ends with a semicolon, and line 25 is a continuation of that line. This use of a semicolon is different from many programming languages, sometimes causing confusion for programmers used to other conventions.

Line 26 reads in the data specified in the preceding 4 lines, storing the values in the variables created earlier. Line 27 converts the user's response to course number to uppercase letters, in order to permit matching with the Grades file.

Searching the database is defined beginning on line 29. First, the course number entered by the user must match a course number in the Grades file (lines 29 through 34). If the course is found, a second loop (lines 36 through 58) processes all records from that course. Lines 37 and 38 define the link with the Courses file. The third file, Students, is linked in a third nested execution loop (lines 50 through 57) that prints a one-line entry for each student in the course.

Printing instructions begin with line 41, which activates the printer, and line 42, which moves the printer paper to a new page. The header information for a course is then printed. This information includes the name of the University, followed by the current date (a system variable "DATE()" is available through a dBASE interface to the operating system). The use of a "?" command at the start of the print lines 43 through 48 indicates that these lines are to be output on the next line available. This heading is to be printed only once for each page. The following lines, 50 through 57, print one line for each student in the selected course. The fields are adjusted according to their length. The program skips to the next record after printing a single entry (line 56).

At the conclusion of the course record for one class, the user is asked if he or she wishes to generate another report (lines 60 through 63). If the answer is not "y" or "Y," the program ends.

Execution of this program is shown in Figs. 4.80 and 4.81, which illustrate the data-entry form and output, respectively. If there is a mismatch in the course number, an error message appears and the user is prompted to re-enter the course number.

In our third example using dBASE III PLUS, we will generate a transcript. The program TRNSCRPT.PRG, Fig. 4.82, demonstrates the creation of a complex report using the dBASE package. A number of features of the language not previously illustrated have been included to extend the coverage of this system. The example was generated with extensive help from a dBASE consultant (M. Shulman).

This program assumes that files have been previously opened and assigned to specific work areas. Later in the chapter, we will describe the master program that is used to invoke this program, in which the files are opened, indexed, and assigned.

```
Program to list all grades for one course at a time

Enter course number:_____

Enter (19__):_____

Enter qtrno (wntr=1,SPR=2,SUM=3,FALL=4):_____
```

Command	\<A:\>|COURSES	|Rec: 1/19	|	|

Enter a dBASE III PLUS command.

Figure 4.80. dBASE III PLUS. Run-time Data-entry form for Course Summary Report.

```
                              Maverick University              7/23/86

Course Report For     C624          Inorganic Chemistry

Fall      19  81

Stud #              Student Name              Grade  Gradepoints

987317211  Catlin, Jerome                      B+       9.90

984669523  Horton, James                       B        9.00

983295827  Michiko, Gail                       A-      11.10

985742759  Poll, Mary                          C+       6.90

984364121  Renoud, Christopher                 C        6.00
```

Figure 4.81. dBASE III PLUS. Course summary output.

In describing this program, we will emphasize those elements that have not been discussed above. Lines 1 through 5 are introductory, similar to earlier programs. Line 6 initializes two temporary variables that will be used to select students whose transcripts will be generated. Lines 7 through 9 describe the manner in which the user will select students, in this case using the identification number range. Lines 11 through 15 create default values for the range to be used. The first record will contain the lowest value, and the last record contains the highest student number in the current database. These values are located using the GO TOP (point to the first record) and GO BOTTOM (point to last) commands.

The next lines (17 through 35) display messages instructing the student to enter low and high range values, or accept default values that are already generated as described above. An error check ensures that the second number is higher than the first.

When this process is complete, the screen is cleared from line 15 to the bottom (statement line 37), and the loop is exited. The next phase of the program provides user options for the manner in which the report is to be generated (screen, printer or both). The SET CONFIRM command waits until the Enter key is pressed to evaluate the answer. This loop (lines 42 through 48) will not permit the user to enter anything but an uppercase S, P, or B.

The next lines (50 through 60) are executed only if printed output was selected, giving the user time to turn the printer on and align page boundaries.

```
Listing of A:TRNSCRPT.PRG          Wednesday, July 23, 1986          Page    1

    1 * TRANSCRIPT GENERATION PROGRAM
    2 * gives subtotals for each quarter for units, gpa
    3 * also requests range of Student IDs for generation of records
    4
    5 CLEAR
    6 STORE 0 TO 1ownum,highnum
    7 a 04,15 SAY 'This program will create transcripts for students'
    8 a 05,15 SAY 'according to ID number range provided by user.'
    9 a 06,15 say '    Enter 0 for low number to quit.'
   10
   11 SELECT GRADES
   12 GO TOP
   13 STORE VAL(STUDNO) TO lownum
   14 GO BOTTOM
   15 STORE VAL(STUDNO) TO highnum
   16 GO TOP
   17 STORE .F. TO Ok
   18 DO WHILE .not. Ok
   19     a 08,10 SAY 'ENTER LOW NUMBER FOR STUDENT ID:   ' GET lownum
   20     READ
   21
   22     * allow user to quit by entering 0 for lownum
   23     If LOWNUM = 0
   24         RETURN
   25     ENDIF
   26
   27     a 10,10 SAY 'ENTER HIGH NUMBER FOR STUDENT ID: ' GET highnum
   28     READ
   29
   30     IF lownum > highnum
   31 * print error message on screen, repeat
   32         a 15,00 say 'RANGE SELECTION ERROR.  High number must be'
   33         a 16,00 say 'hinger than the low number.  Please re-enter.'
   34     ELSE
   35         STORE .T. TO Ok
   36 * remove error message
   37         a 15,00 CLEAR
   38     ENDIF
   39 ENDDO
   40
   41 STORE 's' TO Output
   42 DO WHILE (Output <> 'S') .AND. (Output <> 'P') .AND. (Output <> 'B')
   43     a 20,00 say 'Send output to S)creen, P)rinter, or B)oth: ';
   44         get output picture '!'
   45     SET CONFIRM ON
   46     READ
   47     SET CONFIRM OFF
   48 ENDDO
   49
   50 STORE 'N' TO ConfirmPtr
   51 IF (Output = 'P') .OR.  (Output + 'B')
   52     a 21,00 say 'Confirm:  Is printer ready ?' get ConfirmPtr picture '!'
   53     READ
   54     IF ConfirmPtr = 'Y'
   55         SET PRINT ON
   56         IF Output = 'P'
   57             SET CONSOLE OFF
   58         ENDIF
   59     ENDIF
   60 ENDIF  set up printer
   61
   62 * courses called in area 3 to give full course name
   63 * students file called in area 2 to give name, address info.
```

```
64 * grades file must be previously indexed on studno+year+qrtno
65 SET RELATION TO COURSE_NO INTO COURSES
66
67 DO WHILE (.NOT. EOF()) .AND. (VAL(STUDNO) <=highnum)
68     IF VAL(STUDNO) < lownum
69        SKIP
70        LOOP
71     ENDIF
72
73     STORE STUDNO TO STDTMP
74     STORE 0 TO CUMUNITS, QTRUNITS, CUMGPTS, QTRGPTS
75
76     IF ConfirmPtr = 'Y'
77        EJECT
78     ENDIF
79
80     SELECT STUDENTS
81     STORE GRADES->STUDNO TO TEMP
82     FIND &TEMP
83     ? '                   Maverick University   '
84     ? 'Official Transcript for: ',NAME,'       ',DATE()
85     ? '                          ',ADDR
86     ? '                          ',CITY,STATE,ZIP
87     ?'                           ',TEL
88     ?
89
90     SELECT GRADES
91     DO WHILE STUDNO=STDTMP .AND. .NOT. EOF()
92        STORE QTRNO TO QTRTMP
93        STORE YEAR TO YEARTMP
94        ? '    ',YEAR,'   ',QTR
95        ? 'COURSE #        NAME                    UNITS GRADE   GRADEPTS'
96        DO WHILE (QTRNO+YEAR = QTRTMP+YEARTMP) .AND. STUDNO=STDTMP .AND. .
   NOT. EOF()
97           CUMUNITS = CUMUNITS + UNITS
98           QTRUNITS = QTRUNITS + UNITS
99           CUMGPTS = CUMGPTS + GRADEPTS
100          QTRGPTS = QTRGPTS = GRADEPTS
101
102          ? COURSE_NO, COURSES->COURSE_NAM, SPACE(3), UNITS, SPACE(2)
103          ?? GRADE, SPACE(2), GRADEPTS
104          * advance to the next record
105          SKIP
106
107       ENDDO gtrno
108
109       ? ' Quarter units: ',QTRUNITS,'  Cum.Units: ',CUMUNITS
110       ? ' Quarter GPA: ',(QTRGPTS/QTRUNITS),'  Cum. GPA: ',(CUMGPTS/CUMU
   NITS)
111       ?
112
113       STORE 0 TO QTRUNITS, QTRGPTS
114    ENDDO studno
115 ENDDO eof
116 SET RELATION TO
117
118 IF ConfirmPtr = 'Y'
119    set print off
120 ELSE
121    wait
122 ENDIF
123 RETURN
```

Figure 4.82. dBASE III PLUS. dBASE Program to generate transcript.

Following this initialization process, the program processes each student transcript requested by the user. The active file is Grades. Line 65 defines a relation
between Grades and Courses, which will be linked through the value of

COURSE_NO in each file. The SET RELATION command can be used when there are two files with the same field name in each.

Line 67 initiates the output process, which continues through line 115. This outer loop includes several inner loops, used to generate a subgroup for each quarter and one for each student's transcript. Lines 68 through 71 check records, skipping any whose student number is lower than the starting point specified by the user. Line 73 defines a temporary value of the current student number, to be used to terminate the report for that student when a record is reached with a different identification number. Line 74 initializes variables used to store current and cumulative gradepoints.

The remainder of the report contains variations of commands previously described. Figure 4.83 shows the data input form used to generate this report, and Fig. 4.84 illustrates the output from a request for one student. Notice that the information contains intermediate grade point summaries not produced by the DATAEASE report, although the cumulative gradepoints and units appear in each.

```
        This program will create transcripts for students
         according to ID number range provided by user.
               Enter 0 for low number to quit.

   ENTER LOW NUMBER FOR STUDENT ID:     981425729.00

   ENTER HIGH NUMBER FOR STUDENT ID:    981425730.00
```

Command	|< A:>| GRADES	|Rec: 83/117	| | Caps

```
            Enter a dBASE III PLUS command.
```

Figure 4.83. dBASE III PLUS. Run-time Data-entry for transcript program.

These examples document the flexibility of the dBASE program. Althoug.. may not always be simple, it is possible to generate sophisticated summaries and reports. The language is complicated enough to require training for effective use, a fact that has led to a widespread consultant business for individuals who do gain this expertise.

4.6.5 System Integration: dBASE III PLUS

Although the computer configuration environment can be manipulated in dBASE III PLUS via the SET command, there are no automatic user control options available comparable to those of DATAEASE. User codes, passwords, and protected files are not provided. The operations manager will have great difficulty in achieving effective data security through the language itself.

```
                     Maverick University                     07/23/86
Official Transcript for:  Reid, Jane
                          2003 La Brea Terrace
                          Davis            CA 95616
                          9167927004


    82      Fall
COURSE #            NAME                    UNITS GRADE  GRADEPTS
GEO843 Plate Tectonics                       4.0   C  ,    8.00
   Quarter Units:          4.0    Cum.Units:        3.0
   Quarter GPA:           2.00    Cum. GPA:                2.00


    83      Wntr                                             ,
COURSE #            NAME                    UNITS GRADE  GRADEPTS
CS520  Introduction to Computing             3.0   B-     9.00
E504   Basic Composition                     4.0   A-    14.80
   Quarter Units:        · 7.0    Cum.Units:       10.0
   Quarter GPA:           3.40    Cum. GPA:                2.98


    83      Fall
COURSE #            NAME                    UNITS GRADE  GRADEPTS
E796   Advanced Composition                  4.0   C+     9.20
   Quarter Units:          4.0    Cum.Units:       14.0
   Quarter GPA:           2.30    Cum. GPA:                2.79


    84      Wntr
COURSE #            NAME                    UNITS GRADE  GRADEPTS
M639   Automata Theory                       3.0   A-    11.10
M639   Automata Theory                       3.0   A-    11.10
   Quarter Units:          6.0    Cum.Units:       20.0
   Quarter GPA:           3.70    Cum. GPA:                3.06


    84      Spr
COURSE #            NAME                    UNITS GRADE  GRADEPTS
E925   ComputationalLinguistics              2.0   B      6.00
P709   Optics                                3.0   B      6.00
P709   Optics                                3.0   A-    11.10
   Quarter Units:          8.0    Cum.Units:       28.0
   Quarter GPA:           2.89    Cum. GPA:                3.01


    84      Fall
COURSE #            NAME                    UNITS GRADE  GRADEPTS
CS781  Compilers                             4.0   A-    14.80
E821   Shakespeare                           4.0   A-    14.80
   Quarter Units:          8.0    Cum.Units:       36.0
   Quarter GPA:           3.70    Cum. GPA:                3.16
```

Figure 4.84. dBASE III PLUS. Output from transcript program.

It is possible, however, to write a program that will enable the user to improve the efficiency of operation of a specific database. Figure 4.85 is a program (written by the campus dBASE consultant) that illustrates this type of feature. The basic purpose of the program is to create a menu-driven environment, calling on subprograms automatically as specified by the user. Only a very few elements in this program are discussed here to avoid repetition from previous examples.

Lines 9 and 11 invoke specific color functions if a color console is available (otherwise they are ignored). Header information (in two colors) is displayed by lines 10 and 12, and a wait message appears below informing the user that file initialization is going on, since this process requires several seconds for execution, even in our small sample database. One reason is that the program provides for indexing the files if this step has not already been performed (e.g., lines 19 through 21).

When this process is completed, the initial display is erased and a new display appears as described in lines 49 through 63. This section of the program is an open-ended loop, with options to select different functions from the menu displayed on the screen. The CASE statement (lines 67 through 82) controls execution of the options selected by the user. These options include standard data entry via the *append* command for adding new students and faculty. In addition, however, user-defined programs Grades and Transcript can be invoked. When these options are selected, they will be executed but control returns to this menu program at the termination of the subsidiary function.

Figure 4.86 illustrates the menu created by the execution of this program. This program makes the task of generating user documentation much easier. With options of this sort, the experienced user of dBASE III PLUS can create menu-controlled environments that remove the burden of programming from the end user.

These examples illustrate the major features of dBASE III PLUS as it exists in the form updated in 1986. Updates to the program continue to appear, but the overall flavor of the package remains the same.

```
Listing of A:TRNSCRPT.PRG          Thursday, July 24, 1986          Page     1

 1 * Maverick.prg
 2 * 3/1/84 by MS
 3 *
 4 * will set up database areas once, so each program doesn't
 5 * take so long to run. Will also call other programs.
 6 set talk off
 7 set bell off
 8 clear
 9 set color to u+
10 a 08,36 say 'MAVERICK UNIVERSITY RECORD SYSTEM'
11 set color tro 7/0
12
13 a 15,22 say 'Please wait. Initializing files...'
14 close databases
15
16 select 2
17 use students
18 if .not. file('idn.ndx')
19    a 24,22 say 'Rebuilding file: idn'
20    index on idn to idn
21 endif
22 set index to idn
23
24 select 3
25 use courses
26 if .not. file('crsno.ndx')
27    a 24,22 say 'Rebuilding file: crsno'
28    index on course_noto crsno
29 endif
30 set index to crsno
31
32 select 5
33 use gradepts
34 if .not. file('1trgrd.ndx')
35    a 24,22 say 'Rebuilding file: 1trgrd'
36    index on grade to 1trgrd
37 endif
38 set index to 1trgrd
39
40 select 4
41 use grades
```

Figure 4.85. dBASE III PLUS. dBASE Program for User-defined entry menu for Maverick University database.

Listing of A: MAVERICK.PRG   Thursday, July 24, 1986   Page 2

```
42 if .not. file('stdqtr.ndx')
43    a 24,22 say 'Rebuilding file: stdqtr'
44    index on studno+year+qtrno to stdqtr
45 endif
46 set index to stdqtr
47
48 do while .T.
49    store ' ' to choice
50    clear
51    a 01,00 SAY 'Maverick University'
52    set color to u+
53    a 01,36 SAY 'Record System'
54    set color to 7/0
55    a 01,59 SAY 'Today's date: '+dtoc(date())
56    a 05,32 SAY 'A - Add Students'
57    a 07,32 SAY 'B - Add Faculty'
58    a 09,32 SAY 'C - Process Student Grades'
59    a 11,32 SAY 'D - Produce Transcripts'
60    a 13,32 SAY 'X - Exit to dBASE III'
61    a 15,32 SAY 'Q - Quit to system'
62    a 18,13 SAY 'Enter the letter of your choice:'
63    a 18,47 GET choice picture '!'
64    read
65
66    do case
67       case choice = 'Q'
68          Quit
69       case choice = 'X'
70          Return
71       case khoice = 'A'
72          select students
73          append
74       case choice = 'B'
75          select faculty
76          append
77       case choice = 'C'
78          do Grades
79       case choice = 'D'
80          do Trnscrpts
81    endcase
82 enddo
```

Figure 4.85 Continued.

```
Maverick University                Record System           Today's date:07/23/86




                          A - Add Students

                          B - Add Faculty

                          C - Process Student Grades

                          D - Prtoduce Transcripts

                          X - Exit to dBASE III

                          Q - Quit to system


     Enter the letter of your choice:


┌──────────────┬───────────────┬────────────────────┬──────────┬───────┐
│ Command      │ |< A: >| GRADES               │Rec: 83/117        │      │ Caps │
└──────────────┴───────────────┴────────────────────┴──────────┴───────┘
              Enter a dBASE III PLUS command.
```

Figure 4.86. dBASE III PLUS. User-defined screen for Maverick University System.

4.7 COMPARISON OF DATAEASE AND
dBASE III PLUS: GENERAL COMMENTS

Having reviewed two contrasting DBMS packages in the context of a specific application, it is appropriate to consider these experiences in a more general setting. Neither system is perfect, and together they present only a small subset of implementation options that might warrant consideration in design of an ideal system. This section will treat the general questions of DBMS design from several functional viewpoints, generalizing from the examples cited above and suggesting alternative solutions to certain design elements.

One effective way to consider database package design is to analyze first the underlying design philosophy, then to examine the functional components of a DBMS, following roughly the sequence used in the previous sections. We will adopt this approach, adding some components that did not fit into the implementation example discussion.

4.7.1 Basic Design of a DBMS

Anyone interested in designing a database management system must consider many factors. If the package is to be marketed, there are elements beyond the basic design that influence the process. Some of the key design considerations are the basic file structure, flexibility, user interface, and versatility. Each of these elements also has economic implications, and the final decisions will usually represent compromises between optimal design, timing, funding, and sales. We will not consider directly the economic and timing factors in our discussion. Instead, we will review some of the basic design factors that may affect the acceptability of a DBMS package; these factors will, of course, influence the potential marketability of the final product.

DATAEASE and dBASE III PLUS were designed with markedly different underlying philosophies. dBASE III PLUS and its predecessors were designed to meet the needs of single users or small groups of individuals working together in an open environment. There is an underlying assumption that the users will be programmers, and that there will be many additional features that can be built on to the dBASE package to enance its utility. The design approach may be defined as an "open shop" in which users can, with minimal training, manipulate files and programs at will.

DATAEASE, on the other hand, was designed to be a complete system for a controlled environment in which an operations supervisor is responsible for each database. In this environment, changes can be made only by authorized users, the files cannot be manipulated readily by external programs, and it is not easy to add new program features to the package. The single user is free to work as the operations supervisor of a database and in fact will only see the controls as he or she logs on to the system. However, the database is protected from that point on. Added features require transferring data files to external formats, then, if necessary, returning them to DATAEASE formats, at which time they are once again checked for consistency with the database definition.

These two approaches are mutually exclusive. It is not possible to have an open shop and still control database integrity. Similarly, it is difficult, although not impossible, to augment a controlled environment with programs that add new features. In the personal computer environment, many operations will begin as single user or small group operations. In most businesses, however, the need for control eventually becomes essential, a factor that is less readily accommodated in the dBASE design.

4.7.1.1 Database Model Selected

In Chapter 2, we saw that there are many different models that could be selected for implementation of a DBMS, each with merits and disadvantages. The simplicity of the relational model's file structure makes it attractive to implement; its value is enhanced by the current computer science literature that promotes this model as one of the most effective from a theoretical point of view. On the other hand, the relational model is known to be slow in executing many retrieval functions — much slower than custom-designed hierarchical and network structures, for example.

The designers of both DATAEASE and dBASE III PLUS made a wise decision in selecting an augmented relational model to gain speed and retain the versatility of this approach. Both packages offer relational files. They also offer indexing capabilities that provide rapid access to any keyed field. These index files are in each case B-tree implementations (hence hierarchical structures). Maintaining these indexes slows data entry, but the benefits of retrieval far outweigh short-term delays in the entry process. In the case of dBASE III PLUS, the indexing is also used as an implicit link between files (as noted, only indexed fields can be used for matches between relations). The availability of index fields is an important physical augmentation of the relational model, providing execution enhancement without compromising the underlying approach.

Some other DBMSs for personal computers have been designed using other fundamental models. One commercial version of the entity relationship model is now available on personal computers. A hierarchical model-based system designed for minicomputers also runs on personal computers; this system has been used to implement relational type structures, though the underlying file is hierarchical in nature. The majority of current models on personal computers are relational, but their ability to fully implement the relational concept varies greatly.

Neither DATAEASE nor dBASE III PLUS are complete with respect to the relational model. Some of the operations illustrated in Fig. 2.15 (Cartesian Product, Divide, and one form of Join) are not available in DATAEASE; dBASE is lacking in set operations (union, intersection, and difference), and also lacks the divide operation. In addition, duplicate tuples are not prevented and other integrity checks on data. Limitations on the number of files that can be open at one time further restrict their ability to satisfy all relational elements. However, the most important features (Select, Join, Project, with conditional modification) are available in each. There are also some features of these packages, such as sorting a relation, that are expressly forbidden in the strict relational model, but their utility in many retrieval situations overrides this conceptual violation.

4.7.1.2 User Interface

The two basic approaches, menu-driven (the native mode of DATAEASE) and command-driven (the most effective dBASE III PLUS environment), each requires keyboard input to interact with the package. Other options might include interaction through light pen, mouse, touch screen, or voice. Opinion is currently divided as to whether these alternate forms of pointing to a screen are satisfactory. In at least one experiment, use of a touch-sensitive screen has been used in a highly sophisticated medical data-entry system in which typing is reduced to a bare minimum. Another data input technique has proven successful in the supermarket environment: the bar code reader, variations of which are available for personal computers.

Documentation represents one component of the user interface. The two examples illustrate the straight reference manual to language commands (dBASE III PLUS), the functional organization in terms of database activities (DATAEASE), and the tutorial approach (found in both). Some documentation gives a low-level introduction to commands, then has an "advanced" section with descriptions of more sophisticated applications. A common mistake is the failure to describe escape mechanisms when things go awry. Although there is no perfect solution, combinations of comprehensive indexing, some tutorial information, and functional grouping of features appear to meet the widest range of user needs. On-line help, a feature available in both systems, is also an essential support feature for any complicated package.

The method by which a user will interact often reflects basic assumptions about the user. A menu-driven system requires less understanding of computers than a command driven approach. Interestingly enough, the success of dBASE in the marketplace appears to derive more from timing factors than the command-driven user interface, which tends to scare off the naive user.

4.7.2 File Types

One of the important features of DBMS packages is their ability to interface to other packages, such as word processing, spreadsheets, or other analytical packages. In addition, it often is useful to go from one DBMS to another, for purposes of comparison or to take advantage of different features offered by each.

The DBF format, used in dBASE III PLUS, is a common form of data representation. In fact, DATAEASE provides utilities to convert data files from DBF format to the internal DATAEASE format. Small differences such as allowable name length must be resolved. Another format that is frequently used for data export by spreadsheet programs (such as Lotus 1-2-3) is the DIF format. DATAEASE also has a utility program that accepts and generates data according to this standard.

The two contrasting approaches to file definition (system controlled versus user-modifiable) reflect differences in basic design. Files that can be maintained by external utilities such as editors can also be corrupted by the same methods. On the other hand, systems that do not permit user flexibility in performing many functions must themselves be both comprehensive and error-free. It is hard to say which philosophy is preferable.

4.7.3 File Definition

There is no doubt that data verification at entry is a major benefit in database applications. Many large databases have come to be regarded as worthless because insufficient attention was paid to the input process. Failure to provide comprehensive error checks, whether it be through the file definition or entry process, can result in similar experiences on small systems. In DATAEASE, we see opportunities to build in extensive error checks. dBASE III PLUS offers similar capabilities through programming, but there remains a possibility of bypassing these checks through standard entry techniques, and the obligation of guaranteeing error reliability at entry time is greater on the systems supervisor. There are ways in which this type of control can be exercised, but it is more difficult in dBASE.

Complex files relationships can be specified in both languages through initial file definition (DATAEASE) or program control (dBASE). There appears to be an inherent limitation in the complexity of file interaction in the latter system, brought about by the implicit use of indexing for relationships. The file linkages are more cumbersome as a result of this approach, and there may be limitations in complexity that would result.

A better approach to overall systems design is to have a still higher level package that manages definition of data elements, files, and interactions. Such systems are now under development, although most of them are too large at present to run on pesonal computers. This situation is changing, however, and it is likely that DBMS manager packages will be available on personal computers in the next few years. The designers of dBASE III PLUS include an Applications Generator in their distribution disks, but this package does not serve the function of a design manager as implied in this context. The effective use of such systems will require a sound knowledge of information science and database systems. This text can only provide an introduction to this field; the serious user should consider reading some of the references listed at the end of Chapter 2 to provide further insight. In the long run, practical experience coupled with further reading is essential to master this discipline.

A need exists for new types of files and file interactions. Data such as digitized images, graphic portrayals of information, and text files which include long text passages as well as embedded images represent type of information that are not yet available for incorporation into commercial DBMSs for personal computers. The availability of the memo data type in dBASE III PLUS represents a start in this direction, but it is primitive in its current form. Systems that extend DBMS concepts to more complex data are at the research level now, and may be available in a few years.

4.7.4 Data Entry

The two packages illustrate input forms that are closely tied to screen display and keyboard typing. Options relating to use of function keys are more extensive in DATAEASE than in standard dBASE III PLUS, but the two programs are flexible in their ability to use screens and key in data. Multiple screens are possible with each system. They require clearing a screen prior to portraying the next portion of the form, and in this mode DATAEASE offers somewhat greater flexibility in returning to previous screens prior to accepting all data (a feature that could, with difficulty, be programmed in dBASE III PLUS).

In the section on user interface, we discussed alternate methods for interaction with a DBMS. The need for greater variety in input is most critical at the data-entry phase, since this is the time when most keystrokes or other user-generated codes will be generated. Neither package offers options other than keyboard and screen for the entry process. This restriction is characteristic of most DBMSs today, but it is an unfortunate limitation. Devices including mouse, touch screen, bar code, and voice input are becoming more common on personal computers, and their use in the entry process is desirable for certain applications. Voice input is valuable for data entry in a situation when the hands are occupied with other tasks (sorting through inventory forms, measuring values, or making observations in real time). Touch-screen entry is especially helpful when menu selection is done by unskilled typists. Bar codes on precoded forms permit rapid entry of numeric data, usually with a reduction in the transcription errors generated by manual techniques.

4.7.5 Data Import

Imported data files are of great value when information from two databases is to be merged, or when there is a need to incorporate data from external machine readable files. In hospitals, many laboratory instruments contain their own microprocessors that generate machine readable data. Similarly, generation of data sets from a database may provide useful input into word processors, spreadsheets, or statistical packages.

Both packages offer import and export file capabilities, although the features were not discussed in this chapter. However, each system has difficulties with variable-length records, especially when only partial lists of external data elements are needed. In most cases, these transfers require writing special programs to create new files that will be more closely compatible to the original.

4.7.6 Report Generation: General Comments

There are innumerable variations on the manner in which data may be retrieved from a database system. The examples selected in this chapter illustrate a cross section of reports ranging from simple to complex. The versatility of the two programs in this mode contrasts in several respects. User flexibility in defining reports is greater in dBASE III PLUS if the programming option is used, less if standard report techniques are used. Run-time data entry in DATAEASE is somewhat more flexible in terms of alpha matching capability (it is difficult to do the "wild card" type of character matching in dBASE). The evolution of each package during the last two years exemplifies the inclusion of necessary features to meet consumer demand.

4.7.7 System Integration: General Comments

Users of large systems are accustomed to elaborate security levels of protection, some of them of questionable utility to the end user, but all of them created because a demand for such features is inherent in shared resource utilization. Users of personal computers are accustomed to complete flexibility of access to their files, and such users may find it annoying to have specific users restricted from some types of data access. However, in the case of a database package, it is desirable to provide some form of security. DATAEASE provides security levels, but dBASE III PLUS does not. Security provisions are relatively uncommon in personal computer-based DBMSs.

It is also essential to have user friendly screens that will minimize the learning curve required to use the package effectively. It would appear that both of these packages offer this feature, and that such options are in fact generally available in most database packages running on personal computers.

A factor that influences integration of personal computer DBMSs in a large environment is the relation of that system to other databases, large and small, in the same operation. As soon as it becomes necessary or desirable for more than one user to access the data, the implementation must include provision for different interests, capabilities, and security. The trend in personal computer database applications seems to be increasingly headed toward greater integration. Hence these problems of user interface and security will become even more important in the future. In succeeding chapters, we will explore some of these factors in the context of evolution of personal computer-based DBMSs.

Another important form of integration is the transfer of files to and from other application packages, notably word processor and spreadsheet analysis. Many database applications call for sending form letters to individuals whose names are in the file, adding specific data items in the letter as appropriate (e.g., reminding an individual that a report or payment is due, and noting the specific item required). In this form of integration, both DATAEASE and dBASE III offer useful solutions to linkage with specific packages identified in the user manuals. The two packages also describe how to prepare files for general export, leaving details of reformatting to the user. Although a broader selection of automated interfaces might be desirable, the packages certainly do provide necessary tools in this area.

4.8 SUMMARY

In this chapter, we have reviewed the common functions associated with the care and feeding of database management systems. We have demonstrated different approaches to addressing these functions, and we have pointed out where these different styles lead to various consequences, some more desirable than others. The examples selected contrast in important ways, with neither a clear winner in terms of being the best package, even for a given application.

It is hoped that the reader will, by studying the examples in this chapter, gain greater insight into the choices that he or she must make in selecting a DBMS package. The principal message of this chapter is one of choice, driven by an awareness of the options available as they relate to the application for which a package is intended. Too often, users are bewildered by the literature, even survey articles in magazines, because they fail to point out the real differences between packages. In general, options that are not needed for an application need not figure in the selection process. Variations demonstrated in this chapter illustrate many of the features that will be needed in a variety of applications. It remains for the reader to create a checklist suitable to the particular problem that he or she faces.

REFERENCES

It is interesting to go into a bookstore dealing with personal computer texts and find shelves devoted to books on dBASE II, dBASE III, dBASE III PLUS, and on associate packages marketed by Ashton-Tate (e.g., Framework), and yet to find no texts at all dealing with DATAEASE. There are two fundamental reasons for this discrepancy. First, dBASE is the best seller among DBMSs, and it is naturally a popular item for publishers to seek to support with reference texts. DATAEASE has only recently developed a market share large enough to command attention from publishers, and discussions between several publishers and the marketers of DATAEASE are now under way. However, there is also a second reason for the widespread availability of texts describing dBASE. Since dBASE is a programming language (albeit oriented to database applications), it can be described, with examples, and users will buy these texts so as to learn how to write programs in that language. DATAEASE, on the other hand, is a complete package, with an imbedded query language that, prior to the most recent release, did not have the sophistication required to justify supplemental texts. The package contained sufficient information to permit users to use its options, and supplementary descriptions were not necessary.

DATAEASE

Stanford University Information Technology Services. *Microcomputer Data Base Management Systems: Their Selection and Evaluation*, (Stanford, California: Stanford Press, 1984). 190 pages.

> This text is one of the few that presents a comprehensive review of several DBMS packages, including DATAEASE. It also recommends this package for most applications on the Stanford campus. This text also contains a careful review of the relational features of all products evaluated, including DATAEASE and dBASE II (a more recent version may be available by this time).

dBASE III PLUS

The following references are two of the many available describing the dBASE language. The reader is urged, if he or she wishes to explore this field in greater depth, to browse through the dBASE shelves in a bookstore and look for examples that may be more appropriate for a particular application.

Simpson, A. *Understanding dBASE III PLUS*, (Berkeley, California: Sybex, Inc., 1986). 442 pages.

This text has abundant illustrations and is quite readable. It explains the upgrade features of the latest version and offers guides to conversion from dBASE II to the more recent releases. Of the references I examined, it appeared to be the best written.

Castro, L., Hanson, J., and Rettig, T. *Advanced Programming Guide*, (Culver City, California: Ashton-Tate Publishing Co., Inc., 1985). 664 pages.

This book, published by Ashton-Tate, gives fairly good examples of the dBASE language (dBASE III and III PLUS are compatible), that make the commands more understandable. It is easier to read and contains more examples than the reference manual provided with the package, but at a more advanced level than the tutorial section of the manual. Perhaps not quite as useful as the Simpson text, but it should contain more authoritative examples, since the authors helped design the package.

5

Performance and Evaluation

5.1 OVERVIEW

This chapter approaches the related issues of performance and evaluation of DBMSs from the viewpoint of their ability to meet the functional needs outlined in the previous chapters. It refers to principles outlined in Chapters 2 and 3, citing typical examples. The approach adopted in this book differs from the checklist format of many published reviews. It is intended to provide a framework based on concepts rather than a list of desired features in a database package.

5.1.1 Guidelines for Reading This Chapter

Anyone considering development of a computer-supported database management system needs answers to the following fundamental questions:

1. Will the automated version accomplish all tasks that are required for effective operation?
2. Will the automated system perform more efficiently than current manual methods?
3. Are the total costs (tangible and intangible) affordable?

These questions should be considered, first, with respect to whether or not to automate a given application, and second, whether a particular package or system will provide a better solution than other alternatives.

In order to answer these questions, a systems designer should define the functional requirements of the application, a process that has been sketched in the preceding chapters. Next, the available options for hardware and software should be examined as they relate to these requirements. Two basic measures are used in this context: performance and evaluation. These two elements are intertwined in the discussion that follows, which include factors not discussed in magazine articles evaluating different database systems. We will adopt a slightly unconventional approach to treating these topics, attempting to supplement, rather than duplicate, published articles on selection of DBMS packages. The reader should consider this chapter as one that emphasizes underlying design factors rather than providing checklists to use for all situations. From this review, coupled with articles describing current database packages, the reader should gain more comprehensive insight into the design and selection process.

Performance is concerned with how *well* a system does something, and evaluation asks whether it really *matters*. Each term is broad and can be expanded almost indefinitely. The importance of a performance measure depends on the situation. Slow execution speed may be irrelevant if that operation is done when the system is unattended and answers are not expected immediately. It may be crucial when a user has a deadline to meet. For this reason, it is important to place in perspective the relative significance of a performance measure in light of the anticipated environment. The importance of performance measures will vary with each application. For example, a procedure that requires professional staff to process input documents in an on-line fashion must have timely response during the input process. On the other hand, a system that uses a sequential file as data input can tolerate much slower response times, since the input runs in unattended batch mode.

It is also important to understand the underlying reasons for performance strengths or weaknesses. Sometimes a measure of performance can be improved by minor adjustments of parameters. These modifications often can be achieved through a better understanding of how a system operates. Sometimes, the user can use a different file structure and achieve dramatic performance improvements. Once again, the more a person knows about the principles of the system, the more likely it is that he or she can tune the system to fit the application.

This line of reasoning leads to a third important generalization. There usually are alternative solutions to problems, sometimes controllable by the informed user, that will affect the performance of a package. For example, reorganization of files on a floppy disk to speed execution or incorporation of a RAM disk will dramatically improve performance, even though those techniques are not a part of a DBMS package. The body of this chapter will point out other situations where these principles are important. Since the variations are almost infinite, the user should read this material with a mind open to permutations and combinations of performance measures and system modifications.

5.1.2 Organization of the Chapter

There are several components to performance and evaluation. Some factors, such as the resources required to operate a package, precede definition of performance measures, and comparative evaluations of competing packages are best done when performance issues have been resolved. It is impractical to separate these two components completely. This chapter begins with a discussion of the underlying requirements of automating a database application. Next, the measures of performance are described and their significance is evaluated. The concluding sections consider evaluation from a broader perspective, supplementing the material previously presented.

5.2 RESOURCE REQUIREMENTS

There are many elements besides hardware and software that must be taken into account when assessing the resource needs of a DBMS. Too often, hardware receives the greatest emphasis in cost analysis, even though it is usually the cheapest component of a DBMS. Hardware gains importance only because of tight controls on equipment acquisition that are often imposed in an organization. In this text, we will ignore budgetary and other quasipolitical considerations, concentrating instead on other equally important factors, including especially personnel. The reader should weigh these factors in the context of the total economic and political environment in which a given application is to be introduced.

5.2.1 Personnel Requirements

There are many types of expertise required in the operations of database systems. The degree to which they are involved varies with the application and also with the package selected. The discussion that follows relates the need of each to typical DBMS packages.

5.2.1.1 Systems Analyst

Any database operations will require some sort of analyst to help develop the system. This individual need not be a programmer, but he or she must understand principles of information systems as well as the information flow in the specific application. Initial design of any database system will almost invariably be wrong. This surprising conclusion stems from the fact that neither user nor analyst can completely understand information flow as it will occur after an automated system has been introduced. However, a competent analyst can usually pinpoint major problems in the prototype design and rectify them more readily. Unfortunately, professionals in most walks of life think that they understand their own professional world well enough that they do not require the services of such an individual. Too often, a company or institution wishing to install a database management system will decide that it can go it alone, selecting hardware and software on the basis of external advice and installing the database using a design worked up by the staff available. The concepts presented in this book, especially the fundamentals presented in Chapters 2 and 3, underscore the complexity of these subjects, and it is rare for professionals in other disciplines to understand these elements without special study. It is likely, therefore, that a system installed by amateurs will have serious design flaws that may not be recognized until they disrupt operations.

The need for expertise in the field of data systems analysis does not mean that every DBMS user must have a full-time professional analyst. Professionals in other fields can be trained in the field, and consultants can be hired to help out on a short-term basis, preferably at several steps during the development and operation of a system. Knowledge of the pitfalls of faulty design usually results in a better initial design and allows more flexibility in subsequent modifications. Selection of the right professional to train or the right analyst to hire as a consultant is not a matter that can be easily defined. A good analyst must be a good listener, and one who gives the client the solution without hearing a complete discussion of the problems is probably not going to design an effective system.

5.2.1.2 Content Specialists

Just as a systems analyst is essential in the design of an effective database application, so too is the availability and cooperation of one or more specialists in the content and flow of the information that is to be processed. Systems analysts unfamiliar with a given application may know how to computerize information, but they usually do not fully understand the flow of that information, nor are they likely to grasp intuitively the unstated relationships associated with that information flow. In large corporations, the data-processing staff often develops a system without adequate participation and cooperation of the people who will be served by that system. In the personal computer environment, a comparable analogy would be to have a computer professional create a database package aimed at serving the needs of a particular group, such as private practice physicians, without adequately consulting physicians about their real needs. A single interview is rarely sufficient. This particular example has happened in the design of many systems purporting to solve the problems of this professional group. Few, if any, systems designed in this manner serve their intended purpose adequately.

Interaction between information and content specialists is a complex process. Just as the systems analyst must learn about the specific information needs of the subject area, so the professional will learn, through participation, that some design goals are unrealistic, and others, perhaps unarticulated, are readily accomplished with minor adjustments. The trick is to involve the professional throughout the design and implementation process, so that the resulting package can evolve as the staff gains more familiarity with is operation.

Although we have emphasized the involvement of the professional in the planning process, it is equally important to include clerical staff in the design phase. Failure to do so will produce systems that ignore the local work environment. An editing system that uses commands may work for programmers, but it will probably not suit clerks who prefer using well-labeled function keys. A system that automates a receptionist's file retrieval duties may ignore the human need of that individual to contact other staff members. Any system imposed from the outside or from above will likely meet with resistance. Conversely, any system in which the users participated in the planning process will more likely gain acceptance, and it is also more likely to be amenable to improvements.

All of the statements in this section may appear self-evident, but case studies of the introduction of computer support in large and small operations document the widespread problems that can be traced to these factors.

5.2.1.3 Clerical Staff

Operation of a DBMS is usually a team process, involving professionals, management, and clerical staff with its own levels of management. The opinions of clerical staff and management are vital components in the design of a database system. These opinions will often uncover flaws in design that would never occur to professionals or even systems analysts, yet these flaws may be sufficient to cause an application to fail.

There are several phases of database operations that require different types of clerical expertise. It is important to analyze these requirements and adjust the operations to take advantage of available resources.

The input process is an excellent example. Input can be performed by three types of individuals: clerical data entry staff; clerical administrators who are familiar with the data to be entered and professionals who are responsible for the generation and analysis of the data. Each of these groups will benefit from different input techniques.

There are many forms of data input available, including screen-format, line-at-a-time data entry, and techniques such as bar-code, voice, touch screen, or graphic tablet. Viewed from the perspective of the human resources required to operate such systems, these techniques take on new meaning. A data-entry clerk working all day in that capacity is a very different person from one who understands the data to be entered. Data clerks are skilled professionals in their own area. They work fast, accurately, and automatically, paying no attention to the data flowing through their fingertips into the machine. It is common, in large data-entry operations, for workstations to be equipped with audio channels from television soaps, or else the clerks may listen to their own cassettes while keying in the data. These skilled technicians require a system that minimizes the obstacles to smooth data entry. Entry screens must match the paper forms from which data are to be transcribed. Response times must in all cases be fast enough to avoid annoying delays that will destroy the flow of entry and require the clerk to concentrate on a process that should be automatic. Extensive built-in error checking is usually both unnecessary and disruptive, which means that the data to be transcribed must be accurate before they get to the entry clerk. Numeric pad keyboards, optical scan devices, and hand held bar-code readers would work well in the hands of these input specialists.

Although the accuracy rate of these clerks is very high, errors occur, either as a result of transcription prior to entry, or, less frequently, during the entry process. When these errors do occur, they are much more difficult to correct, since the source data have been stored long before the transcribed results are available. Hence, even though entry clerks may be necessary in large data-processing operations, they are not ideal for small operations. Closer connection between the source of data and its entry is usually preferable, providing that appropriate personnel can be found to key in the data.

The second level of entry personnel is the clerical manager, who might be defined as a clerk trained in the significance of the data and perhaps responsible for its collection and verification. Individuals with this background are ideal entry clerks, since they are both technically proficient with keyboards and they also understand the data that will be entered and can correct obvious errors. Trained clerks require input methods that do provide more extensive error checking. Someone who knows about the data being entered will want to make decisions and think about the reliability of the data being entered; usually, the individual will want edit capability to make changes during entry. Although the preparation costs may be less, the entry costs will probably be higher, because the clerk performing the entry will be higher paid and will work at a slower rate than a data-entry clerk.

Professionals who enter data are likely to be less skilled with keyboards than entry clerks. In addition, the content specialist will be distracted by the data, examining and questioning elements as they are entered. This reflection tends to lead to inconsistency in the entry process, resulting in a higher rate of error than would occur either with data-entry clerks or trained clerical staff.

The packages that we reviewed in the previous chapter can be used to illustrate the point. DATAEASE uses a screen-entry system that could be used by an entry clerk, but it has a few features that are of more value to a trained clerk, such as explicit entry of a completed form (through function key) rather than automatic entry at the end of the form. In contrast, dBASE III PLUS will automatically file a record when the last field is complete, which may be fine for a skilled entry clerk but is often inappropriate for the content specialist. Neither package offers simple methods for incorporating alternate entry techniques, other than interface to externally generated files. Packages that do have such options may well prove preferable in certain applications.

A very different level of clerical support is required in the editing phase. Here, the individual must make multiple judgments with different resulting actions. As decisions are made, he or she must keep track of the actions taken. Accuracy, flexibility, and consistency are key traits in the edit process. They contrast with the entry clerk profile outlined above, suggesting that few persons are skilled both at routine data entry and editing. Professional content experts may be able to serve as editors, but their interest in the content of the data often results in less consistency in documenting changes made during editing.

Editing raises a need for an organizational tool not described in either package: the system journal or transaction log. It is always important to know who made which changes, and when they were made. Manual records can be kept to document changes ordered, but an automated record of the actual changes made is essential in a well-run operation. Few personal computer DBMS packages offer this feature at present, yet it is one that should be a part of all established database applications.

Another clerical function relates to systems maintenance. The tasks associated with this activity include maintenance of disk libraries or other machine readable data files, generation and distribution of reports, backing up files for archival storage, and maintenance of equipment and software. Many, perhaps all of these functions, can be performed by nonprogrammers who have had some training in systems operation. Clerical staff can be trained to perform these tasks, usually under supervision of an individual who knows the operational details. On the other hand, a professional is less likely to perform routine tasks consistently for reasons already described.

This review of clerical functions in database systems illustrates the need for different types of personalities to perform different tasks. Few packages available today offer the kind of flexibility indicated by this analysis. Even fewer take advantage of new technologies such as touch screen systems and bar codes. The importance of the availability of these features will depend on the application.

5.2.1.4 Data Retrievers

The whole purpose in having a database system is to retrieve information in a useful form. As we have seen, the flexibility in retrieval varies greatly, even in the packages we have studied. The two common modes of data retrieval are running predefined reports and using query languages to extract information on-line. The skills needed for these two modes of operation are different. An operations clerk can run routine reports, but query languages for interactive investigation of the database usually requires professional knowledge of the information. The professional will also need to understand the query language well enough to get meaningful answers.

The two packages offer interesting differences in their query language features. DATAEASE appears simpler, since it is menu driven and tutorial. On the other hand, dBASE III PLUS has a tutorial report generator whose characteristics, while more limited than DATAEASE, provide simple retrieval capability without knowledge of the details of the query language. At the more sophisticated level, DATAEASE can be mastered by the professional with training, whereas dBASE III PLUS probably would prove too difficult for most professionals to operate on an occasional basis. In summary, there are complex interactions and tradeoffs in these two packages with no clear definition of the optimal strategy for all tasks.

5.2.1.5 Programmers

The whole idea of a DBMS package on a personal computer seems to be aimed at making the power of integrated data storage and retrieval available to nonprogrammers. Many of the daily operations of a database package can be performed by nonprogrammers. Certain activities, such as complex retrievals, may require special training, but the actual operation can be learned by professionals in other fields.

It is interesting, therefore, to speculate on the degree to which a package such as dBASE III PLUS could operate without programmer assistance. From what we have described, it would not appear that complex reports or error-checking data entry could be readily achieved without this help. Yet we find that dBASE is one of the most widely used packages on the marketplace today. The reason for this anomaly appears to be that a great many individuals have, in effect, set themselves up as consultants specializing in dBASE application programs. By developing general-purpose programs that satisfy many needs of groups of individuals, they have attracted a clientele willing to settle for a package that serves most, but probably not all of their needs. The price paid is the inability to extract the maximum possible information from a database, but the benefit of not needing a programmer is substantial.

There is another option, one that often occurs when motivated professionals develop a keen interest in the operations of the DBMS. Such professionals may take pride in mastering the DBMS package, and they will devote many hours to this task, often to the detriment of their other duties. It is dangerous for a professional in one area to get too involved in the computer aspects of a system. Although the results may be satisfactory, the professional's ego may be wrapped up in the system as he or she has modified it, and necessary changes may be difficult to accomplish without causing offense.

A well-designed database package should provide for the ability to use the package without resorting to programmer assistance. This criterion is especially important if the user has limited access to a trained database programmer. However, it remains important in all situations, since professionals using the database should be able to interact with it in order to derive useful information without having to resort to a programmer as an intermediary.

To summarize, DBMS packages require different types of expertise that vary depending on the package and the application. Not all operations have the luxury of having multiple personnel for these operations, and occasionally, one person may have to perform all these operations. In all cases, it is important to analyze the functional characteristics and match them to the personnel available. This analysis may help avoid mismatches that might threaten operation of a particular system. In addition, selection of a package tailored to the available personnel may prove a wiser alternative than selecting a package that requires changes or extensive retraining of staff.

5.2.2 Environment

Another consideration that is frequently neglected in designing a database application is the environment in which the package will be used. Environmental factors include noise, light, height adjustments, workspace and storage space, power supply, cabling for networking, and access to auxiliary resources, including people, telephones or other equipment, and data. These elements are not unique to database applications, but they are important considerations that may in some cases influence the success of a given application.

Noise factors affect database operations in two ways. For an office that has not previously used computers, the noise level of an impact printer may be unacceptable, and even the buzzing noise of a dot matrix printer may be objectionable. Solutions to these objections include acquiring a noiseless ink jet printer or the more expensive laser printer, acquiring a silencing cover, or moving the printer to a room where its noise does not interfere. The latter choice requires that the printer be within reasonable cable distance (probably 50 feet or less), accessible to the operator(s) who will need to feed paper and retrieve output, and, if confidentiality of output is a concern, it must be protected from improper viewers.

Light factors are important in two respects. The glare on a CRT screen from reflected daylight is often detrimental to effective use, requiring location away from windows or at right angles to windows. On the other hand, there may be a need for bright illumination of input documents, possibly requiring localized (spot) light sources.

A factor not often taken into account in the use of keyboard display units for extended periods of time is the relation of user, seat, and terminal. For example, this author had to acquire a new pair of full lens reading glasses to replace the bifocals that are a sign of his advancing years in order to be able to view clearly both keyboard and screen. Special desks exist with CRT inset at an angle close to table level, to improve the viewing angle. Placing the screen or keyboard too high with respect to a seat can cause chronic back pain. Since DBMS users may spend long periods in front of a terminal, this design factor is an important consideration. Back strain is common in clerical staff, and its causes are complex. It may be necessary to test, adjust, and test again so as to reduce or avoid medical and related problems down the road.

The consideration of space requires more analysis than it usually receives. The first factor to plan for is the new space that is required by the equipment, work area, and associated immediate access factors. The space required often is underestimated, a result of unfamiliarity with the equipment to be installed, or a desire to sell the project to unreceptive management. Storage associated with the workspace is often overlooked, partly because, at the outset of a project, the storage of disks, paper supplies, ribbons, and especially output is not foreseen as a problem.

The second storage factor to be considered requires a review of the current filing system and an analysis of which components will be affected by the introduction of a DBMS. An automated system will, in most cases, increase the storage requirements of an operation. The output from an automated system usually exceeds previous records, creating a need to plan for both manual and automated document storage. Some documents, once entered into machine readable form, may be archived in a different location or even on microfilm. Few offices have a consistent plan for archiving data, and the introduction of automated file support systems will have an important effect on this process. Space is at a premium in most offices, and a well-developed plan for archiving data may capture enough prime space to provide a more satisfactory working environment for the DBMS project. This statement may even apply to a home, where the volume of paper that accumulates is sometimes directly related to the length of time since the last move.

The question of power supply is technically more simple, but it requires a different level of attention to uncertainties in a power supply. An office environment that is prone to light flickers due to momentary power outages is only inconvenienced until a computer system is introduced, at which point such a flicker may damage a disk and render it unreadable. Power surges likewise may result in damage, and lightning storms can cause serious problems. If problems such as these have arisen in the historic past in an office environment, then it is definitely worthwhile to study the power characteristics of an installation and to investigate ways in which problems can be minimized. Line filters are inexpensive (under $20), and they will help reduce power spikes. Uninterruptible power supplies are available for under $700, and they can provide up to fifteen minutes of power at a time of failure. Battery backup is another alternative that will solve small-scale problems inexpensively.

Although we have considered only single-user systems, it is likely that more and more DBMS packages will communicate with other users and other systems. In such cases, access to communication facilities becomes important. There are several different types of cable connections that can be used, and many offices already have provision for one or more of these alternatives. One option is the use of local area networking, a topic that is too broad to cover in this text. However, the field of intercomputer connections is expanding rapidly and is a topic that should be studied carefully as a part of the overall environmental analysis.

DBMS equipment is usually introduced into an environment where the same operations were going on without the automated assistance. Location of the workstation(s) should be planned based on a study of existing and projected patterns of information flow. Individuals are important components of a DBMS, and different individuals may need to access the same system at different times. Use of original paper records may require proximity to file rooms. Hardware may need to be close to some users, farther from others. Access to special equipment (e.g., copying machines) may also facilitate operations. In each case, analysis of the greatest need as well as the most likely problems will help reduce the likelihood of operations friction.

The selected factors cited above illustrate the general environmental considerations that influence design of DBMSs. The single most important rule is to involve the people who will be affected. Using these topics as a basis for a planning session will help the participants to contribute to the design. In addition, their acceptance of the concept will increase the probability of their acceptance of the system. Users will also be more likely to recommend constructive improvements for the system if they identify it as being in part "theirs."

5.3 PERFORMANCE MEASURES

There are a number of factors of varying importance that can be used to measure performance of a DBMS. We will consider a few examples taken from the two packages discussed in Chapter 4. Other examples will be drawn from packages running on minicomputers as well as personal computers.

5.3.1 System Requirements

Conventional thinking with respect to the hardware requirements for a given DBMS starts with the question "Can my system accommodate this package?" This is probably the wrong question to ask, since the basic requirements of most personal computer DBMS packages are similar, and hardware is a smaller cost item than many other long-term operational factors.

A more appropriate subject for investigation is the capability of a DBMS package to utilize fully the resources that are available in a given hardware configuration. The answers may be found in the design of the package itself, or they may lie in full utilization of operating systems options. The IBM PC, for example, can accommodate up to 640K bytes of RAM. Some packages will scan the system to determine available memory, then take full advantage of this space by allocating more buffers, and so on. Other packages do not have any automatic options for full memory utilization, and it becomes the responsibility of the individual to find ways to take advantage of the memory available (RAM disk or more buffers through operating systems calls). The principal difference in this case is the effort required by the purchaser.

There are other ways in which a more comprehensive system may be utilized by a DBMS package. One option is the use of alternate input devices; such use is not provided by the packages described in this text. Another option relates to auxiliary storage. There are differences in database systems that run on floppy disks from those utilizing Winchester or optical disk storage. A flexible disk system could benefit from being able to extend files beyond a single disk, even though there are operational dangers in making such switches. We have noted before that a practical DBMS will almost certainly require a hard disk for volume and performance considerations. Since there are now many different forms of hard disks available, the question of running programs or storing data on such auxiliary devices becomes another important issue.

Optical disks are now available, and some with storage of over 400M bytes may soon be available at costs under $2,000, making them attractive for personal computer DBMS packages. As such systems do become available, it is likely that use of more than one storage medium will be desirable. It is important, therefore, to consider whether existing packages could be modified to accept optical storage devices. In both DATAEASE and dBASE III PLUS, only one storage device can be used for data. Could either system permit splitting of data files between two or more devices? This important question is rarely asked by the potential user.

Another feature that is not covered in the examples used relates to backup methodologies. Both DATAEASE and dBASE III PLUS give instructions for backing up data onto flexible disks, and both rightly state that backup is important. However, there are other, far more efficient backup storage devices, including cartridge tape and video cassette systems costing less than $800. Effective use of backup tapes requires development of an orderly archiving plan.

To these examples of resources could be added others such as bubble memory, extended RAM memory, or the use of storage on auxiliary devices linked through external communications. The central point is that performance of a DBMS may be greatly enhanced by available hardware options. The real question is the adaptability of a given DBMS.

Perhaps the best way to view the matter of system requirements is to consider first, what performance enhancements can be expected from expanded configurations and second, to learn what options exist for attaching other devices to the package. The foregoing examples illustrate these general ideas, but the rapid evolution of technology will create many other choices.

5.3.2 Storage Volume

The question of data storage space is more important in the personal computer environment than with larger systems. Microcomputers currently face limiting volume factors at three levels: internal memory, size of flexible disk storage, and size of Winchester disk storage. We will consider the potential significance of some typical volume measures as they relate to DATAEASE and dBASE III PLUS.

5.3.2.1 Program Size

The version of DATAEASE shipped in spring 1986, required two double-sided, double-density disks to contain the programs and auxiliary text files. The programs and associated Help files occupy approximately 450K bytes, and there are additional files used for configuration and specification of printers, and so on. The version of dBASE III PLUS used in this text, also acquired in spring 1986, required two disks and approximately 555K bytes. However, DATAEASE uses additional space for required buffers and files that require a minimum memory configuration of 384K bytes, whereas dBASE III PLUS can be configured to run in 256K of available memory. These figures are somewhat difficult to interpret, in that the larger package can run in a smaller memory system. However, in practice, the speed of execution is affected by the availability of additional memory, so the real fact is that *both* systems require 394K bytes or more to run effectively, and they will both take advantage of more memory for even more efficient execution.

5.3.2.2 Database Size

In the examples used in Chapter 4, the actual size of each data file was much smaller than a real application. However, it is possible to derive some insight from the examples with respect to possible differences in storage requirements. An instructive comparison is the manner in which information on students is stored in the two systems (see Figs. 4.11 and 4.39). The information in each form is identical. However, the definitions for several fields result in different storage requirements. Dates require eight bytes in dBASE III PLUS, six in DATAEASE. Degree is a choice in DATAEASE, taking up one byte, whereas it is alpha requiring three bytes in dBASE III PLUS. The financial aid information is also a one byte choice in DATAEASE, but three in dBASE III PLUS. These choices were made without studying the storage requirements, and they could be modified to improve certain external aspects of the space required in the dBASE example, but date, for example, will remain shorter in DATAEASE. This example is not intended to invite a designer to employ tricks to improve efficiency, since fancy techniques that are specific to certain systems can often cause problems when new devices are substituted.

The actual storage required internally to record all the information on the students in our file reveals another surprising difference. The DATAEASE file, STUDAAAA.DBM is 1,430 bytes in total size, whereas the dBASE III PLUS file, STUDENTS.DBF is 2,005 bytes. These figures require some explanation. There are ten students in each file, and as shown in Figs. 4.11 and 4.39, the entry sizes for the two files are 143 and 149 bytes respectively. In the case of DATAEASE, the data file is an exact multiple of this value, or 1,430 bytes, and addition of each new record will add 143 bytes. Using the same rationale, we would expect the dBASE III PLUS file to be only slightly larger, or 1,480 bytes. However, the file is one third larger, requiring 2,005 bytes instead. The difference is due to the fact that the header information describing the fields in this file are placed at the start of the dBASE III PLUS data file. In DATAEASE, this information is stored separately in a file that also contains the description for the screen and occupies approximately 700 bytes. Additional records in dBASE III PLUS increment the file size by 149 bytes per record, and the differences in file size decrease as the files grow.

This example emphasizes the potential pitfalls of using a small sample to determine the relative volume requirements of a database. To verify actual storage requirements, it is necessary to examine the differences created by incrementally adding to the file and extrapolating on that basis. In addition, it is important to analyze all files related to a database, so as to make certain that valid comparisons are being made.

There are a few cases where the size of a file can be manipulated to take advantage of internal storage methods. As noted earlier, DATAEASE uses binary and floating-point notation to store integer values, and it uses ASCII characters for text information. The use of binary values can result in saving up to half the length of each field, which could mean significant savings in storage if many numeric fields were used in a database. In dBASE III PLUS, it might be worth while to store coded information rather than text if multiple-choice values are used in many places.

These examples suffice to illustrate the need for careful study of volume results in estimating database growth, and also to point out ways that the user could optimize storage. It is unlikely that these factors will be major determinants in most database applications, since the savings are generally small.

A much more significant potential for saving space lies in the ability to define a data field as being of variable length. If we examine the Student files described earlier, we note that there are approximately 110 characters of text information assigned to fields that would rarely be filled. If, instead, it were possible to define these fields as variable in length, occupying only the space required for each name, then the space savings would be dramatic. A large file could be reduced by more than 50 percent in the case illustrated above. Some database languages do provide for variable-length fields, with a resulting significant improvement in storage efficiency. MUMPS, a language alluded to briefly in Chapter 3, is one example of a language with variable length field capabilities. Another example is the Virtual Storage Access Method (VSAM) available on IBM mainframes.

5.3.2.3 Auxiliary File Storage Characteristics

In the previous chapter, we pointed out the desirability of having auxiliary B-tree index files to permit rapid access by keys. Each of the files created had at least one such index, and some had more than one. One of the prices paid by such an index (in addition to the time required to create and update each index) is the volume of storage space occupied by each, relative to the space used by the original data file. The following table illustrates the size of the index files generated by our examples.

DATAEASE File	Size (bytes)	Index File	Size (bytes)
Faculty	1960	name	1024
Student	1430	name	1024
Course	4896	num	1536
dBASE III File	Size (bytes)	Index File	Size (bytes)
Faculty	2560	name	1024
Students	2005	name	1024
Courses	4417	num	1024

The size of the index is controlled in part by blocking factors used by the B-tree index algorithm. A block of 512 bytes is allocated for an index each time a new split occurs and a new block is required. In each case, the index is large, ranging from one-fourth to one-half the size of the data file. While it is likely that the relative size of the index file will diminish slightly as the file grows, it is also true that they will be substantial components of the total volume requirements of a database, and they might well be targets for special treatment if volume is a consideration. The reasons for this large space utilization can be seen by the illustration of the B-tree growth in Fig. 2.8. Each time a block splits, half of each newly formed block is empty. Hence, using this algorithm, there will be inefficiencies in storage in the creation of a B-tree. In fact, the worst case takes place when a file is loaded sequentially according to the index for which the B-tree is to be created, since each split block will be left empty as the index increases.

A second reason for the inefficiency of a B-tree in many implementations lies in the use of fixed-length keys. Creating a B-tree for faculty or student name, for example, will require a key of length 30 characters. Since the names are rarely that long, there is an exact repetition in the index file of the space inefficiency found in the main file. Once again, use of variable-length keys would greatly improve the efficiency of index files.

Advanced programming courses teach techniques for optimizing the efficiency of B-tree storage. These techniques are sometimes of general utility, but often they require knowledge of the database, and hence would not find their way into general-purpose packages. However, there is a way that the user can improve the efficiency of an index file, by selecting keys that are of smaller size or by reducing to a minimum the alphabetic key lengths when they must be used. It often is adequate, for example, to create a partial field representation that can be used as the index key. In many cases, for example, the first six to eight letters of a name will suffice for most index purposes.

Although there are other auxiliary files used in each database package described, they are of minor significance from a volume point of view. Programs may be large in comparison with small databases, but the size of the program remains fixed despite the growth of the data files. Furthermore, the relative differences between the data files in these packages do not appear to be significant. To take our most complex example, that of transcript generation, the DATAEASE report file occupies 3,056 bytes, and the dBASE III PLUS version requires 3,303. DATAEASE used an additional forms entry file of 427 bytes (with more detailed instructions for name specification), making the total size slightly larger than that of dBASE III PLUS. These programs will handle arbitrarily large files, however, so their importance will diminish as the file grows.

A large number of standard reports will occupy a significant volume on disk, and this space is in contention with data. For this reason, alternative solutions may be required. One solution is to subdivide the data files, grouping them to reflect their use for specific reports. Another approach is to keep backup program disks, loading only those required for a given operation and removing them afterwards. Once again, creativity may be required.

Volume considerations will ease when a user upgrades to a hard disk. However, there will still be limitations. Too often, the recipient of a new Winchester disk system will allow files to remain long beyond their utility. Then, when it comes time to make space for needed functions, the postponed purge is done carelessly, perhaps resulting in loss of valuable files.

5.3.3 Operational Efficiency

Most people, when they think of performance, tend to think first of the internal execution speed of a program or package. This criterion may be of value in some situations, but it is less significant in most personal computer applications than in larger systems. The concern with execution speed is a legacy from large computers and the days when computing power was expensive and had to be centralized and shared to be affordable. Now, with microprocessor chips costing as little as $10 and personal computers costing much less than automobiles (even many used ones), it is possible to consider a personal computer as a resource similar to an automobile, typewriter, telephone, or appliance. They are there to be used when needed, but it is neither sinful nor wasteful to leave them idle or to run them at less than top speed when they are in use.

Viewed in this context, operational efficiency is more concerned with the ability of a system to meet the time demands of the humans using the package, rather than attempting to derive maximum utility from the computer. A function that takes ten seconds to run is admittedly intolerable when a user is waiting for the opportunity to enter the next command in an interactive data-entry mode; it is insignificant if the program is running unattended. It is important, therefore, to place in context evaluations of performance speed. Furthermore, there are many ways in which execution speeds can be manipulated to take advantage of different factors, and so-called standard benchmarks may be misleading. Developers sometimes tune their packages to perform well on specific benchmarks so that they can claim a competitive edge.

The execution examples discussed in this section were selected to demonstrate factors that are likely to be significant. We will attempt to analyze these examples, explaining underlying causes for any differences. The emphasis is on a functional analysis of overall operational efficiency rather than computer execution speeds alone. This viewpoint is more relevant to the true performance of a DBMS, and it offers opportunities for identifying operational bottlenecks.

The literature contains many different measures of efficiency in performance. These parameters can be used to determine relative efficiency of different packages by running benchmark tests on each. Benchmark results often are useful in determining relative performance efficiency, but they can be misleading if the factors that affect the outcome are not understood. The following examples illustrate ways in which performance can be enhanced or retarded as a guide to the interpretation of these numbers.

5.3.3.1 Data Definition

It is unusual for execution speed to play a critical role at the time of data definition. This process usually requires careful planning, and it should not be done hastily. Furthermore, the person entering a data definition into a DBMS will probably want to think as he or she works, taking time to reflect on decisions made. For this reason, measures of performance efficiency are not as relevant in this case as in some other functions.

We noted in Chapter 4 that DATAEASE and dBASE III PLUS differ in the degree of completeness available in the two packages with regard to data definition. Error checks are more automatic in DATAEASE, though the definition process is a bit more lengthy. In terms of performance, these features improve the value of the package because they permit easier automatic error detection and also because they remind the user of the need for these elements. A programmer writing a dBASE data-entry specification may not realize the need for data checks, and there is no reminder in the package that such checks should be incorporated. It therefore becomes the responsibility of the operations manager to actively seek information on error checks from users, whereas in DATAEASE the questions are displayed at definition time to remind the user of the types of checks that can or should be made.

Another aspect of performance measures associated with data definition pertains to the development of interrelationships between files. In the relational model, it is essential that relations be easy to specify, and that relational operations such as JOIN can be readily accomplished. Both packages cited have such capabilities. In the case of dBASE III PLUS, temporary relations can be established between active files, whereas these relations require creation of more permanent definitions in DATAEASE. The overall concepts of the relational model are not adequately discussed in either manual.

Neither package provides a data dictionary approach to database consistency. This is not a problem with small applications, but as systems evolve, it is increasingly important to make certain that a change in the definition of the files is consistent with the use of data elements between files. Changing the size of a key field in one file may require that it also be changed in one or more additional files, but the user may not be aware of the need to make such additional changes. In the last chapter, we will examine the potential for new approaches to DBMS systems that incorporate such features.

5.3.3.2 Data Entry

Whereas data definition is a process in which speed is of little consequence, the reverse is true in data entry. Since it is a repetitive, tedious function, it is absolutely essential that the entry process be as painless as possible. There are several ways in which this goal can be accomplished, or conversely, there are several aspects of data entry that can create unacceptable bottlenecks. Some of the more important elements will be discussed.

In screen-oriented packages, one vital function is positioning the cursor on the screen. The movement of a cursor from one field to the next, and the ability to go back to previous fields are features that must execute rapidly. Both packages described in this text work well in this regard. The use of arrow keys, tabs, and other cursor move features make these functions easy to use.

In the default entry and edit modes, DATAEASE requires an explicit function key to enter data and move to the next record, whereas dBASE III PLUS automatically files a record when the last field is complete. For clerical staff, automatic entry may be acceptable. For professional staff, automatic entry is not desirable. It is natural to pause at the end of a form, check it over, edit if need be, and then go to the next. It is unnatural to have to stop one character before the end of the last field to make this type of check. Furthermore, if one has made a correction, it would be nice to enter the record and move on without positioning the cursor at the last field. Neither of these functions are available in the default mode of dBASE III PLUS. Given a need to accommodate both entry clerk and professional, it is better to require an extra keystroke for the clerk than to frustrate the professional.

Transition into the insert or delete modes should also be natural. Here, the use of a prompt line is particularly useful, as is done in DATAEASE. Another approach, used in some word processors, is to have a template of functions that fits over the keyboard, or transparent labels that affix over standard keys to note their purpose. These functions are valuable for clerical staff, since they avoid the need to learn commands.

A second feature that sometimes causes problems in DBMS packages relates to the user's typing speed. To illustrate the misleading nature of some benchmarks, a large computer manufacturer developed a data-entry package that was guaranteed to accept ten characters per second from each of up to ten data terminals. Since few secretaries type at that speed, it was thought that the system would work for clerical entry personnel. When the system was tested, however, the clerical staff found that, whereas it did accept ten characters per second, they typed certain key sequences much faster. As a result, the system consistently missed characters that were entered in rapid succession, and within a short time the clerical staff refused to have anything to do with the system. The specifications were met, but the real characteristics of the entry process were not accommodated.

Some personal computer-based entry packages read the first character of a field more slowly than the next ones, because the first character may be a control command rather than pure data. In these systems, the time spent processing these initial characters may result in loss of the second character or sometimes several characters, an intolerable situation. To avoid this situation, it is possible to use an operating system's "type-ahead" capability to store characters while the first is being processed. Type-ahead means that the system's keyboard buffer continues to accept characters even while the previous message is being processed. It is an extremely useful feature in many applications. On the IBM PC, the type-ahead buffer is limited to fifteen characters, which should be sufficient for most applications.

Both DATAEASE and dBASE III PLUS offer good data-entry speeds and take advantage of type-ahead to process characters in new fields. It is possible to keep typing when the end of one field is reached, and the characters will appear in the next field, sometimes with a fraction of a second delay while the cursor move commands are executed.

Type-ahead can also cause problems, especially when a command causes an error condition that is then compounded by the remainder of the stored message. If errors occur when a buffer contains commands, recovery may be difficult. It is better to be patient and avoid the use of type-ahead when error-prone functions are being executed.

A feature useful in data entry is the ability to retain fields from previous records for the next record. This feature is handled nicely by DATAEASE, which retains all fields but gives the operator the option of deleting a field or an entire record before the next record is entered. The standard entry mode in dBASE III PLUS does not permit the user to retain data from a previous entry, although it can be done with careful programming.

One data-entry feature available in mainframe DBMSs is the default entry for certain fields. If, for example, a field requires a date that in most cases is today's date, the entry process will automatically enter that date, which the user can override if necessary.

Another place where some database systems are unacceptably slow is in the use of multiple screens associated with a single entry form. The time spent erasing one screen, drawing the entry for the next, and then presenting the current record will vary from a fraction of a second to several seconds. The latter is generally not acceptable.

The time required to file a record is another sensitive point in the data entry process. Many factors can affect this process. The number of index files maintained for a file will have an important effect, since each index may be updated as data are entered. For instance, DATAEASE updates at entry, dBASE III PLUS does not. Another important factor affecting execution speed relates to writing buffers to disk, a process that slows execution but reduces the possibility of database degradation. Both packages display warnings about exiting properly to empty buffers, and they also exhibit satisfactory performance when filing individual records.

It is unlikely that these factors will make much of a difference in files of a few dozen records. However, when the files grow to several hundred or thousand entries, there may be justification for investigating the effects of database size on entry speed.

As noted before, the technique used for data entry can be greatly improved over methods used in today's DBMS packages. Bar codes, touch screens, voice input, and automatic data scanning devices could result in major performance improvements in many applications. In Chapter 6, we will return to these concepts and speculate on new approaches to DBMS packages on personal computers.

5.3.3.3 Editing

The editing process consists of finding records, making the modifications, storing the modifications, and processing any side effects caused by the changes in the database. Both DATAEASE and dBASE III PLUS offer reasonably good editing features. However, one should be aware of the actual manner in which editing is done, and the consequences of different alternatives.

Finding individual records based on content of fields can be done using the VIEW function in DATAEASE, and the LOCATE or FIND commands in dBASE III PLUS. The first difference is in keystrokes. DATAEASE uses function keys for VIEW, whereas dBASE III PLUS requires a command structure. Partial matches are extremely valuable in searching through data files. They are accommodated in DATAEASE; they are not available in dBASE. The speed of these searches is vastly different depending on whether a field is indexed. In the case of a sequential search of an entire file to match a given field, the time may be slow if the file is large. Furthermore, use of many buffers will not necessarily help, since the file is read sequentially to locate the pertinent record. On the other hand, searching an indexed file will be extremely rapid, and the access speed will be increased by having a large number of buffers available. Buffers are useful in this case because the B-tree structure will always retain the first records of the tree in the buffer area, reducing the number of disk accesses necessary to retrieve the desired record.

Replacing fields in individual records is a simple process. The process of updating all records matching certain conditions is much more easily done via dBASE commands rather than generating a complete query/update specification in DATAEASE. An experienced user of the latter system would probably learn how to do these updates rapidly, but the process is inherently cumbersome, since updating cannot be typed in direct command mode.

The side effects of updating are treated differently in these two packages, illustrating some important concepts in the performance issue. In DATAEASE, the user is warned as he or she enters the edit mode that the process must be terminated by a normal exit, and that disks cannot be removed during the edit process. This statement is true because the changes are made in buffers, and because the buffers are not copied to disk until the edit process is exited. DATAEASE automatically updates indexes, and the updated index files are rewritten to disk at the time the editing of a file is terminated. In dBASE III PLUS, editing is done in a similar fashion, with changes made to individual files in the buffers. However, there is no warning given about not changing disks (this author once inadvertently destroyed a data disk by doing just that), and there is no specific checkpoint where one can be certain that buffers have been copied to disk. In order to make certain that the disks have been updated, it is necessary to exit the package, then continue operation.

A much more serious performance flaw in dBASE is the lack of automatic update of index files when keys are modified. There is no master control file of a given database that informs dBASE III PLUS of the relationships between files and indexes in a given application, nor for that matter is there any definition of a set of files as belonging to an application. For this reason, there is no way that the dBASE III PLUS program can tell which indexes are associated with which files. If one attempts to associate an index with an inappropriate file, an error message may appear informing the user that the data file does not match the structure expected by the index file. The end user may be unaware of which indexes are present and may therefore neglect to update one or more of them. The result will be an index that is no longer consistent with a modified database.

5.3.3.4 Sorting

Sorting merits special consideration because it represents one of the major sources of poor execution performance. Approximately 25 percent of computing done in this country involves sorting files. One reason sorting occupies so much time is the need to access the same data files from different viewpoints. Students need class lists of the courses in which they are enrolled. Departments need to know which students are signed up for each of their courses. The same information must therefore be sorted in two different ways in order to generate these two typical reports.

In DBMS packages, there are two basic approaches to sorting. One involves indexing a key that will be used subsequently for searches or, in the case of dBASE III PLUS, for matching relations. This technique usually involves creating a B-tree structure of the keys, with pointers to the individual records. Several such B-trees can be maintained for a single file.

The second approach is to sort a series of records, either in the permanent files of the DBMS or at output time, according to a key that is not necessarily an index to the file. The methods used are different, and the time required is also likely to vary considerably, with differences becoming greater as the file grows in size.

The process of sorting has been studied extensively in computer science research, and there are literally thousands of papers dealing with this topic. This research has shown that different methods work better for different types and organizations of files. The performance differences may be large, and the effect on large files justifies careful study of alternatives before selecting the best fit for the given data. Since this topic is complex and the factors affecting choices may be highly data dependent, we will not attempt to cover it in this text. However, some points can be made that directly relate to performance, and these issues are important in the context of databases designed for personal computers.

Indexing a file is always a good idea if on-line retrieval is to be a major factor in the use of that file. In dBASE III PLUS, indexing is also necessary if the value is to be used to join two relations (this statement does not apply to DATAEASE). The cost of indexing is borne either at input time, as in DATAEASE, or when a re-index command is issued in dBASE III PLUS. Since the indexing is done through buffers in both cases, the process is usually fairly rapid for modest-sized files. Once a B-tree index has been created for a given file, it can be fairly rapidly updated by insertion of new values, since the blocks will tend to be incompletely filled. The DATAEASE system appears to take advantage of this fact in its updating, which is done as new records are entered or when a batch modify is performed. In the case of dBASE III PLUS, it does not seem that the previous index is retained when re-indexing is done.

Sorting at retrieval time is relatively slow. However, sorted output is usually associated with hard copy reports, which are also slow. In addition, most databases stored on personal computers tend to be small, on the order of a few thousand records, and the sorting technology now available can usually cope acceptably with this size file. For this reason, it is usually possible to ignore most sort problems by doing them at times when the machine can be left unattended, such as overnight or during nonpeak usage periods. The designer of a database should be aware that sorting represents a potential bottleneck to output, and he or she should be careful to monitor the operations of an application to make sure that it is under control, anticipating potential future problems arising from file growth or more complex sorting requirements.

One satisfactory solution for this problem, and for others in which there are conflicting demands for use of the DBMS package, is to acquire a duplicate set of hardware that is used to execute time-consuming tasks. This solution is usually not expensive, since the hardware is a small part of the total cost, and it provides a backup system in the event of equipment failure.

5.3.3.5 Retrieving On-line

The retrieval process can be divided into two types of requests: those that are accomplished immediately, and those that can be done in a more leisurely fashion, possibly in unattended batch mode. The requirements for on-line retrieval include the ability to use a simple query language, formulate a query rapidly, and then obtain a rapid response. On-line requests usually start by being relatively limited in terms of the complexity of query formulated. With time, however, people who have received answers to these requests seem to migrate toward increasingly complex queries, and they expect rapid results. This type of escalating demand places an increasing load on the operator, requiring more experience and a flexible query language.

In terms of on-line retrieval, the DATAEASE Quick Reports option works very well for short reports, allowing users to accept default options for output formats and devices. It is, however, not quite the same as having a query language that operates in command mode. On the other hand, dBASE III PLUS is specifically designed to meet this need, and it does it well in the hands of a trained expert. Notice, however, that partial match searches are not as easy in dBASE III PLUS as they are in DATAEASE.

There is a continuous gradation between the one-time search and the complex report. An on-line search usually progresses from the initial simple answer to more specific queries based on preliminary results. Support of the continued search process is slightly different from the straight command structure provided by dBASE III PLUS, and it is also a little different from the stored queries of DATAEASE. What is needed is the ability to store previous queries in a buffer of some sort, then to modify these requests in order to obtain greater specificity in the search criteria. Typing a single command line in dBASE III PLUS accomplishes the first part of this task, but the command is then lost and must be repeated for a subsequent file. Using the report generator is a second alternative, but as noted earlier, there are some limitations to this approach that make it cumbersome and inflexible. Creating a program that is then edited multiple times for the desired result is the next alternative, but this option is slow.

In DATAEASE, moving from Quick Reports to Full Reports is a simple process, and in fact a Quick Report can be redefined as a Full Report, then can be modified to add new features in the query.

5.3.3.6 Batch Report Generation

The requirements of batch reporting are quite different from on-line queries. In the first place, a batch report is usually one that will be run several times, so it warrants the effort to refine the report in order to produce acceptable or even optimal output. In addition, the report rarely requires immediate response. Often, batch reports are more complex. Sometimes, they require a major update of files in conjunction with the report generated.

For all of these reasons, batch reports can tolerate slower performance better than almost any other database function. In fact, since they require time, they are run in a manner where a few extra minutes or hours makes little difference in most cases. There are, however, a few situations in which performance becomes an important factor.

Many database applications operate according to scheduled routines that are dictated by external factors. Certain reports require coordination between the arrival of new input data and the deadlines for the output report. In some cases, this interval may be tight. This situation usually results in haste, waste, and frustration. Incorrect data inevitably appear and require correction. A report partly generated may reveal inconsistencies requiring reruns or patches to the final reports. A variation of Murphy's law seems to pertain to deadlines in reporting.

A second major problem associated with batch reports arises when the computer is needed for on-line activities while a batch report is being printed. This situation is common, since batch reports are slow. One solution to these two problems would be to define places where jobs can be interrupted during execution. Such program stopping points are often referred to as *breakpoints* or *checkpoints*. If a task can be interrupted and then resumed without loss of information, it is sometimes possible to modify data and continue as before. Even better is the ability to pick up a job at a specified location, which implies a starting point other than the one at which the job was halted. Large database operations, the kind that run overnight or all weekend on large computers, usually have checkpoints in the overall execution, and it is possible to restart the job at any one of these checkpoints, using intermediate results to continue execution. In this situation, a second computer will once again be a good alternative.

On the face of it, neither DATAEASE nor dBASE III PLUS offer checkpoint interruptability. Therefore, once a job is started, it will have to run to completion or else be aborted without producing final results. This condition may be undesirable in some situations. However, the performance of many tasks can be greatly improved simply by designing the operation to include separate modules, each responsible for smaller tasks. In this fashion, a long operation can be broken up into smaller ones. This approach is possible in either DATAEASE or dBASE III PLUS, but it requires careful planning on the part of the designer of the system. To cite one example, the programs that generated transcripts in the previous chapter were designed to permit the user to select the students for whom transcripts were to be created. This approach means that the process could be done for all students, or it could be done for a few (even one) at a time if the system is likely to be needed for other applications. Notice that this approach is possible using either package.

A second option that can help the system tolerate a long batch run is to have a "background" job capability. This approach permits a task to be initiated, then run at a lower priority than the "foreground" task. Since the background job is often used in printing reports, it means that the print buffer will be filled when there is time available, and then output as other tasks are going on. In most cases, the printer will hardly slow down, since there is usually ample processor time to move records into the print buffer. When the PCDOS PRINT command is used, the file created for output to the printer cannot be accessed and the printer is occupied, but all other files and devices are available.

Once again, neither DATAEASE nor dBASE III PLUS provide internally for a background task. However, PCDOS versions 3.0 and later do provide this function, and it is possible with either package to take advantage of background printing while using the screen and keyboard for other activities. Using this approach, a print file can be created as a disk file (which will be generated much faster than it could be printed), and then printed as a background job or at a later time. Many packages, including the two studied here, offer this option.

The variety of reports possible in any database application makes it almost impossible to generalize about performance measures. Major factors that bear on performance include file size, the use of index files, the number of buffers, the number and organization of multiple files required, and the manner in which a query is actually specified. Most of these topics have been touched on earlier. Query optimization is one point which has not been addressed; it is a subject of current research in database systems. If one considers the actual file accesses that must be made in conjunction with a search, one can often find ways in which to minimize the number of trips to disk. For example, a search based on two conditions may boil down to searching a large file as well as a small one. If the answer must contain results from both, searching the small one first may prove advantageous by reducing the amount of searching required in the large one. For instance, suppose one wishes to retrieve all employees who live in a certain city and have a certain job classification. If the database is designed to have one index file of cities and a separate index file of job skills, it may improve the search process considerably to know if there are fewer people with the job classification or fewer employees in that city. A company with 3,000 programmers and only 50 employees in Sacramento would do well to start with the Sacramento-based employees and search for programmers among them, whereas one that has 100 programmers overall, but a workforce of 5,000 in Sacramento would be best searched by the reverse methodology.

Query optimization is not generally available in automated fashion in today's DBMS packages, but the foregoing example will illustrate the fact that a little knowledge of the database is likely to enable the sharp user to formulate more efficient search queries.

In summary, performance issues depend on applications, and within those applications, they depend on the specific functions that are being performed. The relative importance of different performance measures will therefore be application-dependent. In addition, an important criterion will be the type of staff available to work with the package.

5.4 EVALUATION

Evaluation and performance are inseparable. In the preceding section, we considered performance measures that constitute evaluations of the suitability of a package for a given application. In this section, we will summarize a few basic principles of evaluation, complementing the check list type of articles that appear regularly in personal computer journals. These guidelines should alert the reader to additional factors that require attention in comparative studies of different packages.

5.4.1 Functionality

The ultimate value of a package is determined by its ability to meet the functional needs of the user. This statement seems simple and obvious. However, the average salesperson will always try to dazzle a customer with the many special features offered by the product, and even magazine articles often dwell on capabilities that are unimportant in many applications. A first-time buyer is usually unaware of the total requirements of an application, and he or she may decide to opt for all choices or for maximum performance just to be safe. In earlier sections of this chapter, we have attempted to place in perspective functional requirements at various stages in database system operations. The prospective buyer may want to reflect on these topics and generate a probable list of functional requirements from that material.

Functional capability implies the ability of a package to perform a task, but it also implies the requirement that the job be done in a timely fashion appropriate to the needs of the application. These constraints differ, and they may require special study, based on guidelines presented earlier.

Selection of the correct evaluation measures to be used for a specific application can be given guidance in several ways. References can help, as can conversations with experienced users or hands-on experience. However, the latter should be done by the individuals who will ultimately use the package in that function, partly to involve them in the decision and partly because, as noted earlier, the professional is not likely to spot features (good or bad) as they are perceived by clerical staff, and vice versa. It is equally dangerous to send a content specialist, a clerk, or a systems analyst to evaluate a DBMS package alone. Reports written in magazines may prove useful, but they are usually done by individuals whose viewpoints may not match all users in a given application. However, using as many of these approaches as one has time for will probably result in a reasonable appraisal of the relative merits of several different packages. Time spent in the design and initial evaluation phase will always pay off in the long run.

5.4.2 Long-Term Considerations

It is easy to overlook the future when planning for a system that is needed to solve the very real problems of the present. One tends not to ask what might happen if the system is a success, although fear of failure is usually present. There are, however, long-term factors that merit early consideration.

A database application on a personal computer is usually designed to meet the needs of a portion of a total operation, rather than the whole. Two groups in the same company may be planning separately for small database applications. Since personal computers are cheap and may already be available for word processing, individual fiefdoms are fostered by the availability of DBMS packages for the same machines. If one of these applications proves successful, it may result in a desire to extend its usefulness. A well-organized application in one section may produce information that is valuable to another group. What happens next? Will the system be duplicated with other personal computers? If so, will the package work as well with the new environment and tasks? Is there another comparable, but different application and package to which the first should be interfaced? Are they compatible? Can they co-exist? These questions represent the tip of the iceberg in the classic conflict between centralization and autonomy, and they can be expected to cause increasing concern in planning. Even an individual who uses his or her own DBMS at home may wish to interface that activity with one at the office, and these issues will inevitably arise.

Another factor affecting the long-term viability of an application is the support that is required from the vendor(s) of a DBMS system (hardware, DBMS, and possibly consultants). It may be less important to have long-term support for a package that has been out for some time and is generally regarded as stable, provided that the user does not plan major changes. Both DATAEASE and dBASE fall in this category. They represent companies with a solid national market base, with products that have been around, and with applications that have been running for some time without serious need for modification, and they run on hardware that appears likely to remain available.

Some users will require more support than others. These individuals should concentrate on the availability of local assistance. Anyone who has sent out software has learned that the demand for support is nearly insatiable. A large distributor may be able to provide a staff for questions on its product, but even large companies find it difficult to keep up with demand. The result for the user is long waits or frequent busy signals. A local source of support is a much more satisfactory solution.

In previous sections, we have mentioned reliability, integrity and security. Reliability is a measure of the accuracy of the data as they are entered into a DBMS. There are many ways in which reliability can be improved, as mentioned earlier. We have also seen that some systems provide better automatic reliability support (e.g., the error checking of DATAEASE), whereas with other systems these safeguards are the responsibility of the programmer and the systems supervisor. Integrity is concerned with making sure that data files are not corrupted by hardware failures, inconsistent updates, and other operational threats to the validity of a set of files. The packages we have seen provide for integrity through backup procedures and, in the case of DATAEASE, through warnings of actions that might impair the integrity of a file. Security has to do with authorized access to a set of files. As we have already seen, DATAEASE allows a supervisor to identify authorized users and to assign them access levels, whereas these functions are not available in dBASE III PLUS. In any environment, an operations supervisor can add other forms of access restrictions, and in some cases it is important to do so. Certain parts of medical records, for example, should be available only to a few individuals (e.g., psychiatric reports), whereas the remainder of the patient file may be more widely shared. Some DBMS packages permit restrictions to be defined at individual record level, although neither DATAEASE nor dBASE III PLUS have this capability.

Cost factors are important components of the evaluation process. In the personal computer domain the costs turn out to be quite different from what one might expect, especially the actual cost of DBMS packages, which typically range from $300 to $1,000. Costs of personal computer software are unrealistically low, the result of many public domain products, the ability to copy without permission, and the reluctance of buyers to spend more on software than on their hardware (which is not a reasonable goal, but we all subscribe to it one way or another). Since costs are unrealistically low, the purchasing process turns out to be quite different from acquisition of software packages for large systems. It is not possible to expect a manufacturer of a $500 DBMS to submit a bid, perform benchmark tests, sign performance contracts, or otherwise accept liabilities that will exceed by orders of magnitude the miniscule profit margin associated with an individual sale or even a modest number of sales. For this reason, the evaluation process is difficult for the personal computer buyer. None of the standard evaluation tools described above apply, or if they do, the buyer will either have to do them himself or somehow involve an intermediate party who accepts these responsibilities for a consulting fee that will understandably be quite high.

While software costs may be unrealistically low, it is also true that the hardware costs are very reasonable, and that most applications will be able to justify addition of a hard disk, to mention one necessary item, without affecting overall costs appreciably. The difficulty lies in obtaining permission to acquire hardware since this type of purchase is one of the few budget categories that can be controlled by accounting processes. The frustrations with this situation often result in individuals buying their own hardware.

If costs of DBMS packages and hardware are so low, then where is the real cost of a computer-supported database application? The largest single item is personnel. As already noted, a number of different types of expertise are needed. If they are available, they must be diverted, at least part time, from other activities. If they are not available, they must be acquired, often at a cost in terms of dollars, space, and impact on the existing staff. This impact will be much greater if hiring people with appropriate skills also means releasing others who were there before. Indeed, the cost and related impact factors associated with these decisions may well preclude introduction of an automated system.

A second cost, exemplified in the case of the dBASE III PLUS package, is in the development cost after acquisition of the package. Development is a service that may be performed by a staff member or by a consultant, and the exact cost category may vary. As we noted, programming costs for the system will be high when the system is first created. They will probably decline at a rate much slower than anticipated, as new applications are developed, enhancements are added, maintenance needs occur, and as the users gain deeper insight into the application. If a decision is made to hire a consultant or outside programmer, this cost may become a nearly permanent fixture in the operating budget.

The third major cost component of DBMS automation is growth. As an application begins to meet its initial design objectives, new ones arise. The volume of information grows. The dependence on the system requires absolute integrity, resulting in more expensive backup procedures. The opportunity to interface with other applications becomes tempting, and as a result the integration of planning becomes more complex and, hence, more expensive.

Growth can lead to several related costs, some of which form the basis of the next chapter. However, the effect is likely to be profound. In many operations that were largely manual a few years ago, automated information handling is becoming a vital component of the process. The database application that seemed small a year ago may become significantly larger precisely because it has succeeded. By the same token, the automation failures will often create a different cost load — what to do with the equipment that is no longer used for the abandoned application. Offices and even homes today abound with tools that no longer serve a useful purpose, and the temptation is strong to try to force this equipment to serve other purposes. Stepping up to new equipment does not necessarily mean that the old hardware or software is worthless in the new environment. However, it takes planning to find the right use, and some of this planning should occur before the first system is acquired.

5.5 SUMMARY

The considerations of resource requirements, performance, and evaluation form a complex web of conflicting demands. Personal computers are small, cheap, powerful and versatile, inviting individual creativity in their use. On the other hand, a database application is by its nature a team process, requiring careful, coordinated planning, and decisions that sometimes sacrifice creativity for the general good. Costs of DBMS packages and the hardware they run on are surprisingly low, an order of magnitude less than they were a few short years ago, yet the process of automating a database application may introduce other costs, especially personnel, that make it prohibitive.

The world of personal computers is unlike that of large mainframes. Control is lost (you can't prevent an employee from buying his or her own system), decentralization is inevitable, and management practices must adjust to these changes. Cost containment is a problem, and the pyramid structure of our hierarchical society is threatened. All of these statements can be considered either hopeful or discouraging, depending on the planning process. Certainly, planning must be different. The question is whether a group can adapt and somehow mange to get a decentralized operation to work cooperatively. The personal computer will play an important role in this process, but it can contribute negatively as well as positively. Humans have the ultimate responsibility in determining how this process will evolve.

This text provides tools that should help to clarify the planning process and indicate how the user can make more informed decisions. However, it provides no guidelines to the effective use of personnel. People are by far the most important components in a database application, and they come in many shapes, sizes, and with different mindsets. The success of a DBMS application is dependent on having flexible, adaptable programs that can meet the needs of many different users. To date, there are few packages that fully meet these criteria.

REFERENCES

The process of evaluating the performance characteristics of database systems involves an understanding of the specific application, the work environment into which the system will be introduced, and the products available.

There are two basic types of reviews on DBMS packages that are found in the personal computer magazines: in-depth reviews of specific products and broad checklist surveys of multiple products. Each of the major personal computers has had feature issues devoted to DBMSs within the past three years (*BYTE* in October 1984, *PC World* in April 1985, and *PC Magazine* in June 1986). These survey articles are of value; however, they usually contain references to features that may only be of limited value in specific cases, and the final ratings often are not significant.

In addition to these reviews, there are often in-depth surveys of specific DBMS packages. Due to its dominance in the marketplace, dBASE has frequent reviews of the latest releases, including dBASE III PLUS. There are fewer in-depth articles on DATAEASE, but they can also be found. The latest DATAEASE version, reviewed in Chapter 4, has not yet been covered in depth, although it appears in the group survey articles.

One of the better in-depth review magazines is *PC TECH*. Its articles are more comprehensive, aimed at a more technically oriented audience, and therefore present more background theory and operational analysis than usually appears in the comparable articles found in other magazines. The article on ZIM referenced at the end of Chapter 2 is a good example.

There are also a few texts that provide quite good information on database packages. Two are cited below.

Information Technology Services. Stanford University. *Microcomputer Data Base Management Systems: Their Selection and Evaluation*, (Stanford, California: Stanford University Press, 1984). 190 pages.

> The purpose of this text (printed from typed copy in three-ring binder format) is to provide a (brief) introduction to data management principles for the staff of Stanford; to review selected products in considerable depth, and to make recommendations for specific environments. It is an interesting analysis, with considerable emphasis given to the relational functionality of various packages, including dBASE II and DATAEASE (one of their recommended products). Since it was published in 1984, it is out of date with respect to the product analysis, and it is possible that an updated version will appear. The technical reviews are informative, although there is an uneven mixture of overly simple material with much more technically complex subject matter.

Emerson, S. L. and Darnovsky, M. *Database for the IBM PC*, (Reading, Massachusetts: Addison Wesley Publishing Company, 1984). 311 pages.

> This text, now out of date because the packages reviewed have been upgraded, has a rather weak introductory description of how and why one should use a DBMS, followed by chapters covering individual packages, checklists, and comparison charts. There are some valuable ideas in the text, and, if it is updated, it may be worth buying for the new reviews. I would not recommend it unless a revised edition is published.

6 Trends in Microcomputer Database Management Systems

6.1 INTRODUCTION

The previous chapters discussed DBMS packages designed to run on personal computers in single-user mode. This frame of reference covers the vast majority of current applications on personal computers. There are, however, features already available on DBMS packages, including dBASE III PLUS, that have not been discussed, and new features are being added as these packages evolve. This chapter discusses positive and negative implications of the more important evolutionary trends.

The word *new* implies "new to someone," but what is new to one person may be old hat to another. In the computer world, innovations appear daily, some of them accepted soon after their introduction, others forgotten despite their potential. The percentage of potentially good ideas that fails to succeed is probably higher than it has ever been. Success or failure depend as much on marketing, financing, contacts, and serendipity as they do on quality. It takes time for a concept, however good, to become incorporated into commercial packages. There is always a gap between the cutting edge of new technology and its availability at competitive prices.

Database Management Systems today are conservative packages, partly because their users are conservative. The naive buyer of a DBMS package will not be prepared for sophisticated improvements; the experienced user may be reluctant to change. The entrepreneur has a hard time selling novel approaches to such a market. There are, however, many ways in which DBMS packages can and should be enhanced. A few of these approaches already exist, even in the packages that we

have examined. The purpose of this chapter is to look at some of the most important trends in evolution of database systems.

There are many ways in which new concepts and features could be treated.
This chapter reviews new concepts and features of database systems in light of the
principles developed in earlier chapters. The implications of current research are
examined as they affect and extend principles already elaborated. There is no
attempt to foretell sweeping revolutions. However, there is a real need for DBMSs
on personal computers to evolve in directions discussed in Section 6.2, and it may
be necessary to consider these trends in planning for current implementations.

The chapter begins with an analysis of the implications of multiuser systems
and the extension of this approach to distributed systems. The next section examines the effect of trends in hardware evolution, and the last section considers new
concepts in database research. Together, these topics form a frame of reference that
should enable the reader to make informed judgments about present-day systems in
light of their short-term evolution.

6.2 BEYOND SINGLE-USER SYSTEMS: PROGRESSIVE APPROACH

The first potential extension to a DBMS application on a personal computer concerns use by more than one person. To begin with, we assume that only one person
is using the package at a time. Although multiple users of a single database have
been touched on earlier in this text, there has been no formal discussion of potential
problems involved.

When two or more people use a database application, questions arise that can
be ignored in a single-user environment. Expressed in simplest terms, who will be in
charge? Who will make decisions about such matters as file maintenance, priorities
in scheduling new developments, and access schedules? Will access be restricted?
What sort of communication channels will be established between the users? These
questions indicate the magnitude of difference between a single user application and
one that is shared. The perceptive reader will see on the one hand a potential loss of
individual control, and on the other, an opportunity to clarify operational details
that are not usually spelled out in single-user systems.

More importantly, the evolution of an application from one user to several
requires fundamental changes in the design of the package itself. DATAEASE provides for multiple users through its access levels and through supervisor-defined
menu sets. By contrast, dBASE III offers no direct means for controlling a multiuser environment. It is not easy to design a front end program for dBASE III that
will overcome this limitation. It is possible in any environment to establish operational rules that will minimize the potential for such damage. However, the ideal
multiuser environment should have built-in safeguards that prevent unauthorized
modification of the data or programs. To date, few DBMS packages on personal
computers offer such features. They will probably become more common in the next

few years as the resources needed to support this environment (faster processors, better multiuser operating systems, networking) become available.

6.2.1 Simultaneous Multiple Use

There are times in the use of a database when it is desirable to perform more than one task at a time. The commonest need for multiple use arises during data entry and during generation of lengthy reports, situations that require substantial time to complete. There are several ways in which these two situations can be accommodated. One way is to use a second personal computer to perform either the input or the reporting task. For small database files, this approach is desirable since it separates the entry process from retrieval. Files can be created using a second copy of the standard DBMS and subsequently merged. In complex situations, this approach can be multiplied as many times as required, so that even remote locations in a distributed system can use DBMS packages for data entry and then transfer the data to a central site.

Using a duplicate system to offload report generation is also feasible. However, there is a much greater risk in this application that the complete database will need to be transferred, or the copy updated frequently, and this transfer time may prove more trouble than it is worth. In addition, there is a much greater risk of running reports based on obsolete data.

A second option for simultaneous execution of on-line and batch reports is to create a background task that runs while the computer is processing another, higher priority task. Foreground/background tasks can run reasonably well even on personal computers such as the IBM PC, provided that the background job is one that is primarily bound to an output device, such as a printer, that uses minimal central processor resources. The relative speed of printing devices is so much slower than internal processing speeds that most of the central processor time is available for a foreground task.

One might think that having a foreground and background task functional capability would be one that any DBMS would want to incorporate. As noted in Chapter 5, it is possible, using PCDOS 3.0, to print files while the computer is being used for other functions. To do so, one must first create disk files suitable for printer output, then invoke the PRINT command with the name of the file. Unfortunately, this capability, while available under the PCDOS operating system, is not built in as a function in either package used in this text. DATAEASE describes how a print file can be stored on disk for later printing but does not provide any internal command to start the printing process while in the DATAEASE package. The user must either exit DATAEASE, start the print file, then return to the package, or establish external calls through the DOS callable functions. In dBASE III PLUS, the functionality is not discussed, and the user must work out his or her own mechanism for doing these tasks.

6.2.2 True Multiuser Systems

The ultimate form of multiuser access to a shared database is to have simultaneous access to the same data files. There are two requirements for effective shared file DBMSs. The first prerequisite is to have a multiuser operating system. Multiuser systems are common on minicomputers and large mainframes, but they are relatively new to the personal computer world. There are several types of multitasking available on personal computer systems. The first is a concurrent operating system, in which a single user can run more than one job at a time. This approach is similar to the foreground/background method described in the previous section. The second approach is a multiuser system, usually involving shared access to a Winchester disk. A typical personal computer version allocates a separate microprocessor board with its own memory for each user, with a single hard disk subdivided so that each has a separate area of disk storage. To date, however, these systems provide limited file-sharing capabilities and limited communications between active users.

Another form of multiuser support permits shared file access, so that two or more users can access the same file at the same time. This capability is just starting to appear on personal computers, and it is not widely used even on minicomputers. Although it is theoretically possible for an 8086/88 microprocessor to support more than one user, it does not make much sense to do so. The preferable option is to dedicate processor boards to single users, but to allocate a separate processor to shared file management for all users. There are several operating systems that permit shared file multiuser access. From the developers of CP/M and CP/M86 come versions such as MP/M and CPNET which offer these features. Third-party developers have also created shared file multiuser systems compatible with MSDOS. Some shared file systems are even available on 8-bit personal computers. Turbodos is an operating system compatible with CP/M (which runs on 8-bit processors) that allows multiuser shared files.

A shared file system is a step forward in database operations. However, it raises some new problems that have not yet been addressed. The next sections examine fundamental issues of database systems associated with shared file access.

6.2.2.1 File and Record Locking

It is statistically unlikely that two users of a database will access the same record at the same time. However, it is a possibility, and sooner or later it will occur. When it occurs, a number of possible results may ensue, some of which can have serious consequences. One of the simplest errors resulting from interleaving access to the same record is illustrated by the following example.

Time	User 1	User 2
1	gets record A	no action
2	modifies record A	gets original record A
3	stores record A	modifies record A
4	no action	stores record A

In an unprotected shared file system, the final result of record A is the one modified by user 2; user 1's modifications are lost when the second update overwrites the first. To make matters worse, neither user is aware that there was any problem with the update performed. The consequences of such a lost transaction could be serious and would in all cases result in unwanted data corruption, the loss of integrity of a file.

The solution to this problem is to introduce a LOCK statement into a DBMS command list. The LOCK command reserves a resource for the exclusive manipulation by a single user. While a LOCK is in effect, no other user can access the designated resource. The LOCK can be done at three levels. The most comprehensive is to LOCK an entire file. An alternate form of a file-level LOCK is to allow users to read data from the file, but to prevent any but the LOCKing program to update the file. The second approach is to permit a LOCK at the record level, so that a particular record is not available to any other user, but the remainder of the file may be accessed. A third, more complicated version, applies to hierarchical structures, in which all components below a particular node are LOCKed, but the remainder of the tree can be accessed by others.

When a LOCK command is introduced, a number of unexpected situations can occur. The first will affect a user who wishes to access a record previously LOCKed by another user. In such a case, the user who is unable to get the record will have to wait, perhaps a very long time, unless there is a system provision for "timeout" of the LOCK request. If a timeout is available, the user will be informed that the resource could not be obtained in the time frame requested, and he or she will have the option of taking other actions.

Many minicomputer systems permit single records to be locked, and this capability suffices in most situations. There are, however, cases in which a transaction requires that two separate records be updated. If record locking is available, this function means that a single user will have to be able to lock two records at the same time in order to complete a transaction. Consider, for example, a transfer of funds from one account to another. The user must:

> Obtain and LOCK account A
> Remove funds from that account, updating the balance
> Obtain and LOCK account B
> Add funds to that account, updating the balance
> UNLOCK records A and B

During this process, neither record should be accessed. If, for any reasons, the transaction is halted midway, the entire transaction should be deleted and reinitiated to make sure that the right actions are performed.

Having two records locked at the same time is a potentially dangerous situation. The most damaging condition that can result from multiple locks is a "deadlock," as illustrated by the following situation. We will assume that user 1 wants to credit account B with funds from account A, whereas user 2 wants to credit account A with funds from account B. Here is a hypothetical series of events that will result in deadlock:

Time	User 1	User 2
1	Request account A	Request account B
2	LOCK account A	LOCK account B
3	Request account B	Request account A

Since account B is locked by user 2, user 1 will wait until it is available. By the same token, user 2 must wait till account A is available; hence, both are tied up permanently! The deadlock situation can occur in even more pernicious forms that cannot be prevented if multiple locks are permitted. One partial solution is to introduce a timeout feature in the request command, so that an error is returned indicating inability to obtain or lock a record if a specified time has elapsed. It is then possible, using programming techniques that take advantage of this timeout feature, to prevent permanent suspension of a process.

The LOCK also poses problems relating to unexpected actions during database operation. For instance, if a user has LOCKed a record or file and then the user is disconnected, the record will remain in a locked state. Special action to correct the situation may be an automatic part of an operating system dedicated to database operations; it is less likely to be available under a general purpose operating system. "Dangling" locks are serious problems in DBMSs. One solution is to have automatic releases of all locks after a certain time period (probably measured in many minutes); but this approach may not be acceptable in all cases.

Another problem posed by the multiple LOCK feature is the action to be taken when a process terminates in midstream before completing all transactions associated with multiple LOCKs. If there is no automatic reversion of records to original state, then funds may be transferred out of an account and never credited to the appropriate recipient, a situation that can cause untold confusion. It is for this reason that many database operations maintain a separate transaction file of every action undertaken and its final status. With such a file, it would be possible to track down the error and correct it.

LOCKS are uncommon in systems running on personal computers. They are, however, necessary in shared file uses. As vendors address these problems, they will need to provide answers to the types of situations previously described. The reader should be aware of these pitfalls as he or she reviews multiuser shared file DBMS packages.

6.2.2.2 Buffer Sharing

The LOCK command is closely related to a second concept important in shared files, that of shared buffers. When memory space is to be shared by two or more users, it makes sense for the buffers also to be shared, so that a block accessed by one user may be available to another. Sharing buffers raises a second set of problems. The LOCK command described above must be coordinated with the buffers, so that the system knows which users have LOCKed which records. If another user attempts to access a locked record in a shared buffer space, the system must know that the second request is blocked.

Another problem that must be addressed in buffers relates to access security. The fact that a block is in buffer does not mean that all users may have equal rights to read or modify that block, so the access restrictions must somehow be available when the block is in buffer. Access restrictions can be defined to limit groups of users to certain types of access, or it can be associated with a particular file or even record, restricting access only to certain groups. Either way, the information must be retained and examined when buffers are shared.

In shared buffer systems, data integrity becomes an important issue that requires careful treatment. Use of the LOCK command is helpful, but it is also necessary to protect against other forms of potential data corruption. For instance, a user wishing to modify a file may copy data into a temporary name area, modify it, then copy it back to the original space. If, in the meantime, another user has modified the original file, there is a possibility that these latter modifications will be lost. It is therefore necessary to develop additional file access restrictions relating to the copy command to safeguard against this danger.

In summary, the functional enhancements achieved through development of multiuser DBMS packages are likely to be gained at a cost of increased overhead, a greater need for operations control, and a risk of compromising data integrity. These features are new to personal computers, and users need to be aware of these problems.

6.2.3 Multiprocessor Systems

In the previous section, we described an architecture in which several processors reside in one box, each one dedicated to a single user, with a separate processor acting as a file server. This configuration is becoming more frequent in the personal computer environment. In many respects, a single box, multiuser configuration is very close to linking two or more independent personal computers together. It would be possible to have several satellite processors accessing data from a single file server controlling a shared disk. One difference between the single box and multibox multiprocessor system is that the communication channels between boxes is likely to be slower than in a single box configuration. In addition, multiple computers linked to one another each have auxiliary storage, and database activities are transformed into much more complicated configurations. For example, if each personal computer has its own database, then the question of accessing data involves a distributed database.

Networks of computers used for DBMSs create new operational problems. It is not sufficient, for database application purposes, to connect two personal computers together. Since the functions to be performed on each system will be affected, it is necessary for each system to be able to send and receive messages that request or furnish data. The most important considerations affecting networks and DBMS packages can be grouped in two major categories: (a) communications, and (b) distributed systems. Network configurations come in many varieties. In this text, we will not go into detail on the choices available for local area networks, even though those options are important in designing distributed database applications. The reader is urged to review descriptions of communication architectures in the context of their likely use for database functions.

6.2.4 Logical Effects of Distributed Systems

When more than one system is used in a database application, there can be several different reasons for communicating between these components. There are at least four different functions that may require network services. The first, and most obvious, is data transfer between systems. A second function might be to transfer programs stored in a central location so that they can be run on a satellite system. The third option, often used in driving special-purpose devices such as laser printers (which have their own internal computers), is to execute a process on a remote device. Finally, one user may wish to use the network to communicate with other users. Each of these network functions has its own special concerns, which will be considered separately.

6.2.4.1 Distributed Data

When two users want to access the same file, it is necessary to introduce the LOCK command to preserve data integrity. If the data are distributed between two or more computers, administration of the LOCK function is more complex. There may be more than one copy of the same set of data on the network. This condition arises if a user wishes to access and process remote files on a local system. All of the problems associated with deadlock and multiple access reappear, only this time in a more pernicious form, since there is uncertainty as to where the data reside and what has happened to copies obtained from a master source. Remote updating or addition to a file is a desirable feature of a distributed operation, but it raises serious questions of data integrity and management.

A second problem arises when data are to be accessed from two distributed sources during execution of a single program. Some of the difficulties are that two files may have the same name but not the same data, or two records may have the same data but different field specifications. When two files have been maintained independently, there may be conflicting updates, and it is often difficult to determine which records are the most recent. Reconciling these differences is usually a complicated process that requires extensive research into the database application and the steps that have been taken in two different places. The use of transaction logs or journals might be helpful in resolving these problems.

Operational problems of this type are not addressed in single-user DBMS packages, where they are the responsibility of the operations staff. In a distributed system, these functions are much more complex and require careful coordination. There must also be automated processes that control data integrity.

6.2.4.2 Distributed Programs

Networked computers can transmit programs as well as data from one site to another. This option is useful if a work station has little or no local storage, hence needs to obtain programs from a central source. It is also useful when programs not usually required at one site are occasionally executed there, or when program updates are sent to all satellites. Transmitting programs presents slightly different communication problems than when data is sent through a network. Source code for programs may exist as ASCII files. However, compiled programs are stored as object code, which uses 8 bits of a byte instead of the 7 bits required by ASCII characters. Some communication protocols do not provide for transmission of full 8-bit data, so that special provisions may be required for object code transmission. Such protocols do exist, but the operations supervisor will have to make sure that this capability is provided if object code is to be transmitted. Occasionally, owing to differences in screen handling or operating systems, the code used at one site may vary slightly from that used elsewhere. These local variations must be dealt with when transmitting programs to remote sites.

6.2.4.3 Communication between Users

An important capability of networks is to provide communication between users. Electronic mail has a value intermediate between postal mail and voice communication. It has the advantage, in a frequently used system, of speed of transmission, and it has one important advantage over the telephone: It does not interrupt the receiver until he or she is ready to accept the message. Effective mail systems can process messages by forwarding, converting to hard copy, broadcasting to specific groups, scheduling for automatic delivery, or archiving. Sophisticated electronic mail systems can play a valuable supporting role in DBMS applications.

In a network, the protocol for communication is usually simple to establish for a homogeneous system. It becomes considerably more difficult when a heterogeneous combination of operating systems and hardware is involved, such as two or more personal computers linked to a central host. It is possible to program around these difficulties, but the responsibility is usually placed on the user.

As with other network features, there has been no incorporation of user communication services into DBMS packages for personal computers. When such a service is provided, it will probably be tied to a scheduling function, so that, for example, a routine report can be scheduled in advance and some users notified that certain items are due for that report, while others are alerted when the report has been generated and is available for distribution.

6.2.4.4 Distributed Execution of Tasks

A network of computers offers the opportunity to distribute tasks as well as data. The problem of managing a distributed execution environment is significantly more complicated than any of the functions discussed in Section 6.2.4. There are two modes in which a process may be invoked on a remote system. In the first, the task is initiated, and no further action is required from the initiating site. This mode is similar to spooling a print file, except that execution is on a remote device.

The second mode of remote job initiation involves a need to maintain communication with the initiating site. Such a case would arise, for example, when a special file is to be created on a remote system, then transmitted back to the originating site. Another example would be the execution of some special computer task, such as statistical analysis of data in which the results are needed for the next operation on the originating computer. In such cases, not only must the job be initiated, but its progress must be monitored, and it must be capable of reporting back results to the originating site. There are infinite variations in this mode of multiprocess operation, each with its own set of special circumstances requiring careful treatment.

Although some specific solutions to pieces of the distributed processing problem have been solved and are available commercially, this field represents an area of current research in computer science departments. It is likely that the results of this research will lead to new features in database systems within the next few years.

In summary, distributed systems offer many opportunities for increased capability. The price in all cases is increased overhead, the need for more careful management policies, and the potential for more complicated and serious problems as a result of the increased functional capacity.

6.3 LINKS TO OTHER SYSTEMS

When a small database application has become well established and is accepted as a part of regular operations, it often is necessary to consider a direct link between that application and other operations. Linking two systems can be done physically, as discussed in the previous section, but providing logical links may be much more difficult. Not only must the types of data on each system be compatible and their integrity maintained, but an interface between two different DBMS packages is also likely to be required. For example, if one were to link data files in two operations in the same office, one using DATAEASE, the other dBASE III PLUS, one would have to resolve several problems. The file formats are incompatible, and the operational philosophies are different. It is possible to use export formats in each in order to transfer data from one environment to the other (the author performed this transfer in preparing material for this text), but there remain decisions as to which system will be required to adapt to the other. For example, what would happen if the error checking inherent in DATAEASE uncovered data errors in files transferred from dBASE III PLUS? The responsibility of correcting them would have to be resolved and the corrections undertaken. Since a marriage of this type usually involves personnel from two different operations, egos and sensitivities will almost always play a role in the resolution of this type of problem. This simple example illustrates the operational decisions and political overtones that arise when incompatible systems are linked to each other.

Ideally, the best type of link is one that maintains the greatest degree of compatibility. Using the same package on two different systems is the optimal solution, since data compatibility is easier to achieve. Things rarely work that smoothly. Usually, if a personal computer DBMS is to be linked to a larger system, the two are incompatible in one or more ways. The programming language, file structures, system limits, entry mechanisms, error checking, and retrieval methodologies may all have subtle or major differences. The challenge in establishing an effective interface between such systems lies in deciding the level of coordination required, and the control to be exercised in the operation of each package.

There are few hierarchical linkages between DBMSs of computer systems in which language compatibility is feasible. Commercial personal computer DBMS programs are often written in assembly language specific to one processor family, or in C. Assembly language programs are not compatible between different processor families. The C language is a high-level language that offers potential for hierarchical compatibility, since C compilers have been written for both personal computers as well as minicomputers. However, to date that compatibility is not complete and problems do arise in converting between different systems. PASCAL, though fairly widespread, is also not standardized, especially when it comes to essential database features such as disk I/O. The MUMPS language is one of the few languages in which standardization from minicomputer to personal computer is widespread, and a general-purpose DBMS called File Manager runs without change on a wide variety of systems in this size range.

Database compatibility is rare across hierarchical architectures. There are ways that translation can be achieved, but it is uncommon for file structures and data-type options to be identical. It is possible to coordinate DBMS designs for interfaced applications and thus minimize interface problems, but many issues must be addressed in the design phase. A review of the data definition, environment, error checking, and access restrictions defined in Chapter 2 will provide a basis for integrated design. One aspect of the database system that will always require special treatment is indexing, since each system will maintain separate indexes, certain to be incompatible, and it is therefore necessary to provide for different index structures when two database files are merged.

System limits will differ markedly from small to large computers. The problem is not serious when going from a small storage environment to a large one, but downloading data to a personal computer may require defining subsets of the database in order to permit remote use of a file.

Access restrictions are particularly difficult to control in a distributed environment. Since two systems usually have different access provisions, transfer of a file from one environment to another will change the access provisions, requiring explicit actions to preserve any desired restrictions.

When a personal computer database is to be linked to a large mainframe, such as a large IBM computer, the actual code used to store information is different, since IBM mainframes use Extended Binary Coded Decimal Interchange Code (EBCDIC) instead of ASCII for character representation of data. Although interfaces exist, the process of linking personal computers to mainframes usually requires detailed knowledge of access protocols linking the two systems.

Despite all these pitfalls, hierarchical links between database systems are often desirable. In many operations, the availability of one or more personal computer-based systems to perform data entry, subset analysis, or report generation will enhance the value and extend the useful life of a central system. Distributed databases are also useful when different users require different subsets of data. A hospital, for example, has many separate services such as laboratory, pharmacy, individual patient wards, and administrative centers, all of which require patient identification information, but each of which has separate data needs not shared by the other. A laboratory needs to maintain quality control information on instruments, and to track passage of samples through the analytical process. The pharmacy maintains inventory, restricted drug control, and formulary data that are rarely needed by outside users. A system that permits local storage of the unique data sets as well as ready access to shared files will probably be most economical and most efficient.

A successful personal computer application inevitably needs to be integrated with other comparable or hierarchical systems. Although few packages available today provide ideal tools for this eventuality, the prudent designer may be able to incorporate flexibility from the outset to facilitate later merger of a small system with others.

6.3.1 Networking: Summary

From this introductory review, we can see that multiuser systems and networked DBMSs offer major rewards as well as posing new problems. For example, dBASE III PLUS offers a networked version of this package, yet this version has no provision for data integrity or security. Database packages for personal computers will usually benefit from connections to other systems, and the designer of a small database application should include plans for growth in this manner. He or she will find little help from today's vendors of DBMS packages, since many of the issues raised in this section have not been addressed by these vendors. Perhaps the best way to begin the long-range planning process is to examine database compatibility between two target systems, then to develop communication links between them. Subsequently, as networks are developed in an office, it may be possible to design communication interfaces that interact between the two databases as an overlay to the commercial packages. This approach ensures a general evolution to integrated systems without introducing rapid changes that might disrupt operations.

6.4 EFFECT OF HARDWARE EVOLUTION

Technological advances in the computer industry offer a bewildering array of new options to database users. In earlier chapters, we touched on some of the important short-term changes that are likely to affect DBMS design, including more flexibility in input techniques; the development of new, cheaper, and much larger storage systems; and larger, faster main memory. Although these developments are well known and already available in many cases, they have not been incorporated into DBMS packages. The enterprising operations supervisor should, however, be on the lookout for new systems that offer direct or hidden ways to capitalize on these features. A system that allows greater flexibility in input may accept new technologies, even though the specific interfaces are not defined. Operating systems enhancements that make interfaces to new options transparent may provide features that are not recognized by the DBMS vendor.

Introduction of new features for which a vendor is not directly responsible requires additional care on the part of the operations manager. Safeguards in terms of error recovery, reliability, hidden limitations, and adequate backup represent just a few of the items that should be considered in enhancing a database system. Increased knowledge of all components, hardware, software, applications, and data flow are important components of this planning process. The early introduction of a new technology often uncovers problems not previously encountered in the operation of a system. For example, very large files, such as might be stored on large Winchester drives or optical disks, may generate problems in file design that were not detected in smaller files.

Optical disks present a particularly challenging design problem in their use on personal computer systems. The volume of information that can be stored is huge, at least an order of magnitude larger than available on conventional disks. The write-once systems offer challenges as well as opportunities in data file revision. Having an audit trail of all actions taken can be very beneficial, but threading through a linked list of deleted files to find the active version may be an operational drawback. Since DBMS designers have not yet provided these features, it may be necessary for the early users of these systems to design their own mechanisms. The potential availability of nonrotating storage devices opens up choices in storage and retrieval strategy that may greatly enhance DBMS applications once their use is understood.

It is dangerous to predict the appearance of new hardware developments. Coprocessors and RISC chips designed to serve database functions appear to be likely areas for near-term research and development. Special-purpose processors dedicated to optimized use of auxiliary storage are already being used, but more significant improvements in this field will have a major effect on DBMSs. Even small improvements in the area of voice recognition and speech synthesis will probably have a profound effect on communication with database systems. New improvements in auxiliary storage technology will probably comprise another potential for major change in database applications. Each of these technologies is already in the research stage; some aspects are in the early marketing phase. It is therefore timely to start to plan for systems that incorporate such features. The difficulty will probably lie in achieving standards in each area, and this aspect may slow down their introduction.

6.5 HIGH LEVEL DESIGN CONCEPTS IN DATABASE MANAGEMENT

Vendors of current DBMS packages are already aware of the need to integrate database applications with word processing, spread sheets, analytical packages and other related functions. Both DATAEASE and dBASE III PLUS provide ways in which their packages can be interfaced to some systems representative of these activities. Ashton-Tate's Framework and Lotus' Symphony offer features of this type. However, the current levels of integration are somewhat primitive and cumbersome, and the integrated packages appear to compromise desirable functions in each of the separate application areas.

A new approach is needed to integrate database applications with other functions. Existing systems have been constructed as independent units. The data types in word processors are different from those in DBMSs or spreadsheets. Conversion between these systems is possible, but it is awkward, requiring knowledge of both systems for effective integration. These discrepancies suggest that a new, higher level design might solve some of the underlying incompatibilities. There are techniques available for such higher level design, and these approaches are now beginning to attract the attention of researchers interested in taking concepts from the drawing board into real-world applications.

The high-level design methodology approach is partially embodied in an approach that has been around for several years: data dictionaries. In its simplest form, a data dictionary is simply a definition of terms that will be used in a database. There is, however, a broader meaning to the term, one that is being studied and implemented in a few experimental systems. In the broader approach, a data dictionary is a high-level, automated design tool that asks a designer questions about the files that will be created and the uses made of the system; then, using program generation tools, it creates programs that perform the integrated functions specified. Systems of this type may ask not only about data types, file relations, and anticipated user viewpoints; they may, in addition, request information on the environments of data collection, responsibilities for maintenance, interface to networks, access limitations, and linkages to other applications. Once defined, the data dictionary system will not only generate the initial code to drive the system, but it will also, by virtue of its "understanding" of the total environment, control modifications to the system, create and automatically update documentation, and maintain data integrity when definitions are changed.

Use of a high-level data dictionary system is probably beyond the capability of the average personal computer user or even some 16-bit personal computer hardware. However, the sophistication of personal computer users is increasing, and the capabilities of such systems are also improving, so new systems offering a very high level of conceptualization may become feasible in the next few years. These new features will probably include the functions now treated separately in word-processing, spreadsheet, and DBMS packages.

Word processing is an interesting extension to database systems. We have already commented on the appearance of a few systems called database packages but designed to manipulate text. Integration of outlines, large text passages, automated indexing, graphic illustration, and reference citation into a single package together with generation of tables, analysis of data, and modern query languages offer exciting opportunities to authors and managers alike. Analysis of the ways in which one might want to work with this type of system represents a challenge in software engineering and the human interface problem. The need for integrated systems is so great that they will almost certainly appear in the next few years.

6.6 NEW TRENDS IN DATABASE RESEARCH

Database uses of computers account for a large percentage of all computing in the world today. Research in this field is active as well, offering promise of important changes in the next five years. A few of the more promising areas of research are noted in the following sections.

6.6.1 Expert Systems and Databases

A major emphasis in computer science research starting in the 1970s and continuing to the present has been in the broad field of artificial intelligence. Because expert systems rely on large databases for support, research on the integration of database technology and expert systems is under way, with promising results in a number of areas. The field is too broad to cover in this text, but a few trends are worth mentioning.

Analysis of the underlying characteristics of information is equally important to databases and expert systems. Knowledge representation is a growing area of research, and techniques are now being developed to improve the definition of relationships between facts or observations. One approach is to express information in the form of semantic nets, linking facts (nouns) by relations (verbs). This approach is unlike standard data representation, but it closely resembles natural language descriptions, and it offers chances for cumulative growth of available information each time a new relation or observation is added.

Study of query languages represents another area of research in which artificial intelligence techniques offer promise. By analyzing queries and storing information about questions previously asked by users, a database system can "learn" what likely paths will be required, and it can optimize retrievals for those paths. The ways in which this learning takes place are complex, but significant research results are starting to appear in the literature.

The manner in which such expert systems are likely to be integrated with database applications is first, to provide a front end that processes queries and decomposes them into elements that can be classified and optimized, and second, to develop new methods for translating those queries into optimal formulations based on the data structure. The interaction between this research and database technology is leading to new file structures, particularly with respect to indexing methodology. B-trees continue to be important elements in these index methods, but they are being refined to provide multiple attribute indexing capabilities within a single tree, an approach that provides reduced search times for complex queries.

6.6.2 New Language Concepts

Another area of investigation affecting database systems relates to the types of languages that can be used in their support. Most languages used on today's computers are based on sequential machines, with the implicit assumption that one step will be executed at a time. For many forms of computation, however, other types of language may be more appropriate. Two major classes of languages are evolving at present that offer potential in the database world.

One type of language begins with an unconventional approach and develops a new form of programs based on that approach. This is the so-called Actor class of languages, of which Smalltalk, developed by Xerox Palo Alto Research Corporation, is the best-known example. In these languages, programming is done by defining "objects" and the manner in which these objects may communicate with each other. An object may be a task, a process, a data element, or some other representation of information. Communication is not constrained to be sequential; the objects can send messages and perform tasks between each other as the need arises. Starting from this premise, it is possible to design totally different program structures that may more naturally represent the ways in which we view the real world. Experiments with these forms of programming, using individuals untrained in conventional computer languages, have developed successful results in a wide variety of applications. The techniques have also shown to be effective in working with children, who are less conditioned by previous experience and who adapt to this form of expression more readily than adults (the term Smalltalk has its origins in this concept).

In the database environment, classifying objects as groups of related data elements and defining communication as tasks that can be performed on these objects requires a totally different approach to the DBMS world, but it may provide a useful tool, especially in the query processing aspect of DBMSs. It is too early to say whether this programming form will take hold, but the increased availability of Smalltalk derivatives offers more opportunities for investigation of this field.

There is a great deal of research going on in the field of parallel (data flow) processing languages. These efforts are primarily devoted to computation problems such as matrix manipulations, but some investigators are exploring the potential for this type of processing in the database environment. Addressing the major bottleneck in database technology, disk access, some researchers are looking at ways of distributing data across disks or other auxiliary memory devices to permit simultaneous searches, and designing languages to take advantage of these architectures. A related area of investigation is in the design of processor chips whose instruction sets are more closely related to data manipulation requirements rather than to arithmetic ones. These new chips are also designed to execute several processes concurrently. The work in this area is not as advanced as the field of Actor class languages, but results should be available in two to three years.

6.6.3 Operating Systems Enhancements for Database Systems

A general-purpose operating system may not provide optimal support for specific applications. In particular, support of database applications requires special solutions to bottlenecks that are not generally well served by general-purpose operating systems. For example, when the MUMPS language runs under a dedicated operating system, it can be tuned to meet the needs of that language (which is designed for database operations). When the same language is placed under a general-purpose operating system, the loss in efficiency means that, despite significant processor speed enhancements, the resulting net throughput is only marginally improved unless ways are found to bypass standard operating system calls.

Buffer management represents another area in which operating systems could be improved for database systems. For example, a sequential file access benefits little from any buffer management scheme, whereas a B-tree search benefits from least-recently-used methodology; hence, any database system that used both types of files would benefit from having a variety of options for buffer management that could be either implicitly or explicitly invoked. Overhead associated with some general-purpose operating systems support is often of little value in database systems, whereas other features, such as integrity and security safeguards or shared file usage may require enhancements. These areas offer potential for dramatic improvements in the performance of database systems on general-purpose machines, and it is likely that research will probably be directed to solving some of these problems in the short-term future.

Database packages as currently implemented usually interpret original code programmed by users for query processing. This approach is slow, since it involves translating the command lines into executable instructions. Once a query has been constructed, found to be syntactically correct, and executed, the interpretation in a subsequent execution could run much faster if the executable code was stored. The process of compiling the commands (translating the request into executable code and then storing that object code) is itself time-consuming, but it does not take much longer than interpretation, and if done only once, it may result in significant time savings in future runs of the same request. For batch processes, therefore, compilation is a valuable option. The designers of dBASE III PLUS now offer a compile option in their package.

These examples illustrate the variety of solutions to operating systems support for database problems. The underlying principle is to search for problems or inefficiencies in current operations, and then to explore in the most general sense the possible solutions to those problems. The best solution may involve a combination of modifications to the operating system, new hardware, and new software. The more a database designer knows about all of these components, the more likely he or she will be to find optimal solutions.

6.7 SUMMARY

In this chapter, we have described ways in which personal computer Database Management Systems might evolve. Some of these evolutionary trends relate to the natural consequences of a successful application in an office environment. Others relate to opportunities, present or under development, that could affect design and implementation of these packages. In all cases, however, the changes are ones that will affect the initial implementation. The enterprising designer needs to think in terms of futures when he or she first embarks on a database application project. In that way, it is less likely that the design will be unnecessarily constrained, and the evolutionary process will take place much more smoothly.

The level at which material in this text is presented is aimed at individuals who may have limited background either in personal computer systems or in database principles. It is clear, however, from the material covered, that the manager of such an environment must learn more about both fields in order to maintain currency in a rapidly changing technological field. This book can only serve as an introduction. If it has whetted the appetite to seek more information, it has accomplished its purpose.

REFERENCES

It is difficult to include current references on new developments in a text that will be published several months after the material has been written. Since this chapter deals primarily with future trends and developments, the need to find the most current information is even more acute than in previous chapters.

In general, the more technically oriented magazines are likely to provide details of new technical developments as they become well enough established that their appearance as commercial products is likely within a few months. *PC TECH* and *Mini-Micro Systems* would be the two best references for this type of coverage.

For more general reviews on new concepts and developments, *BYTE* and *PC World* will often feature areas of interest (some issues are cited below).

MULTIUSER SYSTEMS

Guttman, M. K. (1985) "The Multiuser Dimension," *PC World*, Feb. 1985, pp. 136-143.

> This article describes the Northstar Dimension system, one of the first MSDOS systems extended to provide multiuser access to a shared disk.

The references cited at the end of Chapter 3 on MSDOS and UNIX also contain information about multiuser options under these operating systems.

Greenberg, K. (1985) "The DOS Drivers," *PC World*, July 1985, pp. 122-131.

> This article is a based on discussions with key people in Microsoft about new directions of multitasking and networking. It is a valuable introduction to some of the options that are expected to appear, some of which have since been announced as available.

NETWORKING

Luhn, R. (1985) "The Organization LAN," *PC World*, Feb. 1985, pp. 72-128.

> This issue devotes several articles to reviews of local area networks. The opening article by Luhn is an excellent review of options and factors going into decisions relating to selection of these networks.

Fisher, S. (1986) "Peering into the Future with LU 6.2," *PC World*, June 1986, pp. 256-263.

> This issue contains several network-related articles. The Fisher article deals with IBM's announced network protocol, LU 6.2, which may have a major impact on how intelligent personal computers can access mainframes without having to appear as dumb terminals. An important concept in the mainframe-micro communication domain.

DISTRIBUTED DATABASE SYSTEMS

The literature on this field is expanding rapidly, and new books and articles can be expected to appear in large numbers in the next two to three years. Listed below are just a few interesting references that touch on topics discussed in the chapter.

Draffan, I. W. and Pool, F., eds. *Distributed Data Bases*, (New York: Cambridge University Press, 1980). 374 pages.

> This text contains a number of interesting articles, including one on distributed query processing (by Bracchi et al.) which is particularly relevant.

Ven de Riet, R. P. and Litwin, W., eds. *International Seminar on Distributed Data Sharing Systems (2nd: 1981: Amsterdam, Netherlands),* (New York: Elsevier North Holland, Inc., 1982). 314 pages.

> Another compiled reference of recent articles, with several good ones including one on data integrity in the distributed environment by Leveson and Wasserman (pp. 243-251).

Date, C. J. *An Introduction to Database Systems, Volume 2,* (Reading, Massachusetts: Addison Wesley Company, 1983). pp. 291-340.

> This chapter of the second volume of Date's reference goes into some aspects of distributed systems, but does not deal with personal computers. It is good for theoretical information and some details of mainframe distributed databases.

NEW DEVELOPMENTS IN DATABASE RESEARCH

Bic, L. and Gilbert, J. P. (1986) "Learning from AI: New Trends in Database Technology," *IEEE Computer*, Vol. 19, No. 3, pp. 44-54.

> There are many new directions of research in database systems. This article is an excellent survey of directions in conceptual design changes that are being proposed in current research. Starting with the entity-relationship modification of the relational model this article goes on to describe several other new approaches and their significance. The article is advanced, but still readable by nonexperts in the field. The bibliography is excellent.

NEW LANGUAGE CONCEPTS

White, E. and Malloy, R. (1986) "Object-oriented Programming," *BYTE*, Vol. 11, No. 8, pp. 137ff.

> Each year, the August issue of BYTE is devoted to a new language or group of languages. The August 1986 issue deals with Smalltalk and other object-oriented languages. An excellent tutorial on this innovative concept, including information on the availability of these languages on personal computers.

Treleaven, P. C., Brownbridge, D. R., and Hopkins, R. P. (1982) "Data-Driven and Demand-Driven Computer Architecture," *ACM Computing Surveys,* Vol. 14, No. 1, pp. 93-144.

> An excellent review of Data Flow language concepts. The best place to start in learning about the new parallel computing languages.

Srini, V. P. (1986) "An Architectural Comparison of Dataflow Systems," *IEEE Computer*, Vol. 19, No. 3, pp. 68-87.

   The most recent review article on the subject. The emphasis is more on architecture than language, whereas Treleaven covers more language concepts.

OPTICAL COMPUTING

This topic probably should not yet be mentioned, since it is in its infancy, but processing data optically is now feasible, and there are some reasons to think that optical computing may eventually interface with digital computing. If and when this happens, database systems will undergo a revolutionary change.

   The August 1986 issue of *IEEE Spectrum* is devoted to this topic. Anyone interested in learning why this area holds such vast potential should review some of the material (pp. 34-57), or follow up on individual topics using references cited on p. 57 of this issue.

Index